DOLPHIN
DAYS

DOLPHIN DAYS

The Life & Times of the Spinner Dolphin

KENNETH S. NORRIS, Ph.D.

Illustrations by Jenny Wardrip

AVON BOOKS  NEW YORK

AVON BOOKS
A division of
The Hearst Corporation
1350 Avenue of the Americas
New York, New York 10019

The W.W. Norton edition contains the following Library of Congress Cataloging in Publication Data:

Norris, Kenneth S. (Kenneth Stafford)
   Dolphin days : the life and times of the spinner dolphin / Kenneth S. Norris.
      p.   cm.
Includes bibliographical references and index.
1. Stenella longirostris—Hawaii.   2. Wildlife conservation—Hawaii.   1. Title.
QL737.C432N67   1991
599.5′3—dc20   90-25390

First Avon Books Trade Printing: January 1993

THIS one is for my much loved life-companion, Phyllis. We all call her "Phylly" and we all lean on her for just about everything anybody needs to get through life: food, common sense, devotion to the family, and magical ways with children, plants, and animals. What else can I say?

From her standpoint, of course, all I've recorded here meant dealing with a husband sitting gnomelike in front of a computer screen, or off to sea in some insubstantial craft of his own shaky design. Now that I'm slowing down a little, next comes the part where I apply the same bright talents to things like rain gutters and water systems. But a good woman like Phylly can even handle that.

During the course of this work, members of *Hana Nai'a* used the Hawaiian spelling and pronunciation of place names such as Kealakekua Bay, following traditional Hawaiian usage. My editor, however, suggested the use of the more familiar Anglicized spelling for a general readership.

Contents

Illustrations

Introduction

IN this book I tell two very different stories about a remarkable mammal, the spinner dolphin: one story about its life and societies at sea, and the other about its fate at the hands of man. I have purposely set one story against the other, because that's the way it has been for me.

I'll assume that in picking up this book you share with me at least some interest in the lives and fates of these engaging animals. If so, you will find a good many insights into their lives here, because we were the first scientists to study their wild societies underwater where their lives are truly spent. Their grace and beauty strike any new underwater observer at once. It was only after much looking that we began to understand another key feature of their lives: they are so thoroughly creatures of their schools that they have surrendered some aspects of normal mammalian individuality to the group. A spinner dolphin alone is very much less than a whole animal.

In the first story I describe my original experiences with spinner dolphins, and then how I assembled scientific teams of colleagues and students to study what it means to be a spinner dolphin. These efforts have been wonderful adventures in field science, complete with all the pleasures and trials of finding a place and time where we could hope to see how a wild dolphin lives. We found our window to their world along the shores of the Island of Hawaii, and there were able to piece together our understanding, bit by hard-won bit, over almost two decades' time.

I hope I have conveyed the excitement of such discovery, because it was frequently there as we mulled over the tiny, almost hidden hints that passed before our eyes. A lot happened at dinner in our field camp.

"Why do these dolphins spin?" a team member might say. Spinning occurs when a dolphin leaps from the water and whirls like a top for as many as four rotations before it crashes back into the sea.

Another team member might reply, "I thought I could hear them slapping against the water as they fell back into the water: *crack crack.*" Then a discussion would ensue that set the frame for the next day's observations, and we were brought closer to uncovering a true thing. By the way, spinners do indeed make loud slapping sounds when they reenter the water after a spin.

Spinners emerged for us as mammals that live locked in the geometry of their schools, playing out a lifelong cat-and-mouse game with their predators. We began to suspect that when predators swim near, or when the dolphins sleep, their ultimate defense is to behave like schooling fish. In doing so, their individuality is suppressed in favor of the school. At other times, when no predators were near, spinner schools spread out and the complexities of mammalian life emerged—the young played, and the adults spent much of their time "reaffirming relationships" in what looks like a continuing bacchanal.

Beyond those features of dolphin life, we found that within the protective school each school member seemed to have hourly chores to do that helped maintain the school's integrity. Each animal is a part of an emotionally mediated "phone system" that seems capable of passing a remarkably complex flow of information across a dolphin school.

We became very close to some dolphins, such as Four-Nip, a sort of uncle to the young of the schools we followed. And we got to know a lot about Temple Baby and Mom, whose mother-and-child relationship was engagingly human at times. We had no trouble relating to Mom when her child roared around what we called the "play pen" of a traveling school just when Mom was trying to catch some rest. In all we learned to recognize more than one hundred individual dolphins. We followed one, old Finger Dorsal, for nearly a decade. By patient unraveling of who-swam-with-whom, the organization of dolphin schools began to reveal itself.

The second story in this book is about my own role in the tragedy of open-ocean spinner dolphins, caught and drowned by the hundreds of thousands in the nets of yellowfin tuna seine fishermen. While we worked along Hawaii's shores with our unmolested wild dolphin society, we couldn't escape the shadow of that catastrophe out in the open sea to the southeast of us. The more we learned of the societies of island spinners, the more acute became our desire to apply our understanding to helping their offshore relatives.

Now let me outline briefly where and how yellowfin tuna fishermen work. If you were to go out to the tropical tuna grounds, you would probably leave from some port such as Manzanillo, down where the waist of Mexico narrows, and then sail southwestward for four days and nights. You would find yourself in the midst of a vast tract of open sea where the only land for a thousand miles is a tiny circlet of coral and sea-floor rock called Clipperton Island. Around it the abyssal ocean stretches south to the Galapagos Islands, southwest to the Marquesas Islands, and northwest to Hawaii.

As recently as the 1950s this stretch of sea was one of the least known places on earth. Now, thanks to a tuna fishery that has steadily expanded westward from beginnings along the shores of Mexico and Central America, and to the dolphin kill it has produced, this watery wedge of ocean is a mapped and studied battleground where the currents and bottom topography are very familiar to scientists.

Forty years ago most tuna fishermen used bait fish that were broadcast into the water near feeding tuna, and the big fish were then hooked and muscled aboard. Bait was caught in lagoons along the tropical shoreline and a fisherman couldn't venture far to sea from this source. But the fishermen knew that more tuna schools—sometimes very large—were "out there" beyond the reach of the bait boats. Considering the price of tuna, there were riches beyond imagining in the offshore ocean.

Such a lure breeds experimentation. The imaginative leaders amongst the tuna fishermen began to experiment with giant nets, long enough to encircle both dolphins and tuna. After much experimentation one was made that worked, and the fishery was revolutionized. Small bait boats gave way to giant thrumming seiners capable of engulfing and freezing a thousand tons of tuna or more, and of traveling anywhere in the open sea.

The fishermen learned that to find the enormous schools of fish, dolphins were both beacons and magnets. The tuna seemed to collect near dolphin schools and then swim with them with remarkable tenacity. No matter how violently the fishermen chased the dolphins, the fish continued to follow.

So to find fish, all the fishermen had to do was locate dolphins. This was not difficult because dolphins, being air breathers, travel mostly at the surface, where a good lookout with high-powered glasses can sight them miles away. The trick was to slow the dolphins, "wrap" the net in a circle around them, purse it tightly closed at the bottom, and then scoop out the trapped fish. Later I'll describe in detail how this works.

The trouble with this neat scheme is that the fishermen did

not know how to let the dolphins loose. The troublesome mammals seemed to have no idea of how to deal with a net, and no wonder: they had never faced a solid barrier of any kind in their lives. They rushed the net walls, and tangled by teeth and fins. The vagaries of ocean currents often deformed the net circles and left great canopies of loose webbing that were lethal traps for dolphins rising for air. The dolphins drowned in droves, poking their snouts vainly through the mesh toward the air above.

I will take you through my part in the first U.S. government efforts to stem this slaughter. I will tell you how the efforts of many government scientists and legislators did begin to bring the problem nearer to control in the 1970s. Especially important in this progress were Dr. William Perrin and his colleagues at the National Marine Fisheries Service lab at La Jolla, California. But in the 1980s, as the fishery became more and more dominated by foreign fleets, some under no international control at all, the problem worsened again. Government reports say that in the late 1980s as many as 120,000 dolphins, including oceanic spinners and closely related spotted and common dolphins, were drowned in a single year.

That's not much different from killing entire human populations *every year* in such cities as Arlington, Virginia, Syracuse, New York, or Tacoma, Washington. The full magnitude of this kill comes clear when one reflects that a population estimated at only five to six million animals is involved. Today perhaps no more than half that number of animals remain. And kill figures are shadowy statistics, almost certainly too low.

In this second phase of the dolphin kill, it seemed at first that no one cared much. The U.S. public of the late eighties had apparently grown jaded by the constant drumbeat of ever-increasing environmental problems. But soon there was a response, thanks to dogged efforts, especially of the conservation group Earth Island Institute and the reportage of a young activist, Sam LeBudde. The latter had signed aboard a Panamanian seiner as a crewman and was able to make a damning videotape of the kill at its worst. A film, *The Last Days of the Dolphin,* was assembled from these tapes and narrated by actor George C. Scott. I took part too, as their dolphin expert, and said my passionate piece on behalf of the dolphins.

In this climate of concerned public opinion, certain tuna canners and distributors abruptly announced, amidst much self-generated fanfare, that they were abandoning the use of dolphins to catch tuna. Conservationists exulted and the fishery basked in widespread praise for its actions. I will share with you my concerns that this widely advertised shift may have solved the canner's financial problems in the face of an angry public, but perhaps not those more visceral troubles of dolphins on the tuna grounds.

I have combined my two tales here to let you understand, as my colleagues and I did so clearly, that these dolphins are not mere statistics. I want you to relive with me the experience both of watching the fishery at work and of learning to understand the lives of the dolphins they caught. That is the best way, I think, of conveying our ideas, feelings, and concerns about these animals.

What I tell you here describes many of our scientific findings about spinners, but it is not the science itself. That more detailed work is all but ready to submit to the University of California Press for their consideration.

And as I write we start another phase of my naturalist's work. My students are moving back to those Hawaiian coves again, this time with a new boat that will let us travel offshore with the dolphins, where we can watch, photograph, and listen to them from a viewing chamber we can pull up and down through a cylinder that pierces the ship's hull. We drive out to sea at a comfortable speed, find the dolphins, lower the chamber, and climb down into it. A band of windows goes all the way around the cylinder. When we are through watching and listening, we pull up the cylinder and go home. It works like a charm, except for a little excess water we seem to take over the bow when the wind blows.

THE events of this book span thirty years of my career. More people than I can enumerate have lent a helping hand: students, family, friends, colleagues, artists, secretaries, accountants, pilots, mechanics, officials, funders, fishermen, and patient neighbors of our field camp. A salute to my wonderful team and to Rachel Smolker, Paula Wolf, and Karen Miller, who meant a great deal to us. I appreciate the times and places when all of you gave us help, advice, and more tangible assistance. It's been a real human adventure, thanks to you. I hope that someday soon the *nai'a* will benefit too.

DOLPHIN
DAYS

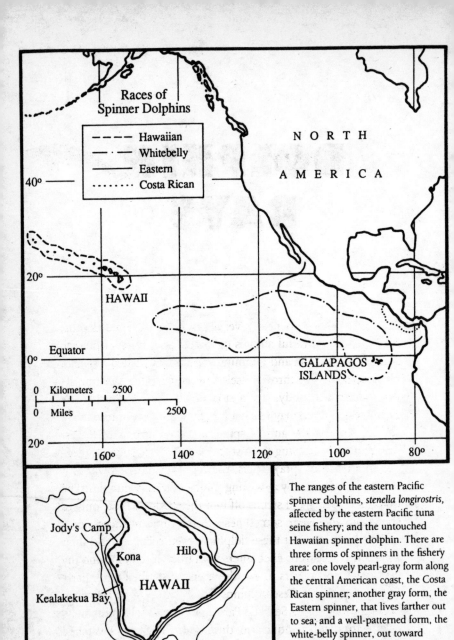

Races of
Spinner Dolphins

- – – – Hawaiian
- – · – Whitebelly
- ——— Eastern
- ········· Costa Rican

NORTH
AMERICA

40°

20°

HAWAII

Equator

0°

GALAPAGOS
ISLANDS

| 0 | Kilometers | 2500 |

| 0 | Miles | 2500 |

20°

160°   140°   120°   100°   80°

Jody's Camp

Kona   Hilo

HAWAII

Kealakekua Bay

| 0 | Kilometers | 100 |

| 0 | Miles | 100 |

The ranges of the eastern Pacific
spinner dolphins, *stenella longirostris,*
affected by the eastern Pacific tuna
seine fishery; and the untouched
Hawaiian spinner dolphin. There are
three forms of spinners in the fishery
area: one lovely pearl-gray form along
the central American coast, the Costa
Rican spinner; another gray form, the
Eastern spinner, that lives farther out
to sea; and a well-patterned form, the
white-belly spinner, out toward
Hawaii. It resembles the Hawaiian
spinner, which ranges into the
mid-Pacific at Kure Atoll.

The inset shows our study area on
the island of Hawaii.

1

Spinners

A DOLPHIN flashes up nearly vertically from the blue depths. Propelled by powerful strokes of its flukes, it bursts from the sea into the air, wet and gleaming. The animal, called a *spinner* by fishermen, has thrown itself into rotation by twisting its upper head and body, like a spinning skater. All during the arcing leap, which may reach a height of almost ten feet above the sea surface, the animal spins: a flickering blur of flukes, fins, and body, moving too fast for our eyes to resolve. It reenters in a crash of spray, sinks, rotating ever more slowly as it descends, attended by a twisting plume of silvery bubbles. The dolphin recovers and swims off into the shadowy blue, only to spin again and again, sometimes a dozen times in succession.

This book is about these dolphins, their societies, and their sometimes disastrous encounters with man. It took me and my colleagues thirty years to live the events described here. Early in that span I met these dolphins as a designer of an Hawaiian ocean exhibit called Sea Life Park, and later, more intimately, as director of its scientific arm, the Oceanic Institute, I watched spinners being caught and trained. I shared the discoveries of a remarkable theoretical biologist, Gregory Bateson, who while working at my institute studied the behavior of the captive spinner school. Gregory's struggles to understand their communication system probably inspired me to seek them out in their true open-sea home.

My first attempts to work at sea were made off the island of Oahu, not far from the Oceanic Institute. But the schools that lived there were small and elusive and swam in waters often roily from storms. More than 90 percent of my time was spent simply searching for them. My resolve and my budget both faltered in the attempt. Ship time is expensive and it seems more so when the major product of one's work is riding the swells over vacant water.

Then an acquaintance told me of a school of dolphins "so tame one could almost touch them" in a crystal-clear bay on the Island of Hawaii. Sure enough, when I visited this bay there was a group of dolphins who, unlike their Oahu relatives, proved tolerant of us, letting our boat travel easily with them. On many days we could watch them underwater through glassy water. This opportunity led to two extended scientific investigations, and to the first extended underwater view by any scientist of wild dolphins at sea.

To a human the most obvious thing about these dolphins is their habit of spinning. That's the first thing you are apt to see when encountering a spinner school. Here and there throughout the school, dolphins burst from the water in those frantic spins. Their mates seem to pay no attention and continue their swimming without reaction.

In attempting to understand what spinning was good for, we assumed from the outset that it was good for *something*. The behavior pattern is too ubiquitous to be explained by chance; it occurs throughout the world wherever spinners live. Furthermore it is too uniform in its expression to be mere play. And when I watched spinner schools and saw that only some animals spun at any one time, while the others went about other activities, it simply *looked* like a job. It was something a dolphin did on purpose and for some good reason.

I knew that other cetaceans leapt from the water, each species performing its leaps a little differently. In fact, I had become so skilled at identifying these leaps and the species that made them that with some accuracy I could shout out the species of a school so far away the animals were just black specks on the horizon. Could the dolphins identify such spins underwater, I wondered? Could they tell a spinner from a common dolphin by listening to that crashing reentry, or by echolocating upon the bubble trails it left underwater? In other words, could spins be markers of some sort?

Like so many observer's tricks, my long-distance identification of dolphin species by their leaps could seem amazing to the uninitiated visitor, but it was not difficult really. I knew that big fifteen-foot beaked whales leapt almost straight up and then fell back without arcing over snout-first. Also they make prodigious leaps that sometimes break the twenty-foot barrier. Any cetacean jumping that high has to be either a bottlenose dolphin or a beaked whale, and the whales are larger. Common dolphins pour from the water in lovely arcing waves of animals, as they speed along. Right-whale dolphins also pour from the water in ranks of leaping animals, but they broad-jump, staying much closer to the surface than a common dolphin, on average. The only other dolphins besides the spinner to spin, so far as I know, are the white-sided and dusky dolphins of both hemispheres, and they do fairly elementary spins, just now and then. No one knew what any of these leaps were good for, though some scientists had mentioned in passing that they might dislodge parasites or the curious sucker fish who hitch rides on marine mammals by sticking to them with a special suction-cup–like fin.

Thinking about spins and what they might mean started me thinking about the spinners' schools as well. I realized that for such mammals to survive at sea their schools had to be much more than simple social groups. They had, somehow, to be places of protection where a dolphin could give birth, raise and instruct its young, find and catch food, sleep; and the schools had to be coordinated in ways we simply did not then understand. Any culture the dolphins could develop had to be carried right along in those schools. The schools were, after all, where a dolphin spent all of its life, and, for spinners at least, the school never stopped moving, even during rest.

Through my musings I began to foresee some of the complexity I might expect from these unknown oceanic animals. That is the excitement of the naturalist's trade: the following of idea trails by returning again and again to nature for her answers to one's questions, and so, in time, building up a view of what the life of a foreign being is like. Look, imagine, ask nature what she thinks, ruminate over her reply, think again, look again, ask a new question, and feel the lift of elation as the bits of truth settle ever more neatly into place, like pieces in a jigsaw puzzle.

Note that in this method of seeing the observer is only a questioner. No truth ever emerges completely from his head. It comes only by checking repeatedly with nature to see if her silent answers fit with the things the naturalist has asked. Nature is the authority, and she gives up her secrets sparingly, bit by bit. So one must look and ask, look and ask, over and over.

Spinner dolphins are beautiful animals, and each part of that form and pattern has somehow been shaped. In later chapters of this book I will fill in some of the pieces, explaining as best I can what I think their exquisite shape and markings are good for. But for the moment let's just look at them in their simple elegance, as an artist might.

Spinners are very different from the robust, nearly unicolor gray dolphins we are used to in oceanarium shows. Their slim six- to nearly seven-foot body is patterned with a glistening dark gray cape laid over their backs from tip of snout to their flukes. Their flanks are paneled with exquisite pearl gray, sharply demarcated from the dark cape above and the immaculate white belly below. Their long, slim, blackish beaks are lined with 180 or more delicate interlocking conical teeth. These splay outward from the jaw line, forming a cage that traps their small prey when these jaws close. Their eyes are ringed with a small black mask that extends as a dark band to their black flippers.

A female spinner in the gliding posture. Note the three parts of her pattern: a dark back, a pearl-gray side panel, and an immaculate white belly.

This pattern, we found, is a complex signal system sending messages about position, intent, and activity to other dolphins. Some patterns send signals quite long distances through the clear water. For example, as one spinner rolls toward another in a passing school, the observer sees the flash of bluish-white bellies even beyond the range where the animal's body form may be easily discerned. The dolphins may use this flash as a signal of affirmation, because when it occurs they tend to move toward one another and often begin to caress.

To the untutored observer, male and female spinners look much alike. But as we watched them they came into focus like a photographic slide being adjusted. We began to learn the subtle markers of sex and age. We began to discriminate the deep muscular tails of adult males from the slimmer tails of females, and ultimately to understand that a peculiar ventral hump of tissue that looks much like a radar dome, set just behind the anus, was also a marker of males. This curious *post-anal hump,* possessed by certain other dolphin species, clearly marks the sex, and to a degree the age, of the spinner dolphin that bears it. Big old males have the largest humps.

The dorsal fins of males also change with age, roughly defining their age for an observer. In old males they become tall, dark, erect triangles that seem to indicate the important social role of their bearers, which is, at least in part, to guard and order the school.

I never get over my surprise that almost none of the features I describe above were, at first, even vaguely apparent to us. At the beginning we couldn't tell male from female, or young from old, unless sheer difference in size marked them for us. (Of course such a subtle learned skill is something we use every day when we watch the faces of our friends for hints of this or that message of acceptance, wariness, trust, disbelief, or whatever.) And especially I shouldn't be surprised that such spinner dolphin patterns and signals are subtle, because these dolphins have reason to look alike. I think their very survival in the face of shark predation depends upon their looking and behaving like a fish school, all of whose members are, for all intents and purposes, identical. That is another intriguing story to which I will return.

Once certain relationships became clear to us, we saw them everywhere in our dolphin schools. For instance, we learned that nearly every time we ventured into a dolphin school we were met by a squad of older adult males, from half a dozen to twelve or more in number. Typically they interposed themselves between us and the remaining school, swimming resolutely, and without the evident *joie de vivre* of other dolphins nearby. They are the oceanic equivalent of what students of primates ashore call *male coalitions,* and they clearly have a job to do.

Calves and juveniles were immediately obvious in these passing schools. Underwater, their swimming patterns marked them as far away as their flashing bodies could be seen. Young dolphins "bounce" through the water, tossing their heads and rolling back and forth as they swim, in obvious contrast to the stately adults. "Just like kids everywhere" is the irresistible comparison with our human experience.

We who study animal behavior feel that there are good reasons for these "metasignals of youth." They indicate the state of "youth," and the little dolphins can play adult games without being taken seriously. Hence they are not challenged by adults. Sure enough, as these young dolphins grow into adulthood they stop juking around, become more staid in their movements. Then they are ready to be "taken seriously" as members of the adult school.

Perhaps I am influenced by a life spent in crowded California, but the sheer aloneness of the lives of oceanic dolphins excites a combined awe and uneasiness in me. To give an example, I once traveled on board ship for five days and nights to reach the Galapagos Islands, and though I looked hard for the first three days I saw no marine mammal. Then, out in that vast watery waste, a group of about twenty dolphins came to our bow, flirted with us for a few moments, and left on some bit of dolphin business. How, I wondered, could the concept "destination" have any meaning for those animals?

I knew from watching them underwater that by eye one dolphin might be able to see a couple of dozen schoolmates while the remainder swam off there somewhere in the impalpable blue. That, too, seemed to me the epitome of aloneness.

More awesome still for the terrestrial human was the certainty that those twenty animals swam their whole lives without ever seeing the sea bottom, since it was down there in the black, twelve thousand feet below them where they could not dive. They were bobbing little corks locked by breath to the sea surface.

We sailed for two more days, and no more dolphins, until we came into the penumbra of the Galapagos Islands and began to encounter the schools of bottlenose and streaker dolphins that frequent the channels between those emergent volcanic cones.

The aloneness of the open sea is muted by events aboard ship. One can wander down a companionway to the galley for a word with a shipmate, and a steaming cup of coffee, while the endless sea slips by. But enter a skiff out there, as I have done, and cast off in your little teacup of a boat, and the aloneness at once closes around you, overpowering and frightening. In moments my sixty-foot vessel churned off, becoming smaller and smaller, until she was an insignificant shape on the horizon, and all around was the heaving sea. Then I was more alone than I had ever been in my life. It was just me, my suddenly precious cockleshell, and the swells. They began to lift me so that I could see the vanishing mother vessel and then to drop me into the trough where nothing could be seen but the domed sky over blue peaks of water. I was assailed by an almost irrational desire to call out and be taken aboard again. I looked over the gunwales into the swirling water and saw the surface foam and the motes of plankton flashing white in the shafts of light that play down into the ultramarine open sea.

I was too far out in that wilderness for most birds to fly by. Most of them are locked near to continents and islands, and only the most far-ranging seek out such oceanic waters. The terrible latent power of the sea stood just at the edge of my consciousness, letting me know my time was brief out there, because sometime very soon the winds would rise, the swells would tower and then crash in cascades of foam so mountainous that I and my insubstantial skiff could not hope to persist.

And so the human, alone in the dolphin's world, looks at those twenty animals slipping by and wonders what they do for company, how they weather the storms that must sweep over them unimpeded, what signals and objects bring texture to their lives, and whether they are as alone as they seem? How is it possible that, floating out there in that limitless space, they have somehow constructed or carried on a society? What might be its depths and nuances? And is there any way for a mere human to look in and learn about such lives in any depth?

There did prove to be a way, because some of these same dolphins use motes of land, islands, or even just shallow reefs, whenever they find them, coming near shore to rest, we think, from the constant attentions of oceanic sharks. At atolls across the Pacific, schools of spinners can be found entering the swift water of tidal passes and traveling into calm inner lagoons. Midway Island, Kure Atoll, Raiatea, Moorea, and Kwajalein, and the Great Barrier Reef, are places where they are known to come. Certain coves along the shores of larger islands host the dolphins too, and they have been coming to them for as long as anyone can remember. At Tahiti, along an open roadstead near Point Venus, only partially protected by a fringing coral reef, a slow-moving school of spinner dolphins comes almost daily. On the Big Island of Hawaii one tiny cove and its two attendant cinder coves is called "the squid place" in Hawaiian, a fisherman's allusion because the coves attract dolphins ashore, as if pulled by the tentacles of a squid. Today the largest spinner school in Hawaii sometimes gathers in this area.

Not far away, down the coast a few miles, is famous old Kealakekua Bay where Captain Cook finally met his demise, at the hands of an angry mob of Hawaiians. It, too, is a gathering place for spinner dolphins, who come there on about 70 percent of calm weather days, and it was there that most of our work was done.

Mark Twain came to that bay in 1877 while writing his famous travelogue *Roughing It,* and there he encountered what were probably the direct ancestors of the spinners we came to know. He seems to have entered the water right in Kealakekua Bay and to have encountered the dolphins a short distance south of the bay at a little cove listed on maps as Honaunau (The City of Refuge). Unlike us, he was not comforted by the sight of dolphins frolicking near his canoe. His account reads:

> At noon, we hired a Kanaka to take us down to the ancient ruins at Honaunau in his canoe—price two dollars—reasonable enough for a sea voyage of eight miles, counting both ways. . . . We turned our eyes shoreward and gazed at the long mountain with its rich green forests stretching up into the curtaining clouds, and at the specks of houses in the rearward distance and the diminishing schooner riding sleepily at anchor. And when these grew tiresome we dashed boldly into the midst of a school of huge beastly por-poises engaged at their eternal game of arching over a wave and disappearing, and then doing it all over again, and keeping it up— always circling over, in that way, like so many well-submerged wheels. But the porpoises wheeled themselves away and we were thrown upon our own resources.

Almost a hundred years later we biologists viewing the descendants of those same animals knew little more than was known in Mark Twain's time, though it is fair to say there was no fear in us as we launched our effort to learn about their lives. The trained dolphins in oceanaria around the world had by that time dissipated any trepidation we might have felt.

But it is also fair to say that science had, up to that time, provided little information about how these same animals lived. As recently as twenty-five years ago cetologists (those who study dolphins and whales) referred to the genus to which the spin-ner belongs (*Stenella*) as a "waste basket" because nobody could sort out the species that comprised it. Almost all that was known came from the skulls and skeletons in museums, collected for more than a hundred years by many people at many places around the tropical world. They came from such places as the lonely island of St. Helena in the mid-Atlantic or the Cape of Good Hope at the tip of Africa; more often the labels simply said "South Seas," without even noting in which ocean the specimen had lived.

About that time the great whale and dolphin scientist of the British Museum, Dr. Francis Fraser, arranged his extensive museum collection of *Stenella* skulls into a graded series and could find no clear indication that they fell into recognizable species. It was not until contemporary workers such as William Perrin began to assemble more precise collections, with accompanying photographs of external appearance, that the story came clear. Then it was obvious. Around the world in the tropics and subtropics were spinner dolphin populations in every ocean. Today cetologists collect all true spinners in a single species, whose Latin name is *Stenella longirostris.*

Another bigger, more robust species complex, and quite distinct from spinners, too, when judged by its pattern and features of its skeleton, occurs throughout the same range. These are the spotted dolphins of the species *Stenella attenuata* and *S. plagiodon.*

Another reasonably closely related species that tuna fishermen call the "streaker porpoise" is widespread in the range of the others, and extends even further into cool water than they. It is called, anomalously, the blue-white dolphin, though the ones I have seen bear no trace of blue. It travels under the Latin name of *Stenella coeruleoalba.*

In at least three places in the world oceans there are strikingly different dolphins allied to spinners. In the warm Atlantic there is a little short-beaked form, *Stenella clymene,* that doesn't seem to spin. And recently a tiny little spinner has been reported from the very warm-water Gulf of Thailand.

The most unusual spinners occur in the eastern Pacific tuna

grounds. A remarkably attenuate spinner lives along its eastern margin on the Costa Rican coast. It is a very slim, pearl-gray dolphin, whose body bears just the hint of pattern seen in the Hawaiian form. Its very slim beak and body are the longest of any spinner. Out in the open sea to the west of this curious dolphin lives the eastern spinner, also lead-gray, but chunkier and with a shorter beak. These spinners are most noted, though, for the strange shape of their old adult males. The dorsal fins of these animals have become tall triangular sails, and, strange to say, they look for all the world as if they had been stuck on backward. The post-anal hump mentioned earlier is also of grotesque size on these two forms, a real radar dome of tissue.

Far offshore near the western edge of the seining grounds and southeast of Hawaii, the spinners are dark and light again, but this time with speckly bellies. Now and then we would see a few speckles on our Hawaiian animals, as if they had relatives far offshore.

These, then, are the principal actors in this book. I knew nothing of them when I encountered my first live spinners swimming in a plastic pool set on a grassy lawn next to a calm Hawaiian bay.

2

Sea Life Park

My journey with spinner dolphins began in 1961 when Paul Breese, the director of the Honolulu Zoo, drove into my parking lot with a load of flamingos standing in the back of his truck. I was curator of a big ocean exhibit, Marineland of the Pacific, near Los Angeles, and he'd come to see me about a similar exhibit he was helping to plan in Hawaii.

There are few formalities in getting to know Paul. Talking a mile a minute, he seemed to assume he'd known me forever. Soon mutual friends were identified. We discovered that both of us had come circuitously to our professions through the improbable route of desert biology. Then we had lunch at my house up the hill behind the oceanarium. There he met my wife Phylly, patted our tame bobcat Hopi, and admired Aristotle the barn owl, who sat stoically on a perch in the back yard. We even took a walk with the owl later on at dusk (Aristotle flew, we walked), and by that time we were in fact old friends, having talked more than most friends do in half a year.

Paul talked on and on. His real message was: Could I help with the new exhibit[1] since they had no expertise at all with

1. The exhibit I speak of here was not at the Honolulu Zoo but a new oceanarium, Sea Life Park.

dolphins? It so happened that I was in the process of leaving my job to join the University of California faculty later that year and I did have a few months in between. I could at least talk to them, I thought.

I learned that the exhibit was the vision of a young couple, Karen and Tap (Taylor) Pryor, and that Paul, who of course knew a lot about animal exhibits, was the third party in the scheme. Finally Paul asked, Would I come out to Hawaii to advise them about the feasibility of their ideas?

A few weeks later Paul and I were driving up Oahu's Nuuanu Pali, headed for Kaneohe Bay, where the Pryors lived. Paul prattled on about how the northwest trade winds blew so hard up on the Pali that trucks were known to tip over when they first met the gust. We were blasted by the wind when we pierced the rampartlike cliff but wound our way safely enough into the verdant valley below. The monologue went on, skipping from cliffs to water buffalo (he knew every one on the island personally), and then to parthenogenetic lizards that clustered around gas station signs at night (the lizards are all females and their eggs don't require fertilization by a male), to taro planting (there are two kinds of taro, dry and wet), to mangrove wood (it's good to use in salt water because it never rots), and finally to Hawaiian dolphins. Paul edged the car off the highway onto a winding dirt road that led down through huge forest trees to the ocean shore at a place called Hakipu.

Even though my navy vessel had sometimes visited Hawaii during the Second World War, I wasn't prepared for the scene that opened before us. We rolled from the tall grass and forest into a broad clearing shaded by giant spreading *kamani* (Hawaiian almonds) and banyans, in the midst of which was an insubstantial little dream house, built mostly of big glass windows. The glassy calm bay ended as a shallow sheet only yards in front of the house, the afternoon apricot sky tinging both the towering cumulus clouds above and the water beneath.

One looked through the *kamani* forest to a fringe of bending coconut palms at the water's edge, and out across the bay to the distant fringing reef penciled by spurting breakers. I was hooked before anyone even said hello.

Under the trees a dozen people milled, and half a dozen kinds of tropical dishes were spread on banana leaves. Tap and Karen sauntered out of the crowd to welcome us. Tap had been based in Hawaii as a marine aviator and had dreamed of returning. Armed only with a knowledge of biology newly acquired at Cornell University, and a collection of pheasants which they planned to raise for a living, he and Karen found their way to Hakipu. It didn't take Tap long to dream other dreams. Slim and boyish, Tap's quiet demeanor was disarming, but under that affable exterior lay a complex and brilliant man.

I would work with him on and off for eight years, and by the time I eventually returned to my university full time he had built and welded together seven companies, including a huge Hawaiian ranch and tourist hotel, a pioneering undersea exploration venture, a feeder airline, a tourist railroad, an ocean research organization (the Oceanic Institute, which I headed for a time), and the most innovative and beautiful oceanarium of its time. He had also been elected a state senator, and had the glue of his empire been stronger he might have reached the governorship of Hawaii. Karen, his partner in this buffeting meteoric ride, was as remarkable as he.

She is a brilliant writer-naturalist and a tough, clear-eyed trainer who came by her talents naturally. Her father, the author Philip Wylie (*Generation of Vipers*), used to have a sign over his office door that read simply "Wizard," and much of that state came to Karen unalloyed. She was soon to reshape the art of marine mammal training, and in the process she and her staff were the first to work with a number of previously unknown dolphins, such as the pygmy killer whale, the rough-tooth dolphin, the false killer whale, the melon-headed whale, and the spotted and spinner dolphins. She eventually dipped into public policy herself, serving in recent years as a U.S. marine mammal commissioner, in Washington, D.C.

Quite a long time before the new oceanarium was complete, which they named Sea Life Park, Tap and Karen began to accumulate dolphins. They put the first four spinners in plastic swimming pools placed on the lawn at Hakipu.

One day Tap asked me where he could find a good dolphin trainer. I replied something like: "Look no further, you're married to her." And so Karen, with considerable trepidation, became first a part-time and then a full-time trainer of those wholly unknown animals. She insisted on reserving time for her growing family, which very soon meant assembling a training staff to take some of the load, but also on being rousted out at any hour of day or night herself. If one added up her hours honestly (nobody did), a commitment of about eighty hours per week would be about right. Her total previous training experience was work with some Welsh ponies, and those pheasants.

She not only succeeded with these unknown animals, but "wrote much of the book" on future marine mammal training. I provided her with the basics of "conditioned response training" through inducing a psychologist colleague, Dr. Ronald Turner, to write a training manual for Sea Life Park. This volume compiled many of the insights and tricks that behavioral psychologists had developed in studies of rat and pigeon learning.

Karen dug into that turgid volume and made it her own, and then went beyond with her own methods tailored to the peculiar personalities of dolphins. Once her dolphins passed successfully through the fragile early days in captivity, she began to try Ron's methods on the new spinners. One method that particularly intrigued me because it reflected so strongly on human behavior is what is called a "jackpot reward." For exceptional behavior an animal is simply showered with food fish. You could see the dolphin startle in a sort of "Oh wow, what DID I DO?" way when one of those jackpots hit the water. Then it scurried around picking up three fish at a time. The motivation such a reward produces is no different from the mesmerizing effect created when silver dollars jingle all over a casino floor. The casino men know that the sound is crucial, just as we found that the splash of a dozen food fish galvanized a dolphin.

Such an overwhelming and unpredictable reward can drive both dolphins and people to work at a task beyond rational limits: in the human case to dump one's last silver dollar down the slot, and in the dolphin's to work incredibly hard at tasks they might otherwise avoid, even to the point where they might not get enough to eat.

Now that I look back on those early events, Karen's success verges on magic. Almost no one has succeeded since in acclimating spinner and spotted dolphins to captivity, and she succeeded with both. These dolphins are oceanic species with no experience of tanks, walls, or people. They live a life almost without obstacles. Instead, by a process called echolocation, they sense fish, sharks, and other dolphins. Strings of very loud clicks are sent streaming off into the unseen sea. Only the faint returning echoes, perhaps a million times less intense than the emitted sound tell of food or roaming predators.

But, emphatically, it is not life in a small tank, being tended by land creatures whose presence is mostly hands and fingers thrust through the wavering surface of the water. Thawed fish are clearly very different fare, to such an animal, from the flashing bodies of the little schooling fish, squid, and shrimps they normally catch and eat.

Karen and her assistants had to penetrate that wall of strangeness, aloneness, and fear to indicate that care and trust were to be had. Most of all she had to substitute, somehow, for the complex society that dolphins had left behind. From the dolphins' standpoint it must have been strange that these humans were around only during daytime, which was exactly the time that a normal spinner needed some rest.

My guess is that those little plastic pools may even have helped. They may have brought trainer and animal into an intimacy that was vital to the transition, and that has been lost in larger and supposedly better facilities. Karen and her colleagues succeeded, I think, because they knew they were trying something that had never been done before and were alert to every signal from the dolphins. A look, awkward swimming, a shy movement away from a trainer, all were watched and respected. Most of all, I suspect the frequent contact between Karen's crew and the animals they sought to understand carried wordless messages between them. A gentle caress from Karen was a message in the body language of the dolphin. As we learned later while watching wild spinners, these dolphins seem to regulate much of the fabric of their school-lives by such tactile communication. As much as 30 percent of a spinner dolphin's day may be spent in complicated caressing bouts that have a syntax all of their own.

To capture these dolphins Tap and Karen had somehow located a most sagacious and capable half-French, half-Hawaiian fisherman, Georges Gilbert. Georges bore indelible marks of both cultural heritages. He could be a joyous Hawaiian, bursting into excited and glorious song when a sought-after animal was netted. And he fit easily into all the intricacies of our western cultural heritage. Georges and I quickly became friends, and I accompanied him on a number of his capture ventures. Georges seemed to know everything about the Hawaiian sea, including lore that had never reached any scientist.

He knew, for example, that you could locate dolphin schools by looking into the sky. If you saw a frigate bird soaring there, most likely there were dolphins underneath. If there were two or more frigates, the dolphin school would be bigger. The frigates, you see, waited until the dolphins scared flying fish into the air and then they could swoop down and catch them. For a marine bird the frigate is singularly maladapted in one respect. It cannot land on the sea because its feathers soak up water and it drowns. So these frigates hover and soar until their food fish are airborne before catching them, or they steal them from other birds, taking them away in midair.

Georges escorted me a little way into his culture, and I took him a way into mine. I was, I think, one of his most exotic friends, just as he served that role for me.

Georges named each dolphin as he caught it, giving it an Hawaiian name somehow appropriate for the circumstances of its capture. His first four were *Mele* (song), *Moki* (a boy's name), *Akamai* (smart), and *Haoli* (this dolphin was pale in color— hence the Hawaiian word for Caucasian). Each time he caught a dolphin Georges radioed news of his catch to Tap and Karen, along with the new name, and then he and the dolphin were met at the Kewalo Basin dock for the ride to Hakipu.

Such delicate, graceful animals those first spinners were! "Dainty" is a word that comes to mind: delicate jaws, lustrous eyes, and a spotless, fastidious raiment of pattern. I watched from the sidelines as Karen dealt with them as they came in. It was, I observed, no simple process for the humans, either. The human-dolphin barrier, especially during such a transition as I witnessed, is full of uncertainty and frustration. First Karen and her assistants had to calm the animals, to make them feel willing to take the next tentative steps. She too had to feel her way, uncertain of the boundaries of her skill, and especially of her ability to communicate across the amorphous human-dolphin barrier, whose very shape and extent was unknown. What meant *anything* on either side of such communication?

I think everyone, dolphins and oceanarium staff alike, felt lifted when a young schoolteacher, Dottie Samson, began to assist Karen. She had a wonderful sensibleness about her, and she was true as an arrow. That honesty of purpose, I came to believe, is about as valuable an attribute as a dolphin trainer can have, since dolphins "pick up" on the moods and problems of their handlers with awesome ease. Dolphins in the hands of troubled human trainers are apt to bite, sulk, and in general reflect that personality at the other end of their communication channel. Dottie was full of love for her charges and it flooded to them via her movements, her touch, and her gentle words, and especially through her steadfastness.

Trainers of all kinds of animals use what is called a "bridging stimulus," usually a blast from a whistle, a tug on a halter, or the click from one of those little Halloween crickets, as their basic means of communication. It means something like "yes." Once its meaning is understood, the animal knows instantly that it has done something the trainer wants. Say a dolphin leaps for sheer *joie de vivre* and hears a blast from the whistle at nearly the same time. To put the exchange in human terms, it thinks to itself the wordless equivalent of "Oh oh, I've done something that is worth a fish." It collects its reward and then it leaps again, and sure enough, there's the whistle again, good for another fish.

I expect that the most difficult time for a new captive dolphin is when it is being taught to understand that bridging stimulus and its uses. If such signals aren't given with great precision, the animal can wallow in uncertainty, unsure of the people who provide its care. The quiet voice, the reassuring and gentle caress are about all that can bridge the gap that early in a wild dolphin's introduction to the human world. It seems that these primal things may serve similar uses for the dolphin and for us. Much later, with one of my students, Chris Johnson, we began to think it possible to recognize the emotional freight of many dolphin signals in such human terms. Many of their signals seemed to transliterate quite directly across the vast gap between us. A spinner's peremptory barks were associated with overt boisterous behavior, and their intimate little chuckles with tête-à-têtes between two dolphins, often male and female. A lot of *sotto voce* signals go back and forth between a mother dolphin and her young.

Isn't it remarkable that this should be so? Why should the signals and messages of an open-sea spinner dolphin bear any resemblance to those we use? The separation between our lineages, after all, is enormous, going back nearly to the origins of modern mammals, and it bridges two entire evolutions, one on land and the other at sea. And yet there it is. The stuff of a human caress, or of a baby in its mother's embrace, the pure emotional bond that speaks of care and safety, and that lets both baby and dolphin calf look out upon the wider world from a central place upon which it can depend, and to which it can retreat, have much in common and can be easily read by either partner in the exchange.

Karen invented a wonderful bit of instruction for her trainers called the "trainer's game." She decided to have her trainers train each other so that they could all experience what the dolphin was going through. A "dolphin" was selected among her training staff, let's say Dottie, who waited out of earshot while the others decided what to train her to do. For example, they might decide to ask her to put on someone else's sweater. Then by use of the bridging stimulus alone they would train Dottie. All the uncertainties of the link between trainer and animal emerged in such sessions. The dolphin (Dottie) might get an idea that she was supposed to put a tablecloth over her head and then proceed to give fifteen incorrect answers in a row before she gave up the idea. The trainers called her "stupid," and she wallowed in frustration. This is superstitious behavior and it is something every dolphin trainer and every captive dolphin knows well. The "dolphin," real or human, has decided, regardless of the signals that could lead to the correct answer, what the correct answer is, and only a blast of dynamite will shake the idea out of her head.

The subject has *predicted* what the right answer is.

The training game shows trainers how sloppy signals can be. A nice crisp whistle given within a second of a behavior the trainer wants to "catch" will be easy to understand, but one delayed even a few seconds leaves time for the dolphin to think to itself, "I wonder what she wants? Was it when I wiggled my flipper or when I jumped?"

Every trainer is a little different in eliciting behavior from animals. Karen spent as much time training her trainers as the dolphins. Together, we decided that a way to avoid much of this uncertainty was to devise a little sound box that could play a dozen very different artificial sounds underwater. Each of these signals could be played with a touch of a finger and the signals would always be the same, or so we thought. Karen could simply assign a desired behavior pattern to a given sound and then organize the show around the result.

Perhaps more important, if more than one trainer was involved they would always give the same signal to the dolphins in the tank. The dolphin would never have to make the intuitive leap to understand the signals of different people.

Aside from the problem of trainers with fishy hands wet with salt water poking electrically actuated switches, the box worked wonderfully. Karen soon found that she was instructing all her spinners at once (which by this time were in a giant show pool). With it she was able to induce them to leap into the air in a glorious simultaneous burst, and she was able to induce them to recreate their spins for an audience. Soon she had the air full of frantically spinning dolphins. But the incident I found most fascinating about that little black box occurred when she tried to replace a worn, scratchy sound tape with a new clean one.

Frustration for everyone, dolphins and trainers alike, followed immediately. The clean new tape failed utterly to cue the spinners into their well-learned acts. No dolphin leaped, no dolphin spun. They merely milled around in the pool, sulking, and obviously waiting for proper instructions. Then it dawned on Karen that the dolphins had learned that cueing tape in such exquisite detail, scratches and all, that a new clean tape simply didn't have the signals they had learned to use. Their learning of the cueing tape had progressed right along with the decay of the tape. Who knew what features of those cue sounds, or of the tape itself, they were using to perform their acts?

Later I thought about this anecdote while trying to make sense of the sounds wild spinners produce. We seldom know what these dolphins are listening to, but it could be aspects of their sounds very different from those we expect. If we are going to understand how dolphin signals are used at sea, we may have to dig deep within their structure, where most things happen much faster than we are used to. The dolphins, after all, may hear frequencies ten times as high as we do, and can probably hear individual sounds at a rate about ten times as fast as we can.

This example also indicates that insights into the dolphin's way of seeing and dealing with the world occur often in training, but they frequently do not come from the trained behavior itself. Instead, they are revealed from watching the way the dolphin does things, such as the way it reacts to a new command. In fact, I began to feel that Skinnerian or conditioned response training, *per se,* often suppressed the animal's real capabilities, rather than illuminating them. The trainer who trained precisely according to the rules was not asking the animal to tell us about itself, but instead inducing it to accept a series of commands that sprang from the mind of the trainer. When a dolphin, or any other animal in training, dared to do things its own way, it would be ruthlessly "shaped" by the trainer. To be sure, the task given a dolphin could build up a set of statistics about the way the animal reacted to this or that command, but the richness of the way that animal normally does things is not part of the Skinnerian experience. For a true bridging of the gap between human and dolphin one must consider the capabilities and expectations of both communicants.

Karen, too, felt the antiseptic nature of the basic method she was using, and one day she decided to let her dolphins into the act. She decided to see if Skinnerian technique could be used to elicit an *intuitive leap* from her dolphins through standard training techniques. She decided to ask a dolphin to do "something new" when it came to her training platform. The amazing result was that the dolphin quickly "got the idea" and did what she asked. Her subject in this test was not a spinner dolphin but another oceanic species, the rough-tooth dolphin (*Steno bredanensis*). I'd be surprised if spinners do not perform similar mental leaps in their wild schools.

Karen started this particular adventure by deciding to let the visitors to the park "in on dolphin training." After all, for a visitor it was clearly one of the wonders of Sea Life Park to ponder how one could instruct a whole school of dolphins to leap into the air, spinning simultaneously. This magical aspect of the show was emphasized because the trainer didn't seem to do anything while the dolphins spun. She just stood up there on the trainer's platform while the dolphins were engaged in frantic activity. The visitors couldn't see the finger touch the button marked "spin."

Anyway, one day Karen took the microphone for the morning show and explained to a stadiumful of visitors how training was done. She told them how the trainer watched until an animal did something that could be a useful building block in a public performance—a leap, a tail slap—and then caught it on a whistle, sounded as soon after the event as the trainer could react.

While she was explaining, Malia, a big, bright rough-tooth dolphin, circled in front of Karen, waiting for something to happen. She slapped her tail in impatience. Karen immediately blew her whistle. Malia startled quizzically at this departure from her normal routine. She circled the tank, and then slapped the water again. Another fast whistle and another fish fell before her. Malia slapped again. As Karen described it in her book, *Lads Before the Wind*:

> That was enough for Malia; she got the message and slapped, ate her fish, slapped, ate, slapped repeatedly. In less than three minutes she was motorboating around the tank pounding her tail on the water, and the audience burst into uproarious applause.

With five shows a day, Karen and her crew, and at first Malia, began to run out of new things to do. Soon everything they thought Malia could do had already been caught and reinforced in a previous show. Then Malia solved the dilemma herself by inventing something new that none of them had ever seen before, perhaps even Malia. Karen described it as follows:

> On the last show of the third day we let her out of the holding tank, and she swam around waiting for a cue. When she got no cues, instead of launching herself into a series of repetitions of old behavior she suddenly got up a good head of steam, rolled over onto her back, stuck her tail into the air, and coasted 15 feet with her tail out: "Look Ma, no hands!" It was a ridiculous sight.

Gregory Bateson, the great theoretical biologist who had become my associate director at the Oceanic Institute, learned of the incident and became quite excited about it. He came to tankside and watched as Malia invented another new behavior pattern, this time a beautiful upside-down leap. The reason for Gregory's excitement was that Karen and Malia had produced a beautiful example of what Gregory called "deuterolearning," or second-order learning. Malia, instead of simply learning things by letting the trainer shape her behavior, bit by bit, had performed a mental leap and had told us that a dolphin could operate on the basis of an abstract concept, in this case a *new behavior*. Malia had understood this need for something *new*.

She also showed that she was no automaton learning only by rote, but instead was reasoning right along with the trainer. Probably this meant that such concepts as *future, old, self,* and *other* were not beyond her. It might mean that she and her dolphin schoolmates used symbols to indicate things.

This second-order learning included a whole realm of possibility for dolphins that many humans, to this day, treasure as their own. I have no doubt that they are wrong, but that is precisely what most scientists thought when Karen and Malia worked together. Now, twenty-five years later, it is clear that many, perhaps most, animals such as sea lions, monkeys, social carnivores such as dogs, and even some birds such as the African gray parrot can deal with abstractions like those developed between Karen and Malia.

When you think about it, the best way to explain how Karen and her dolphins interacted, even on simple tasks, was that both parties were stretching hard to understand the concepts of the other. To be sure, both might suffer from other problems that intruded on the discourse, and this could mess up the dialogue. Dolphins are often timid when you ask them to do curious undolphinlike things. The trainer may end up exasperated at the task of trying to play the trainer's game for real. It can be especially hard when the partners in such an exchange try to psych out what the other intends. These imaginings can do endless dirt to a simple training routine. As master trainer Kellar Breland once told me: "If you want me to train an animal fast, give me a chicken. They have nothing else on their minds."

But as Karen found, when the trainer dares to ask what the dolphin thinks about things, the result can open a whole new vista of understanding between human and dolphin, especially now that we understand that the company of reasoning animals is broad. We humans and the dolphins emerge as just two twigs on the well-branched intellectual tree.

The first evolutionary glimmerings of such a reasoning mind must have emerged long ago in animals very remote from us. If this is true, then we, and our remarkable minds, are not alone on earth, and our visions of speciality that have so easily allowed us to grind the natural world under our heels must, in time, fade. As such understanding spreads, perhaps some of our traditional arrogance about the other living things on our planet will go with it. Wouldn't that be splendid!

3

Gregory's Spinners

THE Oceanic Institute, of which I became the director, was a small, racehorsy sort of place, so different from the often plodding academic world from whence I came. When we wanted to do something, we didn't begin with a committee, or go through a phalanx of deans; we simply talked it over, found the resources, and went to work.

Soon, largely because of Tap Pryor's personal interest, we found ourselves a leader in saturation diving techniques, with a six-person underwater habitat (or house, if you prefer) that could be placed on the sea floor as deep as 560 feet down. Divers could live inside and swim in and out of a hatch that opened into the surrounding ocean, and they could stay down for about two weeks and then bring themselves to the surface.

I had an interest in world food problems, and this led us to early leadership in mariculture—the raising of marine organisms for food. At the same time, and simply out of intellectual curiosity, we carried on my work with dolphins. On some of the shallower dives of Tap's habitat, a trained dolphin named Keiki was trained to carry messages and tools back and forth to our divers as they worked on the sea floor. The divers learned to expect the comradely Keiki to poke his head over their shoulders, a waterproof note pad in his mouth, as they manipulated some piece of undersea equipment. They scrawled grease pencil requests on the plastic slate, passed it to Keiki, and he was off like a shot toward the surface. In moments he returned with the requested gear. Since these human divers were deep beneath the surface, and because they had been living down there for such a long time, quick ascents to the surface were impossible for them. Only after a long decompression period could they surface. Otherwise they would inevitably suffer an excruciating death from the bends. The dolphin, however, proved miraculously free of such problems and could dive dozens of times a day to and from the habitat with no problems at all. One set of tests with a dolphin very similar to Keiki, by my colleagues Drs. John Kanwisher and Sam Ridgway, showed that their dolphin could dive to remarkable depths—at least a thousand feet down—so we probably weren't pressing Keiki very hard.

Keiki was one of our elite group of dolphins who worked untethered in the open sea. We ran tests on them to see how fast they could swim, and how well they could dive, and we trained them to come back to our boats and to enter floating pens for the night, where they could sleep protected from sharks.

Parenthetically, they proved to be lots slower swimmers than the popular folklore usually had it—Keiki achieved a top speed of 17.1 knots, and a spotted dolphin reached just over 23 knots. A knot, by the way, is a nautical mile per hour, and a nautical mile is a mile and a fifth; so Keiki reached just about 20 land miles per hour.

Perhaps most unusual of all, we were the only institution that I know of with a working philosopher as one of its leaders, Gregory Bateson, our associate director. We asked him to reflect on our broad directions as an institution. Beyond that intermittent duty, we suggested that he simply follow his own intellectual bent. That included, as it turned out, the first behavioral observations on a captive spinner dolphin school.

Gregory came from a famous and iconoclastic family of Cambridge University intellectuals. His father, William Bateson, had been a formidable figure in the early and often tempestuous debates over the theory of evolution.

By the time Gregory joined us he was already an important and sometimes controversial figure in the theory of science. His forte was an esoteric discipline called epistemology, which consists of looking for the larger patterns that encompass the small events most of us study. To give an example of how he worked, for years physicians had tried to understand schizophrenia, searching for causative agents such as chemicals, nervous dysfunctions, and the like. Gregory tried to understand the milieu within which this disease occurred and was able to show that one kind of schizophrenia is a communication disorder, implicit within the structure of certain families. These families quite literally choose who is to be the "sick" member, and then create a communication milieu within which the malady appears. This search had a part to play in bringing Gregory to us, because he had sought some of his answers in understanding the communication systems of animals, dolphins among them. He thought that by understanding how animals communicated he might illuminate some of our own pathologies. So Gregory spent much of his time ruminating up in the corridors of his mind, and only occasionally, like a falcon, would he drop down into our world of day-to-day phenomena.

Gregory came to us at the age of sixty-six, and much of his time with us was spent working on a National Institutes of Health Career Development Award. These prestigious grants are usually given to promising young scholars who can benefit by taking time away from their normal duties to develop new lines of inquiry.

"Gregory," we asked, "when is your career going to be developed?" But we shouldn't have been so impatient. In his seventies, and substantially from work he did at the Oceanic Institute, he went on to apply his broad theoretical ideas to the problems of world ecology. He perceived that at their essence these matters were bounded by the same systemic rules as the processes of communication he had studied for so many years. Both were encased in reaction systems made of several major parts, and such systems, wherever they occurred in nature, worked in much the same way. "The system, and its rules, is the first thing to understand because it guides much of what we do, along with the fate of the world," he taught us.

While with us he produced his seminal volume *Steps to an Ecology of Mind,* which led to his being a major theorist in the burgeoning ecological movement, and later becoming a Regent of the University of California, and to the production of his final major work, *Man and Nature: A Necessary Synthesis.*

The way we used Gregory's talents went something like this. One day I walked down the beach to his house and bummed lunch from him.

"Gregory," I asked, "should we be trying to develop world food resources? Isn't the underlying cause of world hunger overpopulation? Won't we simply make things worse in the long run?"

Gregory swung around, raised his sharp little eyes, moved his lips a little in rumination, and replied in his Cambridge accent, "I'll give it some thought."

A couple of weeks later Gregory asked Tap and me down to lunch. Sitting around his giant old walnut table piled with books, we talked the matter over, and after that the discussion went on for months in this or that odd time or place. We finally concluded that the difficult equation we faced in attempting to produce more and better food resources was partly to buy time for hungry people, and at worst we might in fact be feeding into a system that fed the population problem.

In the end we decided to go ahead learning how to raise our mullet and milkfish, but we did so with the realization that beyond this "simple" scientific fix lay other more difficult social problems that could negate all we were trying to do. I came to think that every decent research organization needed a philosopher to help guide it.

I first met Gregory at a meeting of marine mammalogists held in Washington, D.C., back in 1963. He was in tow behind Dr. John Lilly, who was just beginning to cause a stir with his pronouncements about a dolphin language. Gregory had ventured down to Lilly's lab in the Virgin Islands to see for himself, and, like me, came away doubting that dolphins have anything like a human language. A complicated animal communication system, yes, but for an abstract syntactic language like ours, no compelling evidence seemed, or seems, to exist.

Gregory was led to the question of dolphin "language" through his own long history in communication studies. He had at one time or another worked with octopi, otters, and wolves. He and his then wife, the great anthropologist Margaret Mead, had used a movie camera to record and unravel the wordless gestural signals of the Balinese people in what was probably the first major study of "paralinguistic communication" in humans. They found that such gestures are a language all their own that may or may not reinforce the vocal communication going on at the same time. The counterpoint between the two means of communication formed a third "metalanguage," which often indicated the kind of social politesse, politics, or even outright cheating within which the two systems were embedded. That kind of communication system is now well known in higher mammals, and may be important in dolphins.

He and Margaret had met out in the jungle of New Guinea, far up the Sepik River where Gregory was working with a group of headhunters called the *Iatmul*. The ceremonies of these people, he showed, were regulatory and communicatory events of an evolving society. After his work, anthropologists could no longer consider such rituals as static items to be recorded and filed in some musty archive; instead they must be considered as alive and changing communicatory events that helped regulate and sustain the society itself.

Gregory was a great shambling man, perhaps six feet six inches tall, and utterly unconcerned about the clothes that draped his body. His whole world was one of disciplined thought, fueled by conversation, and it had little indeed to do with social pretense. Periodically his wife Lois (his second wife, after the divorce from Margaret Mead) decided Gregory needed new items of clothing and she would bring them home to him. I remember that for one period Gregory sported tennis shoes with bright yellow daisies on them, though I never knew if they were Lois's contribution.

For a major speech, such as the one on dolphin communication where I first met him, he would haul out a great nondescript tie, bend it around under the collar of his sports shirt, and off he would go, pants hitched up and bony ankles bathed by air, to rivet the attention of the audience with the penetration of his thought.

On that occasion his opening words were to this effect:

I stand before you and I have not yet worked with a dolphin. But I will tell you something of what I expect to find, and how I plan to proceed.

The major purpose for many of us here may not be the transmission of science so much as it is to impress each other with our importance. We, like the dolphins I expect, communicate heavily in messages about social context: metamessages. Even though we talk the language of science here, our most important messages may have to do with our relationships to one another, and I suggest that it is like that with the dolphins too.

Soon after his arrival Gregory began to study the spinner dolphin school at Sea Life Park. He set up shop in the lower deck of the ⅝ths scale model of the whaling vessel *Essex* that "floated" (she was set on a cement base) in the midst of the big concrete lagoon we called Whaler's Cove, where the spinners lived. There, Gregory and his assistants could observe from underwater windows and listen to the spinners, learning to know them all at a glance.

One problem Gregory and his team encountered right off was that while we humans can localize the sources of sound in air with some precision, underwater that ability is all but lost. When Gregory's team listened to the dolphins, they could not separate one phonating animal from another. They badly needed to solve this problem to sort out the various sounds that emanated from the several dolphins.

In air we humans rely heavily on the distance between our ears to sort out the direction from which sounds come. The tiny time difference between a sound reaching one ear and then the other provides a major directional cue. But sound travels much faster in water than air, about 4.7 times, in fact. So underwater our heads are effectively too small for our normal directional hearing to work: by that same 4.7 times.

Working with an imaginative acoustician named Wayne Batteau, Bateson set about implementing a simple solution. They would construct a set of human ears 4.7 times human size, submerge them, and listen through them by means of two small hydrophones, one in each artificial ear canal. The ears were mounted on a bar whose length also compensated for the sound-speed difference. The sounds thus received were to be picked up by a pair of stereo earphones worn by the listener.

The result was not the instant success in underwater binaural listening that everyone had hoped for. It turned out that each of us learns to use his or her own ears as we grow up. Given a new set of ears, and in this case they were modeled from Batteau's ears, the human listener had to start all over and learn to use the foreign set. All those folds and shapes we see on people's ears do have functions, and they make our listening system highly individual.

Sad to say, not many of Gregory's observers were patient enough to learn to listen accurately through Batteau's ears, but I think if they had persisted the method might have provided a real revolution in understanding vocal communication under water. Alas, the ears, cast beautifully in stainless steel, are now lost. So if I ever want to carry on that promising experiment I will have to make a new pair.

The observation team, led by Gregory's assistant, Barrie Gilbert, then began to carry out what animal behaviorists call "focal animal analysis." How, they asked, did a given dolphin apportion its time, and with whom did it associate? Quickly, this way of watching sorted out the confusion of a tankful of animals. It became clear that each animal did certain things at quite regular times of day. There were times for rest and times for socializing. Rest for spinners, surprisingly enough, was a late morning–early afternoon pattern, and it was always disrupted by show schedules. Even so, the dolphins persisted in their old ways, breaking up their calm time for a show and then returning to sleepmates and their slow-paced swimming, which is what their sleep consisted of.

Gregory and Barrie began to look more closely at both rest and play. They found that rest was perhaps the central organizing activity of a dolphin's day. It was a very clear and regular pattern. Certain animals regularly slept together in sedately swimming pairs. Perhaps "sleep" is too strong a word for what the dolphins did. They always continued swimming, and it seemed that at least one eye was always open. While active animals caressed each other much of the time, resting ones never did, but instead swam together, each just beyond the reach of their partner's extended pectoral fin.

Gregory could not see whether they closed both eyes simultaneously. But in John Lilly's laboratory he had watched a resting bottlenose dolphin held in a very small tank. Two observers sat, on opposite sides, watching opposite eyes. Nearly always, only one dolphin eye was closed at a time.

How that kind of "sleep" might work poses intriguing questions. How does the dolphin's brain function during such sleep? Not much is known for sure, but brain wave measurements support the idea that these aquatic animals may sleep one hemisphere at a time. What a handy way to be if your world is populated by sharks, night and day! One half the brain can mind the store while the other rests!

Focal animal studies began to unravel the little social groups and arrangements among the dolphins that lived in Whaler's Cove. A society had in fact been established there, and it had many intricacies. This had happened even though the school was not a pure spinner group, but included two spotted dolphins. There proved to be a reasonably clear hierarchy amongst all the dolphins in Whaler's Cove, and the big spotted dolphin, Kahele, was top dolphin. Three of the spinners, the two males, Haoli and Limu, and one restless female named Mamao, typically swam together, but as a group they held lower rank than the lead dolphin.

The hierarchy was sustained by a descending order of threats between the dolphins, and in who caressed whom. Kahele could threaten any other dolphin and remain unchallenged, but others lower down in the order had fewer to pick on. A threat was always an abrupt gesture, usually mild, often involving an open mouth or a slap at another animal with beak or flukes.

Gregory found that caressing took several forms in spinners. They rubbed each other in a variety of artful ways and no part of the body was excepted. One kind of caressing was what Gregory called "pat-a-cake." In this pattern two dolphins "whet" their pectoral fins over both sides of those of the other dolphin, much like a butcher sharpening a knife on a steel. This behavior is often carried out by two animals swimming at considerable speed, belly-to-belly, making it into a remarkable athletic feat.

The slowest caressing pattern was a curious interaction called "beak-genital propulsion," in which one animal pushed another slowly around the tank with its beak firmly implanted in the genital slit of the other. This, like other caressing patterns, was engaged in by both sexes, both as recipient and as the dolphin providing the propulsion.

Gregory was never one to experiment. He wanted nature just the way it was supposed to be when he made his observations. But, as I have said, he worked in a big exhibit tank, which confined most of his work to the early morning hours before the visitors arrived. Once the stands filled with people, Gregory and Barrie retreated to the office for data analysis.

This avoided most conflicts but there was one notable exception. Karen and her trainers had decided to prepare a special Christmas dolphin show. This involved moving Haoli, who was a member of the secondary triad of dolphins in the school. The result was dramatic and instructive. The tight little society that Gregory was documenting simply fell apart.

The sleep partnerships were not changed by the removal, but when the dolphins awoke everything became chaotic. The lead dolphin, Kahele, hung listlessly against the tank wall. He would not play with the others and scarcely took part in the show routines. The other animals were almost as listless and seemed disoriented. The removal of Haoli seemed to have reshuffled the animals so that there were no extra spinner or spotted dolphins left over. Kahele, though dominant under normal circumstances, found no way into the new dolphin society below him. He was shut out, and, with no playmates available, he was miserable. Karen noted this disruption and quickly returned Haoli to the tank. The society righted itself.

I thought back on these intricate relationships when later I watched wild spinner and spotted dolphins trapped in tuna

nets at sea. There, too, spotters seemed dominant over the furtive spinners, which circled the edges of their schools, and
there too events in the school were ordered by aggressive animals that shaped the way the school was formed, not so much
by building a hierarchy that I could detect as by herding sub-
ordinate animals into particular places where the greatest safety
could be found. The walls of Whaler's Cove, I thought, may
have redirected such social forces into a fairly rigid hierarchical
system, while in the open sea the same forces seemed to regulate the form the school took and the way dolphins were arranged
within its fluid outlines. The same thing pertains to chicken
yards. Rigid hierarchies exist inside the confining fence, but in
wild flocks chickens of different ages and sexes tend to segre-
gate in space with only moderate aggressive interaction.

What stimulated me most about Gregory was his wonderful
capacity for looking past the obvious to a larger conclusion.
On one occasion we watched two dolphins in a chase.

"Who is chasing whom, Ken?" Gregory asked.

In the stereotyped way of most of us I had assumed without
looking further there was a chaser and a chasee, and that was
that. But under Gregory's prodding I looked deeper, and it was
soon obvious, by the dolphin's hint and gesture, that the lead
animal was inducing the second animal to chase. There was
flirting going on.

Gregory then launched into a discussion of social processes
as dynamic equilibria. He was always like that. He dwelt mostly
up in what he called "a world of the larger gestalten," or planes
of synthesis above the obvious. Up there he struggled with
relationship, always from the systems viewpoint. Natural processes, physical and social, are typically interacting systems,
and such systems have predictable behavior that most biologists ignore.

I came to see that this business of looking for "larger frames"
enclosed everything from the operations of the cosmos down

to very modest phenomena of dolphin schools. The viewpoint often lets one look past the obvious, as Gregory so routinely did. The rules seem quite uniformly the same and they are those that govern *systems* everywhere. To give a very modest dolphin example, such a systems viewpoint perhaps helps to illuminate the curious circumstances that surround dolphin births in captivity. Many trainers know that the chances of a successful captive birth depend not so much on questions of the health of the baby as upon the social arrangements that have been established between poolmates before the birth. This is not to downplay the fact that birth is a dangerous time for both mother and newborn, especially out in the ocean where it must often occur with predators nearby.

At any rate, if captive dolphins including a pregnant female are kept together, it is good practice to allow the pregnant animal to choose a consort. In bottlenose dolphins these have been called "auntie dolphins," and that's exactly the sort of function they perform, assisting with the birth and then baby-sitting for the mother.

Adult male dolphins in captivity are usually removed before a birth occurs. If left with the mother during labor the male will typically harass the mother and baby unmercifully, nipping the newborn and raking it, and often copulating repeatedly with it as it slowly grows weaker and not infrequently dies. Sometimes, however, the male may press the weakened newborn to the surface for vital breaths of air, or swim solicitously with it, helping it avoid tank corners.

I puzzled long over this conflicting set of patterns, unwilling to accept them at face value. The constraints of captivity, I thought, had somehow warped natural arrangements. But what were those natural arrangements?

Some years later, on the shores of Kealakekua Bay, I sat musing about dolphin school structure with one of my students, Christine Johnson. We had been watching wild spinners from our underwater viewing vehicle and had frequently seen groups of juveniles and young within what I call the *school envelope,* or the outer boundary of a moving group of dolphins. Some were very young animals, obviously only a few days past birth, and they traveled in a group with other young dolphins that were themselves very small, with mothers nowhere in evidence.

Birth, nurture, adolescence, adulthood, and death all must occur somewhere in the school, we concluded. All that it is to be male and female was also there inside the school envelope. We knew so little about the roles each sex played in that traveling society!

Might not the males, when they bit and harassed both mother and young, have been attempting to order the school at what they perceived to be a time of danger? Might they have been attempting to herd these vulnerable school members to a protected place in the school envelope? Might not what I took to be mating behavior be something like the adult male urging the young dolphin to respond to his commands? Because dolphin erections are muscular events that can happen even in the off season—sex being a seasonal thing—could erections have a social rather than a sexual meaning in these circumstances?

The adult male squads or *coalitions* I have described earlier might also have been attempting to order the school into a formation of maximum safety. To the male dolphin the rule might be simple. "If I am here you should not occupy the same space. I will be where the danger is."

Birth possibly takes place somewhere in the protected center of a school, though we haven't yet seen that event. Perhaps those omnipresent male cadres make it unlikely that we ever will, except in the dim blue distance.

Gregory steered me around to such constructs, and he often used the Socratic dialogue as a means of spurring thought. I remember the gist of one such episode. Gregory and I were aboard a vessel anchored in Kealakekua Bay, watching a milling school of dolphins. The conversation went something like this:

Ken: Gregory, do you think dolphins have territories?

Gregory: Well, what do you mean by "territory"?

K: Oh, I suppose they might defend the boundaries of an area.

G: Weeel, would you be happy with a MOVING territory?

K: I suppose I would have to be. Do you mean that the school might serve the same functions as a territory does for terrestrial animals?

G: What functions do you suppose a territory serves for terrestrial animals? Is it necessary for the boundaries to be fixed, or is that something we made up? Is it sufficient to stake a claim to a piece of real estate? Why would any animal want to do that?

K: I suppose an important thing would be to claim a supply of resources or mating partners. But if the boundaries weren't fixed how could we call it territoriality?

G: Why bother if the term obscures the real function? The real issue, I suspect, is that an animal needs to define the circumstances in which the conditions of its life can be met. For some animals on land, geographic coordinates are probably crucial. An animal growing up there can learn every feature, every point of escape, every source of food, and where its associates are likely to be found. But at sea the same purposes need to be served while moving forty miles a day. So where's your term "territoriality"? Territoriality may be another one of our explanatory principles. We humans not infrequently require such things to quell the pangs of our ignorance. Remember Alice's dormouse was made sleepy because of a "dormitative principle." This explains nothing but provides a convenient means to hide the problem, out of sight where it couldn't bother anyone.

And so our dialogues went: the old scholar and the younger field naturalist. They were precious times.

While Gregory was off down the beach writing, my mind turned increasingly toward the sea. If we are ever to learn about dolphin lives, I thought, we need to compare what captive animals tell us with what we learn from dolphin societies at sea.

The two viewpoints taken together would let us compare, and, as a result, see new things; we could observe and experiment in fine detail in an oceanarium tank, but we could only guess what diving to six hundred feet was like.

At sea the world is largely without walls. Only the surface is a constant barrier. In captivity the tightly contained society of friends is incomplete, and it often includes odd bedfellows, such as Gregory's spotted and spinner dolphins. In exhibits, show routines can interdict normal daily cycles. Just when it is the proper time for a dolphin to rest, the shows start, and they don't usually stop until it's time for normal dolphin activity to resume.

It is perhaps remarkable that so much captive behavior seems understandable. Many features of dolphin life do indeed seem unchanged in captivity. These are the smaller structural units of behavior. Captive dolphins probably swim, breathe, caress, threaten, mate, and give birth in ways that are not substantially different from those same patterns at sea. But wherever the dimension of space, of speed, of depth, or the larger arrangements of sociality intervene, the picture tends to become distorted.

I realized that observations would not be perfect at sea either. An observer cannot hide and his mere presence would surely cause a reaction in the wild school. The opportunity to observe a captive society for however many hours one wishes would be traded for vignettes lasting only seconds. Instead of a few identifiable captive individuals, there would be dozens of dolphins, mostly of unknown identity. The events of communication would lack individuality in the general bedlam of a traveling dolphin school.

So, what I sought was comparison, proportion, and to outline some of Gregory's "larger gestalten." After some halting preliminary attempts off the island of Oahu, I heard about the dolphins of Kealakekua Bay.

Kealakekua

OUR boat took us from Kailua-Kona on the lee coast of the Island of Hawaii and then skirted southward past a fringe of tourist hotels that soon gave way to dark and untenanted lava headlands and little jade bays. A fringe of coconut palms bent over the water and inland merged into a jungle of thorny trees sweeping gray-green up onto the immense shield of Hualalai volcano. A dense cloud deck obscured the mountain's crest. Now and then these clouds tatter and break, revealing a high forested ridge, knobbed with cinder cones.

To the southeast was the even more massive shield of Mauna Loa volcano, rising unseen thousands of feet into the clouds. From its crest at 13,677 feet above the water's edge to its base in the abyssal ocean more than 12,000 feet below the surface, this is the largest single mountain on earth. It is so heavy that it actually depresses the sea bed that holds it, so that water around Hawaii is deeper than the average open ocean.

Along the Kona Coast, Mauna Loa's slope, from crest to sea floor, is a single rough plane determined by innumerable lava rivers.

I followed our progress on a nautical chart. The Hawaiian

place names are a mouthful, all k's and w's, a's and u's. The secret is to pronounce every syllable. Then they flow easily enough. Kealakekua Bay, Keawekaheka Point, Keikiwaha Point: *Ke ala ke akua Bay. Ke a weka heka Point, Ke iki waha Point.*

We doubled the navigational light at Keikiwaha and slipped into Kealakekua Bay, an unexpected and majestic cove, brooding and powerful. It is an almost perfect half-circle bay about two miles across the mouth, located exactly at the confluence of the lava shields of Hualalai and Mauna Loa. Its cusps are defined by lava fans, and its back by a massive five-hundred-foot wall of dark lava, punctured here and there with the black mouths of lava tubes where molten lava once spurted into a steaming sea.

A small school of delicate spinners flirted with our bow and then turned inward toward the cliff as we sought a mooring in the north limb of the bay. They were here just as had been promised! I decided to watch them for a while as we rocked quietly on the buoy, and later I would row slowly toward them to see how friendly they were.

The overpowering ambiance of the bay settled over me. Not a hundred yards away was the intertidal lava shelf where, almost two hundred years before, Captain James Cook, the great circumnavigator of the Pacific and discoverer of the Hawaiian islands, had been killed. A mob of angry Hawaiians had discovered that he was just a man, and not their long-absent god Lono, and so he died. A monument to him of cannons and plaques from British men-o'-war stood unobtrusively on the shore, amidst the tangled thorny *kiawe* trees, right abeam of us. Behind, almost obscured in the brush, was the ancient abandoned village of Kaawaloa. Only housewalls, fallen buildings, and a brackish spring remained, sequestered back in the shady depths.

The feeling of history, of Cook, of the Hawaiians before him, and then, earlier still, of that solitary mountain building its massive pile in an untenanted sea, pervades that bay. Our few years with the spinners were just a tick of the clock in a sacred place. The Hawaiians knew the feeling too, for they named the bay *Ke ala ke akua* which means "the pathway to the gods."

Just south of the cliff is a cluster of houses called Napoopoo, and, at its north end, a *heiau*, or stone temple. That huge rectangular pile of lava boulders, carefully laid and mortised together, housed the priests of Lono when Cook first came. One can still see the traces of their thatched house foundations on the flat lava courtyard, where they carried out their ceremonies long before Cook led the vanguard of white men to the islands.

The spinners that flirted with us spanned the entire time. I do not doubt that their original landfall came when the islands originally rose from the sea.

Kealakekua's waters are a reserve now, but many boats continue to use the bay, where they swing at moorings set in the sandy parts of the bay bottom. These boats encroach upon the spinner "sleeping grounds," and if their number increases, if the dolphins' needs aren't considered, the animals will leave, and their span of tenancy, which began before that of any man, will end as they quietly slip away into the offshore sea.

Though the water was glassy when we arrived, when the trade winds shift to the southwest the bay can be lashed with winds as fierce as those anywhere. This shifting face is attested to by the band of flotsam washed high on the lava shelf. At Keikiwaha we found a little sampan nestled among the young palms that fringed the water, crazily tilted and broken, a memento of one of those past storms. I wondered what the spinners did when the storms came.

A huge lee is produced by the bulk of the two coalesced volcanoes, Mauna Loa and Hualalai. This half-circle of calm extends for a hundred miles along the shore and for twenty miles out to sea before gradually giving way to swells and then to the almost-eternal white-capped seas of the open trade-wind ocean. The ocean is very deep close to Hawaii's shore because the island slope itself is so steep. A hidden submarine canyon, formed between the two coalescing lava fans, snakes right into Kealakekua Bay; its inshore tip lay just off our bow.

The volcanoes of Mauna Loa and Hualalai are still building over what the geophysicists call a *hot spot,* a place where molten magma wells up through the ocean crust. Since the floor itself is creeping slowly from southeast to northwest, it has "wiped across" this hot spot, creating a curving chain of volcanic mountains—the Hawaiian Islands. By following the island chain on a map one can trace this movement of the earth's moving surface along a fifteen-hundred-mile path from the oldest island, tiny Kure Atoll (sometimes called Ocean Island), formed about 25 million years ago far to the west-northwest, to the Island of Hawaii at the southeastern tip of the chain that is still building.

For me this meant that the giant mountain over whose shore I floated stood in the midst of the abyssal sea, deep water all around: a lava outpost in the vast open Pacific, and we were amidst the true home of the spinner dolphin. I was, in fact, moored on a pinnacle from which I could hope to penetrate the society of a species that for the most part tended to shun land.

What did this island and this cove mean to them? The answer, I now suspect, lies deep in their ancient invasion of the open sea itself, because that journey was a difficult evolutionary venture, and because the islands provide a bit of surcease: land to return to, a place to sleep near, away for a time from the struggle in the glassy three-dimensional sea where there is no place to hide.

We now know that the spinners are far from alone in that ocean wilderness. A whole fauna of almost unknown large mammal associates is out there with them, arranged in a faintly understood community. I wondered what defined that remote mammal community and how spinner dolphins fit into it.

In time we saw some of these seldom-seen oceanic cohorts at Kealakekua. Perhaps the strangest was the dense-beaked whale (*Mesoplodon densirostris*), a rare fifteen-foot-long mammal, the mouths of whose males hold the only two huge, flattened teeth the species has. Very few cetologists have ever seen them alive. One day, a lazy group of seven, including a scarred old male, appeared at the mouth of our bay and we were able to spend a half hour with them. We've touched but we've hardly met, I thought.

Others of that mysterious fauna swam near Kealakekua, too. Most stayed a couple of miles offshore where the lines of flotsam had been drawn out into wavering slick trails. There several species patrolled back and forth, feeding on fish that hide under the flotsam. There we met our first schools of pygmy killer whales, another associate of the spinner.

Before we first saw them, this species had been considered one of the rarest mammals on earth, known from only three museum skulls. Once seen, the animal proved to be a chunky nine- to twelve-foot whale with a tall black dorsal fin, smaller but not unlike that of the larger killer whale, and we saw them several times after that, and even caught one for the Oahu oceanarium. These ominous little predators possess a formidible mouthful of stout conical interlocking teeth, and they apparently pursue and kill other oceangoing mammals, probably including spinner dolphins.

TOM DOHL and I cast off our little skiff and rowed as quietly as we could toward the spinner school, two hundred yards away. The school rose almost surreptitiously, the dolphins surfacing nearly together. We inched within forty feet or so, and could see them alter course a few degrees away from us. We lay back on the oars, bobbing at the surface, holding our feet still so that no sound from us would enter the water through the hull. The dolphins turned and passed us a dozen feet from our gunwales, dove, and flickered down out of sight in the clear depths. I knew then that we had found a place where the lives of these wild dolphins could unfold for us, and my mind turned to the myriad practical problems such an attempt inevitably involves.

The cliff looked like an ideal place for an observation post from which we could watch the dolphins by telescope. The bay itself seemed perfect for my new underwater viewing vehicle, which a wonderful welder-craftsman named Jimmie Okudara and I had built. This craft, a boy's dream come to life, looked for all the world like a little outboard-driven subma-

The *Semisubmersible Seasick Machine* at anchor off Santa Catalina Island, California. *Bob Given*

rine, only we fervently hoped it would stay on the surface. The observer rode sitting in a comfortable chair down at the bottom of a vertical aluminum cylinder banded all around with big windows. This fixed cylinder pierced the center of the boat and was entered through a watertight hatch at the top.

The craft had its flaws, though. Its engine, set in a well down in the aft part of the hull, made an awful racket when we revved it up. Our concern was not so much for our hearing but that the dolphins might be driven away. In addition, water ballast inside the hull made loud sloshing noises at the slightest motion. Eventually we had to displace it with great basketsful of those styrofoam packing kernels. Even worse, was the curious motion of the vehicle. An observer locked securely in the viewing chamber by a watertight door was subject to seasickness in any but the calmest seas. The air became tinny; claustrophobia crept closer and closer, then pounced. The vessels' detractors soon dubbed her "the Semisubmersible Seasick Machine," or SSSM.

In spite of such calumny I loved her. If I saw something of interest, the craft's faults disappeared and my attention focused on the sea outside, where almost no cetologist had watched.

I wanted to see my newfound dolphins from the cliff, from the water, at sea, nearshore, during the day and night, and from the air. Then, just as a painter blocks in a painting, spinner dolphins might come into focus in something like the totality of their lives.

By flying over dolphin schools, we could brush the broadest patterns of spinner life: how many animals there were, where their various schools lived, how these groups moved with the season and with the weather. I was fortunate that my colleague on these first efforts was Tom Dohl. He was an experienced pilot, eager for any excuse to get into the air.

Before long we made an arrangement with Royal Hawaiian Air Lines, the little commuter service that belonged to Tap Pryor's growing empire. Now and then we took a couple of their pilots away from the routine flights and put them to work flying the perimeter of Hawaii, zooming down for counts on schools, and running offshore legs to see how far out to sea our spinners ventured.

Most of our study had to be carried out on the sea surface, but much farther out than the Semisubmersible Seasick Machine could go. I wanted to follow dolphins at night and offshore, so I enlisted two of the institute's vessels, the stout motor vessel *Hiki No* ("Can do" in Hawaiian) and the big stately barkentine *Westward*.

And then there was the cliffside seat to establish. I'm still not sure who owns the cliffs at Kealakekua. I think it is best just to say "the Hawaiians do," but the land atop them belonged to Sherwood Greenwell, the scion of an old Hawaiian family. He couldn't have been more accommodating to us. We jolted down the lava-strewn trails that pass for roads on that steep mountain in one or another of his battered old Land Rovers. Some of these trails were so rough it was hard for ordinary mortals to detect a road at all. But we found our way to the cliff edge, hacked trails through the dense *hale koa* bushes to the brink, and then, far below, we could see undisturbed spinner schools moving slowly back and forth over the coral sand bottom, five hundred feet below.

Line-of-sight, though, the dolphins were twice that distance away. Those dolphins looked *small*! But over the years I've learned another field naturalist's rule: take what you can get, try to find a better place but always remember to use what you have because the chance may never come again, or may never be better. So we set up camp, established a watch, and began the long process of accumulating information about the comings and goings of dolphins in Kealakekua Bay.

At the first hint of dawn in our clifftop camp we rose in the balmy Hawaiian air to look out across the gray metallic sea. Sometimes, far beyond the bay mouth, we could see a dolphin school making its way toward shore. Only the leaps and splashes gave the animals away, but with a telescope trained on them one could see a broad rank of black dolphin shapes plunging along. As the dolphins neared Palemano Point, at the south cusp of the bay, they slowed, and once within the bay proper they began to move more and more quietly. In some as-yet-unknown sense they seemed to be home.

After long hours of watching, mostly by my two field assistants, Tom Dohl and Dave Bryant, we began to understand something of the daily patterns. Out to sea the dolphins moved rapidly, each cluster (or *subgroup,* as we termed them) within the larger school surfacing somewhat independently of the others. As they entered the bay the subgroups became more synchronized, and finally, when deep in the bay, the school rose slowly as one, in a single tight group. By the time they swam below our clifftop seat they moved almost furtively, tightly bunched, and they spent nearly all their time below the surface.

This latter condition we came to think of as *rest.* It occurred in mid- to late morning, and always over a patch of white coral sand lying close inshore near the black cliff of Kealakekua.

Rest lasted from four to five hours, and ended with remarkable abruptness. On a few occasions when we rowed a skiff near these resting schools, we were able to watch the arousal from "sleep" close-up. Typically, after hours when almost no animals disturbed the surface, one or two would raise their snouts and slap them in a desultory way against the water. A few seconds later another animal might rear up in what we came to call a *backslap.* The inverted dolphin, thrusting its body out of the water above its pectoral fins, flexed backward sharply as it subsided, smacking the water with its back.

Almost at the same time another animal might leap and spin, this time with tense energy. One could almost feel the electricity of this event, especially because it was so sudden and so powerful a behavior after hours of subdued swimming. Those initial spins seemed to send a charge to the animals underwater. In moments others blasted through the surface.

"They're waking up!" I said, breaking our own silence.

Spinner dolphins in rest formation at Kealakekua Bay. The group in the foreground is a male coalition that has interposed itself between us and the rest of the school. You can tell they are males by the swelling on the underside of their tails, which is the same structure they thrust forward when they imitate sharks. *Bernd Würsig*

Within ten minutes the air would be full of dolphins and the cohesive and sedate rest pattern began to break up into individual clots of animals.

All this was reminiscent of the rest and awakening that Gregory Bateson had defined in Whaler's Cove, back at Sea Life Park. He, we recalled, had found that when his animals entered a rest period they abandoned their active caressing to swim alongside special rest partners.

To see if these things happened at sea we waited in the SSSM until a school had settled into quiescence and then cruised slowly toward them. Soon, from the viewing chamber, I began to see the dark shapes of dolphins against the bluish-white sand, and then they came into sharp focus. Each one moved sedately along, about a body diameter from the adjacent animal, often skimming close to the bottom. Then they gathered into a column of rising animals pointing upward toward the silvery surface. They broke the surface seriatim, took quiet breaths, and dove again. In time we found that the habit of swimming spread out, close over the bottom sand, was so regular an occurrence that we gave it a name: the carpet formation. Indeed, the dolphins moved as a sedate flying carpet.

All we heard from those carpet formations were a few faint clicks. We concluded that during rest all but a few dolphins stopped making sounds; visual station-keeping became a substitute for acoustic contact. Such a visual school could only work, I thought, if the water was clear, and even in the near-shore tropical seas of Hawaii that meant a hundred feet or less. I came to believe they had to move in tight to see each other. This explained the tight cohesive formations among the dolphins. It also seemed to explain why, when the water was roily in Kealakekua Bay, we would see schools enter in the bay mouth in the morning, mill for a while, and then leave without descending into true rest.

Why should resting dolphins go silent? Perhaps, after making long trains of intense echolocation clicks for many hours, the dolphin's sound-generation system may require rest and repair. After all, individual clicks can be so intense one wonders how the tissues that make and propagate them stand up. Then, too, noisy dolphins that remain for hours in a single place may be easy for predators such as false and pygmy killer whales to locate. The definitive answer awaits a new and sharper observation.

Unraveling "true" things about these dolphins has frequently taken years. For example, at first we assumed that Kealakekua Bay had its complement of dolphins and that they came each day to the cove. This view was shattered when the logbook of sightings of identified dolphins showed us that there was no "Kealakekua Bay school." One day there would be a school of twenty dolphins in the bay, including a dozen identified ones, and the next day only two of these known animals were with a much larger school. On the third day there might be no known dolphins at all.

To understand this sort of pattern and many other aspects of spinner dolphin life, I knew we had to develop a catalogue of identified individuals so we could follow movements and associations for as long as our work lasted. There were plenty of identifying features on the animals. Some had deformed fins, and others bore evidence of encounters with large sharks. The most common mark, though, was a two-inch circular scar left by an insidious inhabitant of the night plankton, the *cookie-cutter shark*.

I drew a spinner dolphin outline and had it printed up on loose-leaf field journal pages. I asked each of the team to sketch in the scars and marks they saw. These were to be collected throughout our work, along with our voluminous daily field notes. In time, I expected to unravel a series of otherwise hidden stories about the spinners.

The experiment worked to some extent. I have an artist's eye, so my sketches, if I had drawn them directly from a dolphin swimming in front of me, could often be used to identify animals over time. But Tom and Dave, no artists, produced stick figures that left us wallowing in uncertainty.

The dolphins always headed for the same place in the bay— that patch of white coral sand right at the base of the cliff, and right next to the boat moorings. And there, day after day, they swam quietly in the curious pattern of dolphin rest.

As our observations progressed I wanted to roam more widely along Hawaii's shores, to see if the dolphins at other coves did the same things we had observed at Kealakekua, or if we could find instructive differences. So, boarding the motor vessel *Hiki No,* the three of us set out northward toward the fabled fishing ground off Keahole Point. There we found, day after day, the biggest school of spinners on the island, often composed of more than 250 animals. There was no protected cove like Kealakekua at Keahole, but the dolphins seem to "make do" with some little coves and a shallow sandbar that runs alongshore north of the point. The swells frequently come marching in there and we could then see the quiet resting schools lift and fall above the immaculate sand below. Their rest seemed shallower than in the deep calm of Kealakekua Bay. Always some subgroups seemed alert and spinning. Others, we found, were deep in rest, swimming in the same deliberate way as those in Kealakekua.

Why, for heaven's sake, should a bay like Kealakekua house only ninety dolphins, while at Keahole three times that number could congregate? It was as though the Coast Guard had posted a limit on occupancy: "This cove is certified for ninety dolphins," or "This open roadstead is approved for 250 dolphins." Why?

Finally the concept emerged that these shallow places were refuges of convenience for dolphins who made the first landfall after a night's feeding offshore. First come, first served, and a given bay or sandbar could accommodate only so many, according to the size of its sand patch. The dolphins always headed for the same spot in a rest area—that patch of white coral sand—and there they stayed during their quiet period, slowly zigzagging back and forth. (You the reader might well think us obtuse for taking so long to come to this conclusion, but preformed ideas die hard and they can sometimes persist even in the face of obvious evidence to the contrary.)

As we watched school after school come in to these sand patches, another strange feature of rest emerged. If only a few dolphins came to a given rest place, they did not seem to settle down completely, but remained furtive and wary of us. If about thirty to forty animals came, they became much more "comfortable" with us, soon settling in for a good solid rest period with few disruptive aerial episodes. Above this magic number of thirty to forty dolphins, their schools frequently split in two, and there always seemed to be some aerial behavior somewhere, much of it from young animals practicing their spins. Just like human children, some juveniles failed to settle down when the rest of the school was resting. Something was important about that number thirty to forty, and we began to suspect that it represented a "safe" school in which there were enough animals to guard all sectors, while allowing others a good rest. That idea, however, remains to be proved.

After rest was complete, and that wonderful abrupt awakening had occurred, we seemed unable to predict exactly what the dolphins would do. They couldn't seem to make up their minds. They sped up, leaped and spun, and then subsided into quiescence. Over and over, they repeated this pattern. Finally, weeks later, we concluded that we were watching a period of unpredictability and fluctuation, and that this oscillation itself was the behavior we sought to understand. We came to call it *zigzag swimming* because the animals zigged and zagged back and forth between the two cusps of the bay, changing speeds and shifting the compactness of their schools: now swimming tightly together, and now spread in rapidly moving ranks. All that was predictable was that this period would appear after rest was over. I concentrated on those zigzags, trying to come up with a synthetic idea that made sense.

The newly awakened dolphins typically started out with verve toward the bay entrance. At the start, before the school had speeded up, dolphins performed the lowest-energy aerial patterns. One was the *head slap,* in which a moving dolphin thrusts its body part way out of the water and then flexes its head smartly down against the surface, producing both an audible sound and a little splash of water. Later, when the pace quickened, these dolphins leapt free, like salmon leaping a fall, and then crashed back in the direction of travel.

Then the school sped faster and faster, and, as quickly as it had started, the verve dissipated. The school slowed and began to mill, and became almost listless. Often the school turned back into the bay, traveling toward the sand patch. From our clifftop we could sometimes see dolphins move all the way back to the deepest bay to descend again into rest. The next rush might take the school in the opposite direction, toward the north limb, where they might subside once again; the school went back and forth, back and forth, like a blob of mercury rolling in a bowl.

The only word for this was "indecision." Much later, during our second study, we surmised that all this zigzagging was just that: the indecision of a partly awake school in the process of making ready to go to sea for the evening hunt. It was, in short, "dolphin democracy" at work. It seemed to be the way a leaderless school (for there seems to be no single leader in a dolphin school) made up its collective mind about its collective ability to function smoothly and safely in the open sea. Probably it was a way of assuring that all members were alert before they left for the night's fishing. The best analogy seems to be to the tuning-up of a symphony orchestra.

Much of this view jelled later when we listened to the rising and falling sounds such schools emitted as they speeded and slowed their swimming. When the dolphins were swimming fast they were very noisy. Our hydrophone picked up a chorus of squawks, blats, and whistles, and the clicks came in cascades. But when the dolphins slowed they fell silent.

After zigzagging was complete, and the "decision" had been

made to go to sea, one could see a kind of "joy" sweep over the
school. All at once and all together they took off, often enough
directly toward the setting sun. The biologist in a skiff had to
be ready when this time came or in just a few moments the
dolphins would be gone as they sped into the darkening sea.
The dolphins had taken off toward the bay entrance, leaping
high, crashing back into the water, and going twice as fast as
before: seven or eight knots. They became ranks of inky silhouettes bursting from the water, and then they disappeared
from sight.

Typically we lost contact with the dolphins at this point.
And it wasn't until years later that we learned what happened
next. Gradually a few observations piled up, made when schools
left the shore a little early, allowing us precious moments for
direct observation. Once the dolphin school left the bay altogether and reached the drop-off over the abyss, the school quite
literally fragmented. One moment we were traveling with them
in the dim afternoon light, and then they were gone, just plain
gone. Stopping our boat in frustration, we would rock up and
down in the swell, looking for a sign of fins. Finally we saw
them, scattered in twos and threes, spread across several miles
of sea. I was amazed to find juveniles off by themselves, or
mother-calf pairs swimming alone. Then I recalled their sensory advantage over shark predators in darkness. The dolphins
could scan the deep water with their sonar beams for perhaps
three hundred yards in any direction, using bursts of clicks.
But sharks, who seem to depend mostly upon sight and smell
to lead them to their prey, could only hide from the dolphins
against the sheltering bottom. A rush up from behind might
catch a dolphin napping, but no approach in open water was
likely to surprise these mammals.

Once the dangerous bottom had dropped away it seemed
that even very young dolphins could abandon the protective
confines of their schools for a time. Did darkness bring some
measure of safety? Did depth do the same? I began to think so.

Occasionally, at last, we caught glimpses of feeding schools. They move widely spread, in clots of animals. On cues that could only have been acoustic in that dark water, such schools dive almost together over as much as a mile of sea. Subgroup after subgroup ducks beneath the surface and disappears in a dive, and in twenty to thirty seconds they have all gone below.

If we were patient, and traveled slowly in the direction the school had last moved, they would surface four or five minutes later, all around us. What did the school do down there in the black? Why couldn't they simply dive individually? Was feeding somehow a group process?

Clues came from the occasional spinners who died in fishermen's nets, or who were found floating at sea. Each time such an event occurred we took myriad notes about the animal, including an analysis of what it had eaten. Dolphins have storage stomachs, not unlike the rumen of a cow, and in them one can find traces of meals just past—the beaks of squids, the bones and ear ossicles of fish. A biologist can look up pictures of these items and determine what a dolphin had been eating, simply from these tiny parts. We found that our spinners were eating a lot of very small food items: little lantern fish, typified by rows of tiny lights along their two-inch bodies; beautiful red-lacquered deep-sea shrimp; and many many thumb-sized squids.

Some of these squids were of rare bioluminescent species that had seldom been seen in Hawaiian waters. That doesn't mean they were actually rare, though, only that biologists hadn't caught many of them. And no wonder! Some of these little creatures never ventured much closer to the surface than about five hundred feet.

So, we concluded that those synchronous dives must take the dolphins far below any waning light into the wholly black sea, where they somehow catch this tiny food by means of their echolocation or perhaps by watching the lights of the fishes themselves.

These spinner food items are part of what scientists call the *Deep Scattering Layer,* or DSL, referring to the sound-scattering properties of these shoals of organisms. The DSL is a world-wide phenomenon. Vertical migrant communities of such food organisms move toward the sea surface near dusk. During the day these little animals stay deep below the lighted water, probably for protection from visually oriented predators. The DSL often comes toward the surface in bands so dense that ship's fathometers may record a false bottom. For many years its composition was unknown, but it has certainly caused a lot of skipped heartbeats amongst open-ocean mariners whose fathometers showed a hard bottom welling up under their keels where no chart showed it to be. Twenty years before our work, scientists began to understand that there was nothing down there but a cloud of small organisms.

Deep currents tend to pile the DSL against island shores, rather like a conveyor belt, producing a continual concentration of its deep-sea life. The dolphins, and a good many other island-frequenting animals, take advantage of this concentration effect. That, in fact, is why there were so many dolphins at Keahole Point, a promontory that juts into the open sea. An entire biota of marine animals concentrates there because the DSL accumulates against the submerged flank of the island at that point. Birds flock in, marlin and tunas gather in schools along with smaller kinds of life. Biologists have given this phenomenon the name *Island Effect,* and know that it produces a constantly regenerated halo of life wherever islands rise from the deep oceanic sea. I think the spinner dolphins know all about the Island Effect, and travel to the best spots every night.

Everywhere we followed spinner schools we saw them performing their trademark spins. They did it when they woke up, when they went out to sea, and in the dark when their feeding schools surfaced. All true spinners did it, in whatever ocean they were found, but we still didn't know why. The fact

A spinner makes a
beautiful vertical
spin off Kauhako Bay.
R. S. Wells

that the behavior pattern was ubiquitous suggested an important function for the species. I didn't know any animal that had
a coat of arms just for the sake of hanging it on the wall. Spinning could hardly be casual, or simply play, when it was so
firmly a part of the repertoire of an entire worldwide species,
and when it was such complicated and stereotyped behavior. I
decided to devote an entire cruise to studying the question.

My first approach was to see if we could understand which
animals in a school performed the behavior pattern, where in
the school it typically occurred, and at what time of day it
happened most frequently.

The lovely hundred-foot barkentine *Westward* was in between
long-distance cruises, so my observational team and I boarded
and set sail for Kealakekua. We skirted the verdant south

shores of Molokai, Lanai, and Maui islands, and then sliced out into the challenging Alenuihaha Channel, pointing toward the distant blue cones of Hawaii. The *Westward* heeled over in the heavy trades until her rail ran near the whitecapped sea surface, sails and lines thrumming in the wind. I kept a sharp watch for spinner dolphins, because even though they frequent the open sea elsewhere we had never seen them in the open sea offshore of the islands. Did they sometimes cross the Alenuihaha to join Maui animals? No one knew then (or knows now) if all Hawaiian spinners are one population, or if each island population lives pretty much alone. We saw no spinners.

Soon the massive dark profile of Hawaii grew and we slipped into the lee of the giant volcanoes, and finally into Kealake'akua Bay itself, where we took up the familiar mooring a couple of cable lengths from the Cook Obelisk. Only two hundred yards in the other direction we could see spinners quietly surfacing.

My research colleague on this venture was a young psychologist, Bill Arbeit. The two of us watched as the dolphins awoke and began to leap and spin. I pointed out to Bill that one could classify these leaps into a series of fairly discrete kinds of spins. But I also said, "Caution, caution, with the old Aristotelian trap, Bill. It will be very easy for us to subdivide those spins into lots more classes than actually exist for the dolphin."

What I do in such cases—and they arise very frequently in observational natural history—is to watch without making judgment for quite a while; I'm soaking up "the gestalt" of the situation. Only when I have a feel for the entirety of the behavior do I apply divisions where nature seems to have placed them, always bearing in mind that I am imposing a human construct that may or may not agree with nature's patterns. I must be prepared to change my classification if I find that nature disagrees with me.

Spins, though, when we focused on them, seemed pretty distinctive. Just as we thought we were making a real classification, a dolphin would get fancy and leap from the water, slinging its tail over its head right in the midst of a spin. It was a display of athletic virtuosity so intricate that it lacked beauty, like one of those springboard dives Olympic athletes make—something like a one and a half in the piked position with a double twist. It was all elbows and eyebrows, or in this case flippers, flukes, and beaks, flashing by so fast that nothing could be resolved. That idiosyncratic variation, I decided, wouldn't find a place in my classification unless I saw other dolphins do it. I'd just say, "There's one in every crowd," and move on.

After our period of wordless watching was over (mine had already gone on for months) and we thought we were ready to write, our list of aerial patterns had boiled itself down to a small graded series of leaps, arranged in order of the amount of energy the animal put into them. We could also see that these leaps generally matched the energy level of the school. If the school moved slowly, low-energy aerial behavior was common. Dolphins would rear halfway up in the water and slap their heads or backs onto the surface.

If the school moved rapidly, more athletic patterns appeared. In fact some leaps were seen only in fast-moving schools where the very momentum of the school seemed to be imparted to their leaps. Instead of rearing halfway out of the water, a moving dolphin might broadjump a dozen feet over the surface before falling back.

The lowest-energy aerial patterns were ones we came to call *nose-outs* and *tail slaps*. Typically these were seen in slow-moving schools deep in the rest coves. A tail-slapping animal might crack its flukes against the water several times in succession, or lie on its back flicking its flukes up and down against the water surface several times in succession. One could hear the *pop, pop, pop, pop, pop . . . pop* across the water. We came to

An arcuate leap. Spinner dolphins use this leap when they travel fast.

A back slap. This pattern is given when a school is moving right along, often when they go out to sea at dusk.

An inverted tail slap. If the dolphin makes a series of such slaps in a row, we called it "motorboating."

A tail-over-head leap. Only very active dolphins perform this leap.

A head slap. These are usually given when the dolphins are moving briskly forward.

call this pattern *motorboating* because it sounded for all the world like a little outboard motor on idle, putting along across the bay.

In nearly stationary schools the earliest signs of high activity to come proved to be nose-outs. In the midst of the quiet school a dolphin would lift its snout from the water, or sometimes two would fence beaks with each other. Then we knew that in a few minutes the school would speed up and animals would begin to leap.

Fast-moving schools, especially those making that last dash out to sea at dusk after all the zigzagging was over, usually contained some animals engaged in what we called *salmon leaping*. This leap looks much like a salmon trying to jump up a waterfall. The dolphin's body is arched as it bursts from the water in the direction of travel. Very high and very rapid spins were seen in these schools too. The spinning dolphin sometimes rotated as many as four times before crashing back into the sea.

Another frequent high-energy leap was a strange one we called a *tail-over-head leap*. The dolphin burst from the water head first and slung its tail over its head, sending a great spiral of sea water into the air. At the last instant it smacked the top of its flukes onto the water with an audible *crack*.

So Bill and I counted and arbitrarily classified leaps by their energy level throughout the day, for as long as we could see. We stood on the foredeck, one person calling out the kinds of leaps he saw and their numbers, and the other recording. Then we asked the *Westward*'s skipper to haul up the anchor and take us to sea. Even before we added up the numbers, the patterns began to come clear. Aerial behavior, and the specific kind of leap involved, was an excellent gauge of the activity level of a dolphin school. The most athletic patterns were far more abundant in very active schools than during times of lesser activity. Later we put real numbers on this behavior, by using a surveyor's instrument to track dolphins, which also let us calculate their speed and hence activity.

At dusk we could see that spinning was a common pattern out on the feeding grounds. This was later confirmed when we spent several nights watching a captive school. Spins were even more frequent in the dark than in daylight hours. So, spinning and those other aerial patterns were tied to activity level, and they became even more abundant in the dark. Hmmmm.

The next question was, Did spinning occur at some special place in a school? In the back of my mind was the possibility that spins might be used to mark the edges or front of a school for its members. But this supposition was soon blasted when we found spins in every sector of a school—the lead, the sides, the middle, and, often enough, by the last dolphins in a school.

Was it some age or sex class that spun? Was leadership somehow involved? Those ideas, too, failed, as we frequently saw very young dolphins spinning, and in captivity both sexes spun. I remember one young spinner leaping about thirty yards off our bow one evening. It was a tiny animal, seemingly intent on learning its spins. Each spin brought it closer to the ship. While we counted, the little dolphin performed fourteen spins in a row, and finally the last one was so close aboard our vessel that the animal fell back into our curling bow wave. Startled from its concentration, it raced off, as if to say, "How did that boat get here?"

None of our constructs seemed to fit. Somewhat desperate now, my colleagues and I wondered if spinners were shaking parasites loose from their bodies. Remora fish, for example, often cling to dolphins. These curious fish possess a dorsal fin that is modified into a suction disk that operates at the will of the fish. They can attach one moment and be towed along by their host, or they can let loose to zip around their host, picking up scraps of food missed by the larger animal.

Another animal a spinner dolphin might want to shake loose

is that insidious Cookie-Cutter shark, *Isistius,* that I mentioned earlier. Scars from encounters with this fish were common, even open wounds not yet healed. This strange twelve-inch-long bioluminescent fish may be a mimic of a squid. Perhaps it is mistaken for food by a dolphin who approaches it. The little shark may then race in to attach its curious mouth to the dolphin's side. It then proceeds to force the sharp-toothed arc of its lower jaw through the dolphin's blubber, and even into the muscle below. In this way it can scoop out a disk of flesh about one to two inches in diameter.

We watched each spinning dolphin to see if it bore remoras, and occasionally we saw them, but the large majority seemed glistening and clean of any such hitchhiker. Later, when my later colleagues Bernd Würsig and Randy Wells had accumulated boxes full of slides of individual spinning dolphins, we were able to inspect them at our leisure and a surprising number, about 30 percent, were found to carry remoras. This number seemed far greater than the percentage we observed from below the water surface. So it began to seem likely that one cause of spins was, indeed, an attempt to deal with these pesky fish. Clearly it wasn't the only reason or even the major reason they spun, because the large majority of dolphins leaped with no attendant fish at all. I'm not even sure a dolphin can shake or slap a remora loose by spinning.

There's another possible utility to spins. They may allow other dolphins in a school to localize the spinning animal's position. A similar effect has been suggested for the breaches of whales, and for the leaps of the dusky dolphin of the southern hemisphere, but no one had really pinned the matter down. One much-respected team of bioacousticians had cast doubt on the entire idea because they had been unable to record any sounds from leaping spinners.

Finally, on one of those night-long sessions with the Sea Life Park spinners, I heard the reentry sounds repeatedly—on every spin, in fact. As I watched through a big viewing port, one of the dolphins spun over and over in front of me. Each time it landed a loud percussive *smack* issued from its sinking body, presumably because its fast-revolving dorsal fin or some other part of its body hit the surface as the animal reentered the water. The longer I watched and listened, the more convinced I became that these leaping patterns were exquisite athletic feats, certainly honed through much practice, in which the goal was not only that smack of sound but a bubble trail as well. *Smack, smack:* the sound was so sharp that it could be heard clearly through the ports of the tank where I watched. I could see the reentering dolphin "hunch its shoulders" at that last instant of reentry, accentuating the impact, and then draw a long twisting trail of bubbles down with it as its rotations slowed. I can only surmise that the inability of my friends to record such sounds came from the distance at which they attempted to record. The sounds were very distinct in my listening gear at Sea Life Park, and we have since heard them on occasion in wild schools when our recording boat drifted near to a spinning dolphin.

Perhaps more revealing than these sounds were the other patterns of behavior associated with spinning in the captive school. Each time a dolphin was about to spin it announced the fact by diving down a few meters and barking in a characteristic way, as it rocked back and forth, stationary in the water. Then with a few powerful strokes it thrust itself upward through the surface into the spin. As it fell back its rotating body drew that long plume of bubbles ten feet or so down into the water. These bubbles drifted slowly upward, dissipating in a matter of minutes.

I TURNED to my companion in the observation room, Randy Wells. "Randy," I said, "I finally think I've seen and heard what spins are all about." Randy, having lived through several versions of my speculations, cocked his head skeptically. "Yes?"

I replied to this effect. Spins and most of those other variant aerial patterns are probably used by dolphins as local geographic markers. In aggregate, they mark out the dimensions of the school. The barks at the start are made well below the surface and can inform other dolphins when and where a spin is about to take place. With a listening dolphin's attention focused in the proper direction by the barks, the reentry slap confirms that it was indeed a spin, and the bubble plume makes an excellent echolocation target, providing range and bearing for an echolocating schoolmember.

The barks, reentry slaps, and bubble targets of several dolphins in a school, given continuously, should easily define the disposition and changing shape of the school as a whole for its members. In this scheme the sounds of reentry may be no more than identifiers of a true spin for a listening dolphin who has already turned their way because of the precursor barks. A slap, even a rather faint one, may be discriminated easily because the listener's attention has been engaged to expect it, and when followed by a bubble trail it won't be confused with a crashing wave. A given dolphin could then know where all the other nearby dolphins were, even in the dark, and from any place in the school, even as the last dolphin.

Randy nibbled at his knuckles and looked sideways at me.

Not letting him off the hook, I continued: "And don't forget that spins are made most frequently in the dark, when the dolphins are spread, and most active."

"Well, sounds pretty good . . ." allowed Randy.

And there the matter stands. Some spins seem involved with remoras, but the majority may well be crucial geometric organizers of the traveling society. Such facts as there are seem to fit. So, you young scientists, here is a theory of spinning (and the other leaps and slaps cetaceans make) for you to take out to sea and test.

5

The Alisa S. J.

WHILE we were building our camp atop the Kealakekua cliff, another, more tragic story was taking place. One of my doctoral students, Bill Perrin, had been attempting to gather specimens of spinners and spotted dolphins so that he could establish how many species there were in the warm oceans of the world. He found that these dolphins sometimes ended up at tuna canneries at San Pedro and San Diego, California, carried in the brine tanks of tuna seiners and frozen along with the tuna. Bill got his specimens all right, but he was appalled by the numbers of dolphins that the tuna fishery seemed to be killing. After some sleuthing he published a paper putting the kill at about 350,000 dolphins a year! This finding caused a sensation, especially among those considering national legislation to protect marine mammals. By that time I had become involved in the legislative effort.

We were all part of the larger worldwide realization, during the 1960s, that we humans were dealing with our world, and all the things in it, in ways that had to be changed. The days of the hunter-gatherer were coming to an end and the days of the citizen-ecologist were just beginning.

I began to make regular trips from Hawaii to Washington, D.C. Some scientist friends and I were hatching a plan for a nationwide research effort to perform the necessary biology related to the worldwide conservation problems of marine mammals. Our leader was my longtime friend Dr. Carleton Ray, then of The Johns Hopkins University. We were joined by Bill Schevill of Woods Hole, and later by others from the Smithsonian Institution and elsewhere. Carleton had lined up an office for us in the Smithsonian, so I flew in from Hawaii, arriving all bleary-eyed with jet lag; for the first day I went to sleep on the office floor in a vain attempt to equilibrate. I still wonder how politicians and diplomats can speak any sense at all with the peripatetic longitude-crossing lives they lead.

Carleton comes from a family of lawyers and was able to move easily into the Washington milieu. He told us that a move was underway, sparked mostly by a consortium of animal welfare and conservation groups, to produce a "Marine Mammal Protection Act." Their special target was the whaling industry, which for four decades had driven species after species of giant whales into decline throughout the world's oceans.

As a west-coaster I didn't know much about the inner workings of the U.S. government, so I watched Carleton carefully, soaking it all up. He explained that this proposed act, like most other legislation, was primarily the work of legislative assistants who put it all together for the senator or representative. The politico would then nod sagely and push the bill through the intricacies of the House and Senate.

Mostly, I found out, the politicians wrote nothing at all; they didn't have time. So anybody with real expertise found himself or herself sought after in Washington. Information has its own kind of power in the nation's capital.

One evening Carleton arranged a dinner with Frank Potter, a legislative assistant who was working on drafts of the Marine Mammal Protection Act. Potter proved to be a bright, caring lawyer, eager for us to add the scientific perspective to his work, and he asked endless questions about how ocean animals such as the whales and dolphins might be protected.

We happily trotted out our prejudices, and soon began to learn about the curious way that the nation's laws are drafted. One thing Carleton and I agreed upon was that marine management in general suffered because all conservation efforts focused on *species* and not on the environments of the animals involved. A lawyer writing a new law typically constructed protective rules for a given species but forgot to protect the world in which it lived.

I had strong opinions about an inappropriate concept that was being drafted into the act. It was called the MSY, or *maximum sustainable yield,* and it was widely used as a measure of how many fish could be taken from a population. In the final law this measure would determine, in some fashion, how many dolphins, whales, or seals the fishery would be allowed to kill.

The MSY said that it was OK for a fishery to strip off all of the animals in an exploited population, be they fish or whales, down to the bare number needed to sustain the species reproductively. The MSY, I thought, failed in two crucial ways. First, one could not apply the same criterion to whales and dolphins as to fish. A single fish might spawn a million eggs a year, while a whale gave birth to fewer than two dozen calves in its entire life. The way these very different animals responded to being hunted was, as a result, vastly different.

And, second, MSY said it was OK to strip away all the animals in a population that weren't actually required for reproduction. I didn't believe this. I knew that there was compelling evidence that the "surplus" animals in an unexploited population weren't just waste animals, but actually served vital functions. For example, they might provide a buffer for the species against unpredictable environmental change.

So Carleton and I came up with a substitute concept, which

we called the *optimum sustainable yield*. Our idea was that a figure would have to be calculated for how many marine mammals could be taken from a population without compromising its long-term ecological health.

This new idea immediately drew the fire of just about everyone, conservationists and fishermen alike. Then, to my surprise, the legislators solved the situation by compromise! How can you compromise on a definition, I wondered? But that being the way of lawyers, they did it anyway. They finally evolved a new concept thought to be halfway in between the views of the fishermen and the conservationists. The conservationists insisted on doing away with the idea of *yield* because they were against the killing of whales, and the fishermen bought the notion of *optimum* because it seemed undefinable and harmless.

What found its way into the act that was passed by Congress was a measure called OSP, or the *optimum sustainable population,* but no one knew what those words meant. In the curious way of laws, depositing this undefined little pebble in the resource manager's shoe fomented debates and symposia for the next four or five years. During that time, attempts were made to devise legal ways of dealing with the amorphous concept, and of defining what it meant. Strangely, in this process our mission was well realized. We had shifted this part of fishery practice away from an outmoded and dangerous concept— the maximum sustainable yield—that had contributed to the decline of fishery after fishery, and we had spurred a search for what "optimum" meant. It caused a lot of soul searching about how living marine resources should be managed.

Another thing I learned was that most lawyers didn't know a dolphin from a draft horse, and they wrote laws about them anyway. I remember one especially luminous example in which the legislative lawyers defined everything on the ocean floor as a mineral and regulated it as such. This meant that for a time the Alaska king crab fishery had been dealt with as if crabs were manganese nodules. Those lawyers needed our help, and they still do.

We also insisted that the act should somehow assure that the best of scientific talent be brought to bear on management issues such as the whale fishery or the dolphin kill. The whole history of ocean management was a sordid story of economic interests coopting scientific expertise to support their unimpeded exploitation. The scientists needed a way into the political process where their words would have some clout.

So the ultimate Marine Mammal Protection Act of 1972 became, in a modest and often awkward way, the first U.S. ecological management law. The ramifications of this are still playing themselves out, since most fishery biologists still try to manage wholly on a species-by-species basis, rather than giving consideration to the health of the ocean in which the animals live. It's a lot easier to do things that way, even if in the long run it makes little biological sense.

Frank Potter brewed up legalese that accomplished these and other subtle but crucial matters. He assured the scientist's place in decision-making by drafting in a Committee of Scientific Advisors that had a true policy-making role. He made the head of the Marine Mammal Commission a scientist, when such posts are typically filled by political appointees whose primary job is to make sure the results of their commission follow the party line.

To an extent all this worked. The commission ended up as a unique entity in government, a gadfly commission allowed to comment, unfavorably or otherwise, on the work of the various other agencies of government that dealt with marine mammal issues. This lack of conformity has caused endless irritation and placed the commission under a continual drum beat of criticism from other agencies in government, but for a time it also provided a "breath of spring" in some dark corridors. More recently, as with a rocky promontory on an exposed sea coast, the waves of political opposition seem to have eroded the commission's force, and bit by bit it has been edged toward more "acceptable" blandness.

Soon the Marine Mammal Protection Act became law. I was asked to join the first Committee of Scientific Advisors of the newly formed Marine Mammal Commission, and found myself back in Washington trying to make some operational sense of the law I had helped to shape. Because I was an "expert" on spinner dolphins, I headed the subcommittee established to deal with the thorny "tuna-porpoise issue," as it was then called. For me this task proved to be an exotic and sometimes almost frightening amalgam of passions, politics, money, and sheer legal force.

Until then I had no inkling of the power that a single administrative law judge sitting in an undistinguished courtroom could wield, nor of the power of an impassioned public constituency. But in 1976 Judge Charles Richey, after consideration of the very high annual dolphin kill and of the public outcry against it, ruled that the tuna fishery was in violation of the Marine Mammal Protection Act. He temporarily closed down the U.S. tuna fishery. His decision had been made after a flood of testimony from more than twenty conservation groups, mostly under an umbrella group called Project Monitor. I remember feeling surprised and elated that our governmental process could work with sufficient force to stop the nation's second-largest fishery in its tracks. Most remarkable of all, the decision was based on a new law that for the first time was designed to protect marine mammals, not a fishery.

Not long afterward an apparently chastened fishery set to sea under the law's new regulations, and the problem began to edge back toward some semblance of control.

Despite the evident progress, however, a new problem developed. Augie Fellando, the Tuna Boat Owners Association head lawyer, had told me that as we pushed the fishery toward social responsibility, they would react against the new laws and begin to think about "going foreign," and that is just what happened. In the years after the landmark Richey decision, boat after boat and crew after crew has slipped out of U.S. registry to appear under foreign flags such as Panama, Costa Rica, Mexico, and Venezuela, thus freeing themselves from the irritating U.S. regulations. When Richey made his ruling the fleet was about 70 percent U.S. boats and 30 percent foreign. Today as I write, the numbers are reversed: only thirty-four boats, or about 30 percent of the eastern tropical Pacific tuna fleet, remain under the U.S. flag. Independent-minded, primarily foreign-born tuna fisherman could not stomach going to sea from San Diego, California, to watch the Panamanian, Mexican, or Costa Rican boats circle tuna schools without adhering to the law that had been imposed upon the U.S. boats. After all, these men hadn't gone to sea in the first place to be told how to do things by a bunch of lawyers and scientists.

If they stayed under U.S. registry they had to install something called the "super apron" on their nets: a kind of chute in the upper edge, or "corkline," of the net which the skipper could pull underwater and through which he could sluice the apparently stupid dolphins who wouldn't jump over the corks of their own accord. The fishermen also had to have a man in a skiff down along the net edge who could help animals escape, and they had to line the place toward which dolphins were maneuvered for release, or "backdown channel," with fine mesh net that would keep the animals from tangling. Finally, they were no longer allowed to set their nets at dusk, when it became difficult to see well enough to guide the release process, and when dolphins seemed particularly unable to help themselves.

One of my contributions to this struggle might have caused particular irritation. Nowhere in the plans of the National Marine Fisheries Service, the agency charged with dealing with the tuna-dolphin kill, could I see any real experimental effort designed to solve the problem. Under Bill Perrin's propulsive leadership, the problem had been defined, but at that time scant help for the trapped dolphins had been developed. The reason, I sensed, was that the National Marine Fisheries Service is positioned to "help" the fishery, not to regulate it, and most of its staff survive by conforming to the wants of the fisherman rather than by confrontation or even by experimenting with new methods that might work better. These matters are usually left to the fishermen themselves, who rightly think they know more about fishing than anybody else. If the agency people present too much of a challenge, the fishery can be depended upon to use its significant political clout to bring "the feds" back in line. Once again I found that fishermen don't much like being told what to do.

So the Marine Mammal Commission stepped in. My subcommittee fought for a budget that would let the fishery people experiment with ways of releasing dolphins. It proposed a "dedicated vessel program" in which the fishery was asked to send a couple of its "top-of-the-line" seiners to sea with a team of scientists (myself among them) and fishery specialists aboard. The mission of these cruises was to seek an understanding of the dolphin kill in behavioral terms, to look at the netting process and its gear, and otherwise to contribute a scientific basis to possible solutions.

The National Marine Fisheries Service had advertised among the fleet for vessels willing to take part in the program. The deal was this: the ships would operate on contract, and could keep the fish they caught. Since the fleet was now under strict quota—so many tons of tuna were allowed per season—this permit had the advantage of letting participating fishermen tap a special "research quota" of tuna. We researchers were given control of the design and operation of fifteen research net sets per cruise.

That putative control, as it was played out at sea, involved a series of little compromises that I for one hadn't expected. But, fortunately for me, my counterpart from the National Marine Fisheries Service was Dr. Bill Perrin, who understood the needs and attitudes of the fishermen with considerable subtlety. Both of us knew from past experience that the primary motive of good fishermen is to catch fish, and that the tinkering, inefficiency, and complications that typify field science would be foreign matters to them. So we sought every opportunity to help our fishermen fill their ship's brine tanks with tuna, at the same time trying to complete our own work plans.

We were lucky: the chance to fish from the research quota and the genuine interest of many fishermen in working toward a solution of the industry's problem induced some of the best boats in the fleet to apply for the program. The boat selected for my cruise was the magnificent *Alisa S. J.,*[1] a nearly new vessel of 260 feet that could chill and carry 1700 tons of tuna. More important, her crew were professionals to the last man, amongst the top producers in the fleet. Every aspect of their operation went like clockwork. In six weeks at sea, few parts of the complex machinery of that giant ship failed, there were no serious accidents, and we half-filled the holds with tuna. Though we handled hundreds of tons of fish, only eleven dolphins died (the kill on many vessels for a cruise like ours numbered in the hundreds, or even thousands, of dolphins).

My first view of the *Alisa* came in early October 1976, as I stood on the dock at San Diego, bags in hand, looking up at the rakish bow of this immaculate sea-foam-green fishing ship. She was, I thought, beautiful. Fishermen, accompanied by wives and children, straggled aboard in what must have become a ritual goodbye for the men about to go to sea.

The men spent nearly three hundred days a year at sea on

1. I have changed the name of the ship and her crew in order that I may speak graphically about events and people without offending anyone.

half a dozen voyages. So as I boarded and walked down the broad companionway to my cabin, the reason for a women's powder room done in gold-flecked wallpaper became clearer. It was used only during these ritual goodbyes and then it stayed closed during the weeks at sea. On the other hand, the religious shrines built into the bulkheads of the vessel would be tended throughout the voyage. They came to seem like an almost tangible presence watching over the ship, I thought.

The *Alisa S. J.* in the midst of a seine set. Note the captain's lookout on the mast and the little helicopter atop the wheelhouse. *Edward Mitchell*

My gear stowed, seaman John Bregante took me on a tour of the ship. My unfamiliar eyes caught mostly strangeness, and superlatives. Only later would I see how everything aboard meshed together—the huge bridge fitted with the latest electronic equipment, where up-to-date weather maps were printed out on command; the ship's position bounced down from a

satellite and flashed in red neon; the little Bell helicopter dogged
down tight atop the bridge; the palatial skipper's quarters abaft
the bridge. In its anteroom a curving red-tufted vinyl bar arced
beneath a mural of home: a twenty-foot-long representation of
the Point Loma breakwater at San Diego. That breakwater was
the first thing the skipper would see of home port each time
he returned.

We wandered through the seldom-used game room and the
spacious airy galley where, soon enough, exhausted men would
pile in after the net was in and stacked to slug down half a
tumblerful of Canadian whiskey. The wiry little cook, who
looked for all the world like a scaled-down version of the dap-
per film star Adolph Menjou, would soon cause meals of quite
amazing abundance and variety to materialize. The ship, operated by owners of Portuguese descent, served many spicy dishes
completely unknown to me.

It was easy to see these amenities as "high living," but for
men who literally spent their lives at sea it was a way of guar-
anteeing the best crew members for the skippers and owners.

John and I clambered down to the tank deck, which stretched
nearly the length of the ship. Here were the chilling tanks that
during the course of the trip would exchange a load of diesel
oil for tuna. Deeper still were the engine rooms, bright with
paint and light, where twin 2800 horsepower engines would
push us at seventeen knots toward the fishing grounds.

That tremendous power was no luxury, though. It meant
two things to the fishermen. It gave a crucial advantage in turn-
around time. With the tuna grounds thousands of miles from
port, the owners of such a swift ship could hope for an extra
trip over their slower competitors. What is more, the faster the
ship the more easily it could "wrap" schools of dolphins and
their attendant fish. Out on the grounds most dolphins were
wise to approaching ships. They moved away, stealthily at first
when the noise of ship's engines reached them, and then

speeding away in full flight as the ship turned toward them. But with top-of-the-line vessels such as the *Alisa,* the first sound the dolphins heard were the flailing blades of the helicopter that rode above them.

Speed also meant that the fishery traded diesel oil for tuna. This fishery, like modern agriculture ashore, is high-tech and heavily consumptive of fuel, with all the ecological ramifications implicit in those few words.

On the broad working deck of the *Alisa,* booms, cables, winches, and a giant net pile as big as a small house dominated. Above it all, the vital hydraulic block hung from the boom tip. This winch, built like a big rotating truck tire, allowed fishermen to draw in the huge net in a small fraction of the time taken to do it by hand. The net pile was topped by a huge squarish open skiff, resting up there at a slant, like a mother hen trying vainly to cover her chicks.

I soon learned that a net set is a dynamic thing. The giant net is payed rapidly into the sea, but it doesn't simply stay where it is dropped. Instead, the net rather quickly sinks, its bottom, or lead line, changes shape, and begins to pull together. Unless the fishermen act with precision and dispatch, it will close completely and kill everything within it. Such net collapse can also create an unholy tangle that may take many hours to unravel. For this reason, the net skiff's powerful diesel engine is as critical to this way of fishing as the main ship's engine itself.

A net set starts upon a preemptory command from the skipper. A pelican hook is whacked open by the skiff operator and the skiff slides down backward off the net pile and into the ship's wake to pull the net out. Once the mother ship has raced in a circle, paying out leaping flakes of net, any gap that is left is winched closed, and later, as the catch is being encircled, the skiff drops the net end and reattaches itself to the outboard side of the mother ship to pull this way and that to keep the big ship from drawing itself into the dwindling net circle. That maneuver is critical to the entrapped dolphins; if the big vessel creeps into the net circle, great canopies of netting develop that sometimes kill whole dolphin schools. These sloping underwater sheets of net block dolphins from rising for a vital breath of air. At times like these the dolphins may come up underneath, probing the mesh frantically for a breath, and die in windrows.

We clambered up from the net deck to a small half-deck above, astern of the ship's bridge. There amidships nestled six speedboats, called *pongas* on this boat. Each had a single bucket seat and a wide seat belt, an outsized outboard engine, and little else. Each was the personal domain of a skiff operator who tended it with much care. It and he had to work flawlessly when, during the net set, these speedboats were launched over the side of the rapidly accelerating mother ship. No slipups were condoned. A crewman whose engine coughed and died, or, worse, ran out of gas, would first find himself cursed in Portuguese and then out on the San Diego dock when the cruise ended. The speedboat drivers and their boats were the cowboys and horses of the tuna fleet, and they would herd the dolphins and fish during the entire netting operation, regardless of the sea state. Later, I watched from the helicopter deck as these crewmen worked in a blur of action to launch their boats: each motion, each line, each knot precisely right lest the vessel be swamped and a crewman dumped into the open sea.

At launch each crewman sat strapped in, wearing a helmet inside which shouted radioed instructions were received direct from the skipper. More important, the crewman couldn't talk back. He could only take the verbal abuse as ship, skipper, and net became predatory instruments in a single exquisitely coordinated effort. A debate over tactics would be as out of place in those emotional moments as two wolves discussing which one should hamstring the caribou.

John finally brought me back to my cabin, where I sat on the bunk trying to take it all in. The one place he hadn't taken me was the crow's nest. That was the skipper's command post, and his alone. No one clambered up a ladder to get there, either. Instead, once the chase was underway the captain left his bridge, went aft to the mast, entered a little door at its base, and was carried aloft by elevator to the enclosed room at its top. There, with windows all around, he could see and command everything. No visitor such as I was allowed there. The smooth functioning of that nerve center was too critical for extraneous diversions of any kind. The captain needed to be alone with his shouting. This was finely tuned predation: men against all the senses and skills of tuna and dolphins. It was, in the last analysis, our complicated version of wolves and caribou.

Into the midst of this smooth operation came our crew of scientists. Another contingent of scientists traveled on the much slower and less elegant government research vessel *David Starr Jordan,* and together these two ships tried to work in concert. Life on the *Jordan* was another world: one of ship's schedules and civil service rules. It was, however, in its own bureaucratic way as dedicated to its mission as the *Alisa* was. It was a place of experiment, a platform for the probing scientist who could gather his data, tinker with his equipment, and ponder a thousand unanswered questions. There was little of the immediacy of the *Alisa.*

Scientists came aboard with odd experimental gear, snarls of wire, and things carried in buckets, which because they had never been honed through long practice not infrequently failed to work well. Once the scientist had solved a given problem, such gear was apt to be discarded as he moved on to something else. Precious ship time could be spent tapping one's fingers on the rail while a technician tried to keep salt water from leaking into the seagoing radios designed to be carried by dolphins.

To the fisherman all this must have seemed vastly unprofessional, but it was not. Science is tinkery business. One must conceptualize, design, test, repair and modify, discard, and above all try to perceive without bias what nature has to say as a result of the test. And it all takes a lot of time.

Once the tinkering is past and things are known with some assurance, there is little reason for the scientist to tarry, except to do it all over twenty-five times to convince his colleagues through statistics.

The fishermen had their science too. Their whole fishery was a tribute to experimentation and innovation. But instead of dealing with budgets on grants, they had to deal with the bottom line. They needed a nearly immediate payoff for their ideas. Among the fishermen, the large conceptual risks were taken only by the brave, the foolhardy, or the geniuses. The difference between their science and ours was that they had evolved their methods under the natural selection of economic promise or some crisis in the fishery, and it had taken them decades for that evolution. Their goals, of course, were also different. They were centered on tuna, and how much fish could be stuffed in the chill tanks, and not with the integrity of wild dolphin societies. We instead sought openings of the mind, visions of new ways to solve the problem of dolphin release.

I intuitively knew that my task as one of the project leaders was to try to keep these disparate activities and attitudes focused on the single goal of learning about dolphin behavior in the net. In this task I was part of a leadership troika, including two others from the National Marine Fisheries Service. Bill Perrin was there, as was behaviorist Warren Stuntz, my cabinmate. Buddha-like, Warren said little, but his sharp eyes seemed to miss nothing as he wandered the ship. Together the three of us trod the thin line of balancing the histories and needs of these two ship worlds, and hoped that the result might be progress in understanding what went on in the net.

Probably most important, however, our team included Jim

Coe, whose job was to look at the netting operation and at net design for clues that might reduce the kill. Jim, physical and powerful, is half fisherman. He spoke curtly if he said anything at all. Mostly he was simply there ahead of everyone, pulling dolphins over the corkline, or sculling around the net with a face plate on, watching animals below water. Finally, when our trip was over, some of his suggestions meant the most to the dolphins.

A major equalizing factor, and one that finally brought the *Alisa*'s fishermen and our scientific party a little closer, was the fact that we and they worked equally hard at our jobs, and it finally showed. Mutual respect ultimately hung on that simple fact.

"What's he saying into that tape recorder?" I was asked by a crewman craning over the deckhouse rail at Ed Mitchell, a well-known Canadian marine mammalogist whom we had invited to participate.

Ed said *everything* into his tape recorder, and then at night he transcribed the whole shebang onto paper. No detail of dolphin or fish, or of the ship's operation, was too small for his chronicle. When Ed did put down his little hand-held recorder, he immediately took up his camera to take hundreds and hundreds of photographs. The whole structure of what we saw or did ultimately lay in his notes and slides.

The *Alisa* headed south from San Diego, and by the fourth day we cruised in calm subtropical seas southeast of Clarion Island, Mexico. Big puffy cumulus clouds were scattered around us, with veils of gray rain hanging down, caressing the glassy sea below.

A lookout manned a pair of giant swivel-mounted binoculars cradled in an elastic cord to damp ship's vibration. Soon he sighted birds. I could not at first see them. But finally there they were, masked and brown boobies swooping and circling over a distant area of sea. The helicopter, released from its deckhouse fetters, rose off the cabin roof and soon flashed back the words: "Fish and porpoise."[2]

The *Alisa* heeled over and headed for the area. The skiffmen rushed to their places, and as we neared the feeding school they were lifted with amazing dispatch over the rail and released, motors already roaring. Their first task was to race ahead of the dolphins and to turn them back toward the *Alisa*. As the dolphins began to pass us going in the opposite direction from our course, their school poured from the water in low-angle cascades of fleeing animals. The *Alisa* heeled over at flank speed and churned in a broad turn that took her outside the track of the dolphins.

SOMEWHERE down under the speeding dolphins traveled the tuna. Why don't they leave? one wonders. The answer to that question is still shrouded in controversy, but I feel reasonably sure that the tuna follow the dolphins and that the mammals find food for both of them with their sonar systems.

I was intrigued by the *Alisa*'s public address system. It reached every cranny of the ship: the engine room, the vacant powder room, our bunks. And it always blasted at full volume during a net set. We heard what the *ponga*[3] operators heard, and I cringe for the ultimate fate of everyone's hearing. Rapid-fire instructions were given to each of the boat operators, often rising to a crescendo of pure emotion as this or that driver was sent pounding over the swells to corral a little knot of dolphins that threatened a dash to safety. All the fishermen knew that such little groups of escaping dolphins could siphon off huge gouts of tuna, and at $750 per ton the affair became personal for each of them.

2. The fishermen use the term "porpoise" for all small cetaceans.
3. Some fishermen call the speedboats *pongas* and others say *pangas*. *Panga* is the Spanish word for skiff.

I was immediately in awe of those *pongas* and their drivers. During my time aboard the *Alisa* they corraled tuna and dolphins in all sorts of sea conditions. In rough weather one could see them out there vaulting from wave crest to wave crest, motors snarling wide open, audible to us even half a mile away.

The *Alisa* circled in, and finally an explosive command blasted from the PA system and the net skiff was whacked free. She slid off the sloping stern into the sea, anchoring the end of the net as the *Alisa* churned away.

About this time the dolphins abruptly stopped their flight, two or three hundred feet from the net wall, and began to mill in a desultory way. A kind of hopelessness seemed to emanate from their slow movements. They, and the fish they carried,

Pongas race ahead of the seiner after being launched. The big seiner follows and will then encircle the dolphin school in hopes of catching its attendant yellowfin tuna. *Edward Mitchell*

were trapped, and they knew it. The intensity of the half-Por-
tuguese, half-English on the PA system began to moderate too.
I was interested to note that the commentary slid back into
predominantly English commands. Before, during the high speed
flight of the dolphins, Portuguese had the upper hand. I suspected that for pure emotion Portuguese was the preeminent
language, and I wondered what the translation of some of those
commands might have been, but I didn't ask.

It took fifteen sets, but over the course of the trip I began to
understand how the dolphins were trapped. It was not what I
had expected. The dolphins were not simply being run down
in a sea chase and corraled. The method worked because it
thwarted the sensory capability, especially the echolocation, of
the dolphins, and I wondered if the fishermen understood fully
what they had evolved. If they didn't, I thought, wasn't it awesome that they had arrived at their subtle, intricate, and very
precise method of netting? At the least it had involved empiri-
cal observations as precise as those of any scientist. At the most
it had evolved by trial and error, leavened and guided by "what
worked." The only major difference I could see between their
way and mine was that they looked first for results, not causes.

What they did, I found, was to locate dolphins and fish and
then come up behind the school as the *pongas* rushed ahead
and turned the animals onto a course opposite the big seiner.
Then, as the ship turned to curve around outside the animals,
and now traveling on their course, the *ponga* operators began
to harass the dolphins from a position ahead of them. The
dolphins continued the curving course of their flight in response,
the turning vessel following outside. Gradually, gradually, the
flight of the school of dolphins and fish, and the ship's course,
became an inward-twisting spiral, tightening, tightening with
each turn. The big ship beat a deep spiraling wake of bubbles
and turbulence around the fleeing animals. This, to the dolphin's sonar, was an impenetrable wall. Unlike storm waves at

sea, which simply punctuate the sea with deep cascades of bubbles with long stretches of clear sea in between, this wall was continuous, though it did dissipate slowly as the bubble veil rose toward the surface. I suppose a dolphin could "see" no way around it, especially as it became a spiral and the animals found themselves inside a maze as escape-proof as those of any English garden. The dolphins did not dive beneath the veil. I suppose that might be because fleeing dolphins travel shallowly, using long leaps in the air to increase their speed.

A look at the drawings on page 113 will help show why I was so amazed at what the fishermen had evolved. I'm not sure any of the designers of this exquisite maneuver even knew that dolphins have sonar. At least no conversations aboard ship revealed that they did.

Another thing the skipper did was to send some of his *ponga* operators out to guard the places where the ship's wake was weakest. There they beat the sea to a froth in tight spirals of noise and bubbles, effectively filling the gaps.

From time to time we saw little dolphin schools skinning along just inside the ship's wake, and then we realized that it was a true wall for them. To enter those frothy waters was to have one's sonar shut down. Nothing can trap and dissipate a sonar signal more completely than a dispersed veil of rising bubbles. Each bubble resonates with every dolphin click that hits it, sending signals in all directions. The upshot is that no usable information about anything but bubbles can come from directing echolocation clicks at a wake. To stick one's snout inside a wake was to go acoustically "blind." No shark, no schoolmate, could be detected. So it was not surprising to watch dolphins in the last tight turns of the spiral swim toward the wake two to three hundred feet away and simply stop dead, and then begin a listless mill, the tuna presumably stopped beneath them.

In those last spirals the dimensions had gradually reduced

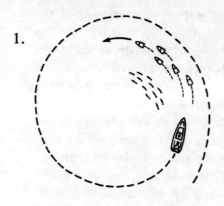

1.

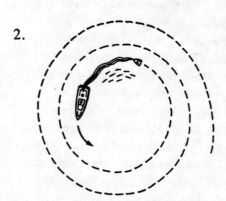

2.

1,2. A tuna seiner corrals a
dolphin school and sets its net.
3. The seiner backs down, spilling
dolphins out the end. The skipper
ties one side of the net to the
seiner and backs away from the
net in an arc. This pulls the
remaining net out into a long
finger, the backdown channel,
which often contains both tuna
and dolphins. When the fish
come toward the ship, the skipper
backs hard, sinking the end of the
backdown channel a little and
spilling the passive dolphins out
the end.

3.

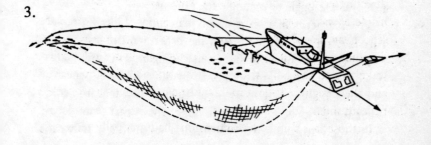

until finally the circumference of the spiral came to match the length of the net the vessel carried.

There were more complications that the skipper had to deal with, not the least of which were the wind and current. He took great pains to gauge the wind direction before he gave the command to let the net skiff go. He did this so that his spiral would finally bring the *Alisa* to rest with her net closed and with the wind on her port beam, blowing her away from the net. This was a crucial judgment, because a set net is a dynamic thing, in the process of sinking and collapsing of its own weight. Temporarily, it is held open only by the frictional drag of the sea passing slowly through the three-quarter mile of net. The vessel tends to be pulled by the huge weight of this collapsing net right into the open net circle. So, having the wind press outward against the great flat bulk of the ship's side and superstructure served to counteract this process and went far toward keeping the net open while the fishermen worked.

They have no time to waste, though, because in spite of everything they can do, the net finally closes and collapses on itself and its clasping mesh then kills everything within it. Any dolphins must be released before such collapse, of course: any hitch in this complicated procedure can kill dolphins. For example, sometimes the net will catch on a burr in the cable, and because cables tend to spin under tension the net will roll up like a long sausage. Such "roll ups" kill many dolphins because the remainder of the net inexorably collapses while the fishermen struggle to untangle the sausage.

When a net is first set it simply hangs down like a circular curtain. And the curious reason the fishermen can seine tuna in the eastern tropical Pacific is that this gigantic net wall hangs down through the warm surface layer into cool water beneath. The tuna, it seems, are like people sticking their toes into cold water and deciding not to go swimming. They won't swim down out of the warm water very far into the cold, and so they can be caught.

Some dolphins, such as the oceanic bottlenose, do swim right down through the net bottom and thereby escape, and so do some other groups of dolphins that fishermen call "the untouchables," who have learned to escape.

Finally, all escape, even for untouchables, is cut off when the fishermen "purse the net." To do this they winch in a thick cable that runs down through steel rings the size of small tires that are lashed along the bottom margin of the net. The net puckers closed and soon these rings and the net bottom begin to come up out of the water, dragged by the enormous tug of a big winch. The rings are carefully stacked on a long projecting metal pole called a "ring stripper." This orderly pattern allows the fishermen to set the net again without fear of tangles. I was amazed to see the air dusted with powdered rust from the rings as they were pulled aboard. The enormous tension of the operation had simply popped off any scale that had begun to accumulate. By this time the net was a huge saucer floating in the heaving sea.

Once the net is drawn in to about one-fourth its maximum diameter, the skipper begins the "backdown operation." This is presently the major way dolphins are released alive from a tuna set, for they won't jump out themselves. The net is lashed tight against the bows of the mother ship and the skipper begins to back away from it slowly, in a long backward arc around the net perimeter. This draws the remaining net out into a deep curving channel. If the skipper has made his move correctly he places a special shallow apron of net, a piece sewn into its upper margin, at the very end of a long finger of net. Tuna tend to shun such shallow water, but by this time the dolphins are inert, their school structure destroyed by crowding, and they can be slid passively onto the apron if the skipper is a skillful ship handler.

This is usually the first time in a set that one can see the tuna very well. The skipper watches, eagle-like, and when he sees the tight ranks of tuna heading his way he revs the ship's engines, backing hard against the finger of net, so hard that those net corks out on the end of the net channel are pulled five feet below the surface and dolphins begin to spill out willy-nilly, sometimes in great gouts of animals. But should the tuna turn and head for the apron, the skipper stops pulling immediately. The net corks pop to the surface and the net closes before the fish can reach its margin. The skipper watches. Once the fish turn and head back toward the vessel, he pulls again, spilling more dolphins. The maneuver is repeated again and again until the living dolphins are all free.

Once the dolphins have been released the net is drawn in tight alongside the ship, with only a fifteen-foot circle remaining. This is held open by the big net skiff and the fish "brailing" operation begins. Into the shivering mass of tuna a heavy dip-net called a "brailer" is lowered, scooping out a half-dozen or more of the big fish at a time. These are dumped into metal sluiceways on deck to slide belowdecks into the brine-filled chilling tanks. Fish blood is in the water at brailing time and sharks come furtively along the drifting odor trails, flashing pale just below the working fishermen. They've actually been there all the time, patrolling along outside the net waiting their chance.

We scientists had to learn everything that went on aboard a seiner and in the net with extreme rapidity. If we were to suggest new ways of doing things, we had just fifteen net sets to understand both what the fishermen did and what the dolphins faced, and nobody was telling us. Most of all we needed that *gestalt* of chase and netting in order to think constructively. We needed to watch events both from the deck and in the water where the dolphins and fish were. It simply wouldn't do for us to try to learn about this desperate drama from the deck of a ship alone. We had to don wet suits, masks, and snorkels and dive in those net circles. We had to watch the dolphins from close up, when they were crowded in the backdown channel, and we needed to discover if they made any moves to help themselves that we might exploit.

I was determined that somehow I was going to poise myself at the end of the backdown channel so that I could watch what the dolphins did as they were being sluiced out of the net.

Back in San Diego, before the trip, I'd thought about the need to see and work underwater. I asked the Fisheries Service to build me a little boat with underwater viewing capability. When she appeared amongst the equipage we loaded onto the *Jordan,* I knew she was both one of those awful scientific jury rigs, full of angles where people hadn't had time to smooth the corners, and a gem that would let me get my eyes underwater. Because I could remain in air I could observe as long as I liked and record everything I saw. The craft was a seventeen-foot fiberglass skiff whose bottom had been cut out and replaced with a rectangular plywood box, big enough to lie down in. My head would be just below waterline. There, if I could stand the inevitable crick in my neck, I could observe all I wanted through a boxy bow made of heavy Plexiglas. This ungainly boat had been slapped together with admirable speed by the shop people at the National Marine Fisheries Service lab in La Jolla, California, and little did they, or we, think that after this cruise we would take her to Hawaii, rechristen her *Maka Ala,* for "watchful one" in Hawaiian, and use her for three more years of uncomfortable observation.

The NMFS craftsmen realized as they were assembling her that she was going to turn over upon launching if they didn't ballast her heavily. After all, they had in essence built a big air-filled box that was supposed to project down under water. Since they had had only a few weeks to put her together, she came equipped with dozens of bags of lead birdshot to be used as ballast: 2200 pounds in all. I tried to arrange these little floppy pigs so that an observer could lie down among them. But it was always a lumpy bed until we sent her to Hawaii.

Then I melted the bags down into flat leaden slabs and arranged them along the walls of the viewing box in racks. Remembering my discomfort on the tuna grounds, we also slid a nice comfortable foam mattress in the box to lie on, but even so the crick in the neck always remained as a necessary aspect of work in the *Maka Ala*.

Underwater observation was only one part of our research plan for the cruise of the *Alisa*. In fact, the scientific scheduling of precious dedicated-vessel time was so tight that some other program was going on most of the time, day or night. One team recorded the underwater sound produced during a net set. It proved to be a remarkably noisy event, with the big seiner and her satellite craft projecting a veritable concert of sound underwater.

A second, less successful, attempt was to find out where the dolphins went at night, and where the animals came from that made up the big mixed schools in which we found them during the day. We wanted to know if the big schools the seiners chased were family units, or more casual assemblages, as our Hawaiian work had indicated they might be. Dolphins were tagged as they were released from the net, and some others were given radio tags and followed at night. The samples proved too small for definitive answers, but it did not seem that we were dealing with tight, structured schools of dolphins in the tuna seines. In other words, these schools seemed to be built generally like the Hawaiian ones.

Our final task was to turn Jim Coe loose on the netting process itself. He looked at the way the net and the dolphins interacted. Even though no one knew the nets, boats, and fishing process as well as the fishermen themselves, we needed to use our own eyes.

In the end there seemed to be two viewpoints we could contribute. First, we scientists were outsiders. Our very differences gave us fresh eyes. Perhaps, just perhaps, we could note something the fishermen hadn't seen, because our experience had been different from theirs. Perhaps we could put together a "two and two" which only we could see, because we were trained observers. And second, some of us were dolphin advocates, not emissaries sent to increase the catch of tuna, and the dolphins needed us badly.

Our behavioral observations began on the *Alisa's* deck. Bill, Warren, and I spent much of our time just watching the encirclement process, and trying to see what the dolphins did in response to it. We simply looked for regularities. Gradually patterns began to emerge from the original chaos as our eyes and minds sorted out the patterns before us.

We saw the dolphins slow in that last hopeless resignation as the bubble spiral entwined around them. Once in the net circle they always came up as far away from us and the *Alisa* as they could manage—a quarter of a mile out from our beam, and about seventy yards inside the distant cork line. There they formed a tight forlorn school that seemed to react to every disturbance. A passing speedboat caused them to move away, and why not? These wasp-voiced little boats had just harassed them and finally destroyed their chance of escape.

If the big net skiff gunned her throaty diesel engine, I could see the school move away. But curiously a diver in the water was treated as just another trapped dolphin, somebody their capture had crowded them in with, and not a source of fear. I concluded that they were circled in a ring of fear, and that they balanced the sources of fear in such a way that the fishermen could probably move a school this way and that inside the net, and, with ingenuity and commitment, figure out how to let them go.

As we watched it became apparent that other regularities existed, and curious ones too. Not infrequently all the animals of a trapped school traveled in one direction, and yet the school as a whole didn't move relative to the net. Only when we dove with the dolphins in the net did we realize that those traveling animals swam the length of the school on the surface, dove at its far margin, reversed course underwater, and swam back down the school to surface again. The school was a wheel, rolling this way and that, depending upon the source and strength of external stimuli.

What moved the school was fear. If a *ponga* roared past outside the net, the school moved away. If the mother ship's engine was being used to maneuver the ship and the net, the dolphins stationed themselves as far away as they could manage. I watched as these forces moved the milling dolphins back and forth for long distances inside the net, and always away from the major disturbance.

It slowly became apparent that there were two more-or-less-distinct parts to those trapped schools. One was a group of very slowly moving or still dolphins that often hung at or near the surface, with tails down at 45 degrees. The other was an active, quarrelsome matrix around the less active dolphins.

Only when the school's position began to change did the quiet animals begin to move slowly with their more active schoolmates. We called these slow ones "rafting dolphins."

More or less around the group of rafters was the highly fluid matrix of active, quarrelsome dolphins. The water in their areas of the school was frequently white with the tail slaps and lunges of dolphins chasing one another. When I finally dove in the net with the dolphins, I could see that aggression was vastly more prevalent in this active group than we remembered from undisturbed Hawaiian schools, or than existed in the quiescent core of rafting animals. These aggressive dolphins approached each other with snapping jaws and slicing pectoral fins. Even our divers were challenged by dolphins who exhibited the peculiar S-shaped threat posture that we had seen from time to time in the Sea Life Park spinner dolphin school. In the net these aggressive animals seemed to be predominately the ones that swam back and forth beneath the tiers of rafting animals floating near the surface.

I dubbed this highly fluid three-dimensional moving mass of dolphins a "teacup formation," contending that it could well be the functional unit that dolphins used to defend their societies at sea. It seemed possible to me that what we were seeing was a cadre of aggressive adults attempting to herd the more vulnerable parts of the trapped school generally toward the protected center of a "teacup" of aggressive adults that swam around and below them. With threats coming from every direction, and changing from moment to moment as *pongas* raced by, or when the mother ship's huge engine roared to life to maneuver the net, the dolphins might have been hard pressed to decide how to array their defenses. This might account for the high degree of fluidity we saw in the trapped school.

This formation had been seen once in a free-swimming school. The report came from the middle of the Gulf of Mexico, where a school of dolphins had come up alongside a research trawler. The scientists aboard noted that the school was being attacked by sharks and that the school arrayed itself against the side of the boat, a quiescent group including mothers with calves next to the boat and a half-circle of aggressive adults out on the perimeter somehow fending off the sharks. The dolphins stayed by the boat for four hours, until a heavy rain squall had overtaken the boat in the midst of this drama. When it passed, all were gone.

Only when I dove in the tuna net could I see the tiers of animals circulating under the more quiescent dolphins above. But others pointed out that rafting animals often enough appeared at the edge of the school, rather than in its center, and no clear separation of age, sex, or species could be assigned to rafters or aggressive dolphins. I wondered if the confining net and its many sources of disturbance was distorting a behavior pattern.

This highly dynamic formation of dolphins would resonate in my mind as I later watched undisturbed Hawaiian spinners, and when I finally recognized that cadres of adult males frequently arrayed themselves between me and the remainder of their school. Perhaps they were players in the teacup that would take exaggerated form inside a circle of fear formed by a tuna net.

If the teacup formation is real, it did not survive the ultimate crowding of a seine set, as the net narrowed down into a backdown channel. By that time, even if there were as few as fifty animals in the net the school became a melee, and many dolphins seemed clutched by a kind of catatonia. Many of them simply sank to the bottom of the channel and stacked there like cordwood on the sloping net wall, the white of their bellies flashing up through the water. At first, like everyone before us, we assumed that they had drowned.

Backdown is indeed a dangerous time for dolphins. Records gathered throughout the history of the fishery showed that thousands of dolphins sometimes died at backdown in a single net haul. We soon learned that it wasn't necessarily because these catatonic animals were truly dead. Much of the death seemed to occur when the skipper looked at all those stacked inert dolphins, and sighed in frustration that these maddening "dead" creatures had failed to help themselves. He threw up his hands in resignation and drew the net in, sure that all the sunken animals had drowned. And in fact, by the time the backdown channel had been hauled in they were dead, so his view was neatly confirmed.

Along with the rest of us, Jim Coe wondered about the odd helpless sinking of the dolphins, but he alone did something about it. He slung a little rubber raft over the rail into the backdown channel and climbed down into it. Then, sculling by hand (I can still see him flailing along, breast stroke fashion), with a face plate and snorkel he watched those sunken animals gleaming up from twenty feet down. Once back on board he announced laconically, "They aren't dead. I watched their eyes follow me."

I had to see for myself, and so on the next set I observed in the backdown channel with Jim. Sure enough, not an animal in that cordwood stack was dead. As we watched, animal after animal bestirred itself and rose for a breath, sometimes to sink again into the mass of stacked animals below.

We immediately realized that if the skipper waited a little while for these supposedly dead dolphins to rise, they could be sluiced out to safety. Jim once again took the lead, stationing himself out on the backdown channel looking through his face mask underwater. With his free hand he signaled to the skipper on the bridge. The once quiescent dolphins rose, and then, on Jim's signal, the skipper pulled hard, sluicing them out of the backdown channel. Such a simple thing, but so important! Perhaps 15 percent of the total kill of the fishery was involved in those sunken animals.

Swimming in tuna nets is an eerie and dangerous business, given the large sharks that were not infrequently seined with the dolphins and fish. Nonetheless, much that we needed to know was underwater in the net, and so on almost every set some of our team swam there, observing and talking notes into cranky little underwater tape recorders. Much of the time these divers came from the scientific team of the *Jordan,* or were one of our two photographers, Joe and Little Joe Thompson, a father and son team who seemed unburdened by fear. Bill Rogers, a brilliant young naturalist graduate student from University of California Berkeley, was there on nearly every set too, in spite of a healthy level of apprehension, and so were marine mammalogists Steve Leatherwood and Don Ljungblud.

On some of our sets the seine brought up sharks. They swam below the tunas and so they usually weren't seen until the net was nearly aboard. I watched while an oceanic white-tip, a

Galapagos shark, and on one occasion a ten-foot brute of a hammerhead surfaced in the net. We also looked with awe at one dolphin that died early in a set, sank, and was all but eviscerated by the sharks swimming out of sight below.

Most of the sharks had been excluded during the netting process and later began to gather around the floating stationary net as it was being pulled in. Joe Thompson, always looking for camera angles, decided to swim outside the net so he could get the net's mesh in his pictures. That was a mistake. In moments he clambered hastily back into his tending skiff after a close encounter with a white-tipped shark. The shark, prowling the net perimeter, had to be fended off with Joe's camera. Once I understood what I was seeing, I often noted the flickering forms of these sharks outside the net, probably attracted by the blood of dying tuna.

In spite of this obvious deterrent to going in the water, I had to see events in the net from the dolphin's perspective. So I spent some time in the net too, and my major sensation was not fear of sharks but the unreasoning apprehension of swimming in the open sea with the bottom twelve-thousand feet down. A person can handily drown in six feet of water, but to have those unimaginable depths below my sculling feet stirred up an almost overwhelming sense of dread. Irrationally, I was comforted by having the net below me defining a piece of that open water column. It provided a "place," a set of dimensions small enough that I could grasp them, and an enclosing wall. I guess we humans need boundaries like those. Certainly I felt a palpable sense of comfort at having the net around me, even if it did contain sharks. But it is also fair to say that I was accompanied most of the time by anxiety and the frequent need to swivel around to look behind me.

But when the dolphins were crowded around me, all my attention became focused on the animals. The rafting dolphins seemed to regard me as one of them: something curious but not hazardous that had come up in the net. I didn't frighten them enough to induce flight, and sometimes I could even reach out and touch one. I watched rafters hang at the surface, and then I watched them sink and dive into the tiers of dolphins who swam beneath, usually, I thought, to rise once again into the surface rafting group.

Things were very much different among the active animals that formed the amorphous teacup. They were purposeful and often irritable, not only at me but toward each other. I saw dolphins with bodies arched in anger, pectoral fins slicing back and forth, snapping and raking their exposed teeth at each other, or engaging in chases that took long, spiraling courses down into the blue water and out of sight. Squads of old males with thickened tail stocks and tall erect fins seemed to patrol in that part of the school, as was later described in detail by the behaviorists Karen Pryor and Ingrid Kang, who replaced my team on the next leg of the dedicated-vessel cruises.

Outside the heavy central concentrations of spotted dolphins (the most abundant species in tuna net sets, by about threefold), we sometimes saw the ghostly pale forms of eastern Pacific spinner dolphins. They swam around the perimeter of the teacup, often down near the limits of vision. They were almost always like that: satellites to the central and more abundant spotted dolphins. The two species, although they formed an obvious association together, were not equals. They didn't seem to mix in a real sense; the spinners were followers, and typically peripheral.

Why, I wondered, were these dolphins of such different species pulled together in this vast sea? They and the tuna seemed locked in a powerful and enigmatic affinity.

Only once while diving in the open net did I see tuna. On that occasion a small group of spinner dolphins swam in front of me and behind them trailed a single line of about twenty small tunas, each perhaps twenty pounds in weight, following everywhere the spinners went. There was no question in that observation about who followed whom.

But in the backdown channel as both net walls emerged out of the murk, swift yellowfin tunas began to appear in large numbers. They flooded back and forth in front of me, swimming in tight ranks. They are lovely animals in life, the blues, bronzes, and lemon yellows of their terete bodies as beautiful as paintings, and their full bodies are the embodiment of power. To me they seemed much more at home out there than did the dolphins. Even a slight tear in the net was enough for them to escape, and the entire school would flood through to safety. But that was after their mysterious bond with the dolphins had broken. Before, in the open sea, they were satellites, and little could dislodge them from their dolphins. Not even a flank speed chase by a huge tuna boat could do it.

One morning I had the chance to see those fish from the air. The captain agreed to send me up in the helicopter when a dolphin school had first been sighted. I clambered to the wheelhouse roof, bending down under the *whup whup whupping* blades, and strapped myself in the copilot's seat of the little chopper. We were set free by a crewman and immediately rose, tipped, and shied away from the ship in a climbing turn. Soon, a thousand feet below us, the pilot sighted the plunging dolphin school, flanked by flashing fish. The tuna seemed to swim below and to the sides of the dolphins, though sometimes they raced a little ahead of the plunging mammals. But to my eyes the dolphins were clearly nuclear and the fish were the followers, just as were those little tunas I saw in the net.

Down below, the dolphin school began to speed up. Two hundred dolphins poured from the water in hurrying ranks, splashing back in bursts of white water. The tuna followed below, and we could see them as flickering flashes of gold. I began to perceive how an experienced spotter could tell at a glance what tonnage of fish was involved, and then radio back that vital knowledge to the skipper, who would make the decision to set, or not set, the net. We called in the pilot's estimate: twenty tons of fish.

Seven miles away, and just a gray mote on the horizon, the *Alisa* responded to our call. The nearby *David Starr Jordan* responded too, plodding along after the faster vessel. The pursuit by the two vessels took place amid towering cumulus castles that cast vast gray shadows on the shining disk of that tropical sea. We could see the white wake suddenly spurt from the *Alisa*'s stern as she turned, picked up speed, and headed toward the dolphins. Our task over, we descended between the giant dark clouds and settled again, like a dragonfly, on the deckhouse roof. I mused that maybe the gyrostabilization of the *Alisa* was not primarily for the comfort of the crew but a way of providing a good place to land for the returning helicopter. After all, not all days were flat calm like this one.

Once back aboard I was scheduled to observe dolphin behavior in the backdown channel, so I quickly ducked away from the helicopter, her blades still slowing, and made my way to the ladder inset in the ship's hull that let me drop into a skiff pitching alongside. Once aboard the smaller craft, we circled the *Alisa,* coming around her bows to view the giant net circle that rose and fell in the swell.

Soon the awkward shape of the viewing vehicle, which had been launched and brought over from the *Jordan,* appeared alongside the net. I leapt aboard and moved down into the sweltering viewing vault. I quickly ignored all the lumpy bags of shot that formed by bed as I looked out below the surface into the ultramarine sea.

There, curving away into the blue murk, was the wall of the net. It arced down, first tan and then fading to pale bluish-white as it deepened. The last of it that I could see dove straight down toward the distant invisible net bottom. Bright rows of yellow corks bobbed on the surface just above my head. At first I could see no fish or dolphins, and so my eyes turned to smaller things. That remote sea was full of life: tiny crabs zigged by, and planktonic jellyfish danced slowly in the swell. I recognized little Portuguese man-of-wars, strange colonial animals equipped with little gas-filled sails and whose tentacles were lined with potent stinging cells. A good thing, I thought, that our divers were well encased in rubber wet suits.

I tethered my craft to the corkline on the net section that would become the "superapron" of the backdown channel—the low spout of net that formed when the captain pulled hard with the *Alisa*. That was a landlubber's mistake. In moments a flood of pyrotechnic Portuguese blasted over all the speakers. Not understanding that I was the culprit, I stood up in the cockpit trying to see who was getting chewed out. Only when one of my crew came alongside and said the message was for me, and to "get the hell off the corkline," did I understand. I quickly cast off, and the flood of abuse subsided. The skipper had seen me tied up out there and knew that when the full force of his huge vessel pulled against the net it would submerge me along with the corkline.

I quickly repositioned the viewing vehicle at the edge of the channel so I could continue to watch backdown events as they developed. Soon I saw the channel, a long canyon of net filled with dolphins and fish. The fish patrolled the net wall in disciplined legions, hurrying back and forth, alert for any route of escape. The dolphins, on the other hand, were helpless and disorganized. They faced every which way, and down below in the pale blue I could see some of them beginning a pile of inert animals. Their cordwood pile soon became four deep. As Jim Coe had insisted, I could see those eyes moving. I watched as from time to time an individual awkwardly shook itself free of the pile, rose to breathe and sank again, often tail first. What a strange difference! Somehow the vaunted intelligence of the dolphin stood in the way of escape, while the fish, not so encumbered, could take advantage of any opportunity. Something fragile in the dolphin's social organization had been blasted by encirclement in the net, while the fish's simpler responses as a cipher in a school were still intact.

Only spotted dolphins were present in this particular cordwood pile, but deep down behind them a half-dozen spinners flashed into view. They were ghostly bluish-gray against the dark water, and as usual they swam separate from but near the spotters. The small group of spinners rushed blindly at the net wall, bending it outward in a motion muted by the weight of water, and then they rebounded back. I understood now why net designers had reduced the mesh size in the region of the backdown channel. Otherwise those frantic dolphins would have thrust their long beaks through the webbing, tangled, and died.

Backdown reached its culmination. The channel had been properly shaped by the skillful maneuvering of the skipper, and dolphins began to collect in pathetic piles just inside its opening, right in front of me. The tuna appeared briefly, turned, and hurried back toward the ship. At once the skipper pulled strongly astern. I watched as the outermost corks just to my side submerged deeper and deeper, a current sluicing up through the opening. Up from their piles came some of the dolphins. Headfirst, tailfirst, and sideways they came, all but inert in the current. They rolled and straggled over the corkline beneath them. A mother and calf spotted dolphin drifted into view, their mutual bond stronger than any of the fear that surrounded them. They swam aimlessly, trusting only one another.

Dolphins eased close to my viewing window, and just over the corkline were immediately galvanized into purposeful action. The instant a dolphin passed the corkline it *knew* it was free. It burst forward, propelled by powerful wide-amplitude tail strokes. Such animals then dove, swimming at full speed beneath my viewing vehicle, down and away into the dark water, only to burst from the surface in a high bounding series of leaps two hundred yards behind me. Not until the animals were a quarter of a mile from the net did they slow and reassemble their school. I wondered how the mother-and-young had fared in that frantic flank-speed rush.

The instant change from helpless apathy to full life was startling. Even though I had already seen it from the ship's deck, only now did the full force of the change hit me. I knew then without any possible equivocation that the net, the *Alisa*'s speedboats, and the mother vessel represented an overwhelming ring of fear. The dolphins had known all along that they were trapped, and knew instantly when they were released. Nothing in their oceanic lives, where no complete barriers at all existed, had equipped them to jump the corkline that bobbed two inches above the surface. I emphasize this fear because a scientific debate went on at the time between those who saw the dolphins as dealing calmly with net encirclement, and those of us who felt that they were deep in the grip of fear.

My view was underscored by the many dolphins that were sluiced out of the backdown channel tailfirst. Some of these, with a wall of net still in view ahead of them, even though they were actually free, did not perceive this freedom and sculled slowly back into the net. They had to be slid out a second time before they would come to life like the others.

Soon our fifteen net sets had been made, our data gathered, and we headed for home. We scientists of the *Alisa* transferred to the *David Starr Jordan* for the long cruise to Manzanillo, Mexico, leaving the *Alisa* out there to complete her load before she too headed home. Much of what we had accomplished would only appear when the reams of data sheets, films, and notes had been digested. And much would depend upon the dedicated-vessel cruises that would follow us.

Our science is slow stuff and it would take more time than we had at sea to "prove things." But I felt that we and the fishermen had joined forces a little in the way we had to proceed. Rigid proof was a long way away from anything we had achieved, but we had experienced seining first hand, and we now had those fifteen sets to think with.

I went back filled with the need to know much more about wild, unfished dolphin lives. We had to spend more time up close to them to see how they lived free of nets, and then we had to set such knowledge in a framework that would show how those hapless netted ones, with their inadequate teacup defense, might be helped to free themselves. The crowding of the subtle dolphin society until it loses all semblance of organization, leaving the animals unable to help themselves, is not the way to go. This method was derived from the understandable fishery viewpoint that tuna in the hold is the primary aim. But it does not consider what the dolphins face. It was, I thought, time to "think dolphin" for a while.

6

The Hukilau

MY time on the *Alisa S. J.* reminded me all over again how fearful dolphins can be in strange situations. The tuna had paraded in their restless ranks in the backdown channel, alert for the slightest opportunity to escape, while the dolphins in the same channel had stacked in those forlorn windrows. If we understood this difference, we might be able to let the dolphins go with the same speed as tuna escape. Knowing the dimensions of dolphin fear might just provide us with the key.

What I knew of dolphin fear had come from a lot of small observations of captive dolphins over the years. I knew that every oceanarium dolphin trainer spends long hours training his charges to go through gates between big exhibit tanks and the smaller pools where they are trained or isolated for one reason or another.

It doesn't matter which way the dolphins are asked to go. It's no different for a dolphin to be asked to go into a holding pool or to go back into a million-gallon exhibit tank. The gate's the thing. And for this reason no exhibit designer builds little dolphin gates anymore. They are built just as wide and just as deep as trainers can easily handle. This usually means an opening about six feet square. Dolphins hate going through such restrictions, and that's that. Even though they can see their buddies on the other side, they buck and fight against going through, and even if they have done it a thousand times they always go through in a burst of speed. The fear of death is somehow involved.

One experiment at Kealakekua showed us that they are also wary of new things. The premier team of marine mammal bio-acousticians, Bill Watkins and Bill Schevill, both of Woods Hole Oceanographic Institution out on Cape Cod, Massachusetts, wanted to use our spinner school to test a new experimental tool they had developed. It was called a *non-rigid listening array* and they wanted to station it on the bottom near the sand patch where the dolphins rested. This array consisted of a spiderweb of cables, four hydrophones (underwater microphones), little sound generators (called "pingers"), and other things such as anchors and skiffs. The pingers were used to describe the geometry of the array at any given moment. By making a ping from one of them and then recording how long it took to get to each of the receiving hydrophones, the two scientists could tell you with great precision exactly where every listening station was located. This information was then turned about to describe where all the dolphins who decided to make sounds were swimming.

Somehow the scientists unsnarled all this rat's nest of equipment and set it in place in about 120 feet of water offshore of the main cliff face. Dolphins came regularly to this little area and it was hoped that they would swim between the hydrophones. Then, by laborious computation, the two biologists could prepare a detailed track of the members of a school in three dimensions. Plots of passing schools might reveal many details of dolphin school structure. It should be possible to hear individual dolphins as they exchanged signals with one another, and it should be possible to describe the geometry of the passing school by plotting the sounds of its members. In short, if it worked, the snarl of wires and listening gear could help us unravel much of the intimate discourse within a dolphin school. Like many such hopeful scenarios, it proved much easier said than done. For five of the six days the array occupied the bay bottom, the dolphins avoided it assiduously. They came into the bay as before, and when their sonar beams revealed the array, they skirted around it like kids tiptoeing past a cemetery at night.

Only on the sixth day did a few dolphins approach the array within good listening distance, and even then their sounds were furtive and sparse, as if communicating near that strange tangle was dangerous.

Sadly, on the seventh day the two Bills had to pick their wires from the bay bottom and leave for the east coast, their testing complete. Two events from this brief scientific foray stand out for me. First, the Watkins-Schevill array, if it had been used for months instead of only six days, could tell us many things we do not know about how dolphin schools work and what the phonations of these animals mean. In fact these two workers have since used a similar array to give us our first insights into the behavior of sperm whale schools that sometimes swim thousands of feet down in the deep sea. Such listening posts can indeed provide "acoustic eyes" underwater.

And second, I was fascinated by the caution of the dolphins. It seemed not to be the simple fear of individual animals, but a group process in which the whole school stamped "danger" on a little piece of previously friendly sea. It was also clear that the dolphins of Kealakekua knew their underwater world in considerable detail and anything new in it was a threat that "had to prove itself innocent" before they would swim near.

Why didn't we build an array of our own? Well, reducing its data is an incredibly complicated process which only a specialist can do well. To this day, amongst biologists only the

Woods Hole team is effective in the arcana of its use. One day soon a bright young behavioral scholar with time on his or her hands and a solid knowledge of electronics will revolutionize what we know of wild dolphin signaling with something like the Woods Hole array.

As for dolphin wariness, it clearly wears off in time. The many boats anchored over the Kealakekua sand patch had once been strange and dangerous objects too, and now they were accepted as parts of the landscape. The resting dolphins frequently came skinning along close to them, much closer than they did to the Woods Hole array.

Somehow, this dolphin caution seemed to me more complete than I would expect from a deer in the forest. Faced with the unfamiliar, dolphin schools tighten, become more fishlike, and routinely flow around the offending object like so many anchovies. Anything new requires getting used to. The "getting used to" is, I think, a process in which individuality is submerged in favor of what's good for the group, a point we will return to when I discuss what we learned about the mechanics of dolphin schools.

The fear exhibited by a dolphin school can include the most unlikely things. One day we were dragging a rope behind our vessel to straighten out its kinks when we encountered a spinner school. Much to our surprise the dolphins seemed to regard that tiny snaking rope as a stone wall. They would not cross under it even though a hundred feet of clear open water lay beneath it. We split the school neatly in two merely by towing that rope through the middle.

Observations like these led me to explore further. What were the dimensions of a gate through which a dolphin school would move easily? If we knew this it might be possible to maneuver a netted school to such a gate and let it go.

Of course like most simple questions there are complexities to solve. For example, fishermen would have to learn to maneuver the dolphins reliably to the chosen release point. Knowing how entire trapped dolphin schools avoided fearful stimuli such as net skiffs and the big seiner itself, that might be simple. Then gear designers would have to develop a way of temporarily opening a big gate in the side of the seine. Because of the huge stresses on an open net, that would have its own problems.

Though I watched a dolphin school split when a single rope snaked along at the surface, I doubted that that simple expedient would work as a way of guiding dolphins in a net. There is too much else that is fearful in a tuna seine, and fears are balanced against each other. Witness the fact that inside a tuna net I could swim up to a trapped dolphin and touch it, something that would never be tolerated at sea. No, there were priorities of fear inside a tuna net. A swimmer was of far less concern than that thrumming mother ship. A thin line would, I predicted, also be ignored under such circumstances.

For a long time I wondered how I could test the fear reactions of an entire dolphin school. I couldn't set a net around them for fear it would collapse and drown the animals I sought to save. Then I remembered a method that Hawaiians had used to solve a related but different problem.

Over the prickly coral reefs around all tropical islands there are teeming shoals of fish, but no net can catch them. A net dragged across a reef, or thrown onto its surface, instantly entangles and is then torn to pieces on the myriad glasslike projections jutting from the coral.

To counter this problem, the Hawaiians reeve a row of long palm fronds into the twist of a rope that floats at the surface. When this contraption, called a *hukilau,* is dragged across the reef, it does not entangle. The frond tips simply brush across the rough coral surface like a row of feather dusters, chasing the fish ahead of them. Then the fishermen steer the fish to a sand patch free of coral and set a normal net around them. After that they generally have a splendid *luau* on the beach.

Would something like this work on dolphins? I wondered.

So at the University of California where I then taught, we devised my version of a *hukilau* for testing at Kealakekua. I had it built just as insubstantially as I could. For the top or "cork" line, which I wanted to float at the surface, we selected approximately four hundred yards of thin half-inch-diameter polypropylene line. I had my team affix a series of little floats along its length to help buoy the line when we pulled hard. Then every six feet we attached quarter-inch lines sixty-four feet long, weighted at their tips with smooth blobs of lead, just enough to sink them vertically from the corkline. These lines, about the diameter of the average clothesline, and much too weak to resist the charge of a large frightened dolphin, might, I hoped, inhibit them from swimming through.

That was it. I was betting that this spider web, featuring a regular series of openings six feet wide through which any dolphin could swim, could catch a dolphin school. Generally it wouldn't reach the sea bottom, so if a dolphin didn't want to go between the vertical lines it could escape by diving under the danglers. We bundled the dolphin *hukilau* up at the lab and sent it off to Kealakekua. My grad student Sheri Gish flew with the *hukilau* to our Kealakekua camp and performed a series of tests on the wild schools of the bay. Here is an excerpt from the scientific description of these tests:

With this insubstantial barrier we were able to encircle whole schools of spinner dolphins in 20–40 m (66–131 ft) of water and to crowd them severely. In one case when the *hukilau* was reduced to a surface area of about 6 × 10 m (19 × 33 ft) a school of 40–60 animals refused to leave through the wide openings but continued to mill inside. Even when two of the thin vertical lines were removed, leaving a "door" 6 m (19.6 ft) wide, the school continued to circle, "eyeing" the opening but not passing through it. Only when the area was further reduced did the majority of animals pass

The *hukilau* that trapped a whole dolphin school. Thin polypropylene lines dangle six feet apart, except for the place where we removed one line and they still wouldn't go out.

through the wide opening. They had been held captive for 3 hours and 50 minutes in this fashion.

This demonstration involves wild and free dolphins faced with an unfamiliar obstacle. It is not necessarily what might happen in a tuna net, though that test has not yet been run. My guess is that if a *hukilau* is used in a tuna seine to crowd dolphins toward a waiting gate, the danglers will have to be much closer together than at Kealakekua, because of the many other fears that impinge upon trapped dolphins.

Whatever is used, it will have to be a "dolphin sieve": a device that lets tuna through and somehow prevents them from going back with the dolphins, while the latter are being maneuvered to a gate big enough to let a whole school of dolphins swim free.

How to design such a sieve is a problem for experienced fishermen and gear experts. They will have to decide how to open the net to let the dolphins out, and how to separate dolphins and tuna. I'm hopeful that such a team could solve these problems. After all, they have already devised the backdown maneuver and all the clever bits of gear that go with it, and the intricate seining method itself.

My scientist's vision (i.e., layman's vision) is of a "crowder net" attached inside the big net as it is set. It would be equipped with "tuna ports" that let the tuna flow through into the main seine, but which don't allow the fish to reverse course and rejoin the dolphins. I see it as positioned out on the far net margin away from the seiner where the trapped dolphins always congregate. Probably its end can be released by the speedboat men, using quickly operated snaps, and then pulled around the dolphins by other boats that are already in the water. Its circle could automatically bring the dolphin school up against a release point.

I have no idea how this rig might be built,

but I do think the "circle of fear" that surrounds a trapped dolphin school can be used to steer them to an escape point, and this very likely is not especially difficult to do. I also know that it is best to maneuver the trapped dolphins before their schools lose their coherence and internal order, and when they are separated to some degree from the tuna.

If experts from both the scientific side and the fishery come together, I believe that a smooth and simple dolphin release system can be devised. If it succeeds it might well save both dolphins and fishing time. The backdown operation, after all, is a difficult and tricky maneuver suitable only for the best of ship handlers, and the time saved could be spent catching tuna.

What none of this answers is, How much seining, even if release is simple and effective, can a wild dolphin population put up with and still carry out the necessary events of a normal life? So far they have put up with a remarkable amount of such disturbance and their tattered schools seem to be hanging in there.

There are other mysteries, too. What is lost when a dolphin school is crowded? Why should they be so inordinately disturbed when arrangements within their schools are disrupted? These questions set me to imagining the inner dynamics of dolphin schools, and this line of thought became a major theme of our next attempt to learn about the lives of wild Hawaiian dolphins.

7

Hana Nai'a

IN 1978, I left Washington, my term on the commission completed. I planned to return to Hawaii to do a real in-depth study of the spinners. My excitement was almost palpable, like that of a little kid on Christmas day with a pile of new boxes to be opened. Of all the treasures to be had, most of all I wanted to spend more time with my head underwater, down there in the real world of the dolphin, down where they disciplined their young, where they caressed and quarreled, and where they all met the desperate challenge of living in the open sea. I wanted to know where they found food, how they slept, how the traditions of their lives were played out, and how their babble of clicks, whistles, groans, banjo twangs, and barks made sense in their lives. I wanted to go to sea in that awkward viewing vessel that I had so inappropriately tied to the backdown channel of the tuna net and to lie in her belly watching dolphins until the crick in my neck drove me topside.

Not that I was disappointed with what we had accomplished in Washington. By the time I left the land of lawyers, a sixfold reduction in dolphin kill had been achieved. Even so, twenty-four thousand dolphins a year still died in tuna nets, a far cry from the goal the Marine Mammal Protection Act had set of "kill and serious injury rate of insignificant numbers approaching zero." But the affected dolphin species were no longer in danger of extinction, according to National Marine Fisheries Service calculations. That was our most important achievement.

Once free I immediately began to plan the new dolphin field effort. This time I wanted it to be much more than a reconnaissance, and so I turned to the twin tasks of building a solid field team and finding money to finance my dream. Fortunately for me, I can take pleasure in these things, the assessment of skills and limits in people, the construction of a group that can go into some foreign situation and fit in enough to wrest precious truths from nature. My colleagues and I were to be tested severely, because times had changed Kealakekua radically since Tom and I had worked there. It had become an active and poignant battleground on which the cultural patterns of ancient Hawaii were pitted against the predatory sprawl of commercial America.

Kealakekua Bay now lies gemlike and seemingly peaceful only half a dozen water miles south of the nearest tourist hotel, where every weekend a pig is roasted and local Hawaiian boys dance in their flowered loin cloths and blow the conch shell, and where local girls and boys, barefoot and lithe, jolt out the sexually explicit rhythms of the Tahitian hula. The docile tourists watching all this in matching flower-patterned muumuus and shirts do not understand that the accompanying chants are sometimes filled with local jokes full of anger and insult to the visitors, any visitors, because their Hawaiian way of life is being swallowed up in the banalities of a tourist culture that often mocks, and, worse, ignores the dignity of their past, making cardboard cutouts of their lives and history.

In 1980, precisely at Kealakekua, the roots of the conflict

reached the surface. On one side was the island culture whose source was, ultimately, ancient Hawaii. The village of Napoo-poo (*Nah-po-o-po-o*) had been home to a few fishing families for generations. Other similar families lived a little to the south, near the Painted Church (a wonderfully decorated little church, complete with dusky Jesus, painted by the Hawaiian congregation long ago), and near Honaunau (the City of Refuge), and on down the coast to the village of Milolii near the south tip of the island, where the best outrigger canoes were still built. As a local half-Hawaiian lay minister told us in his deep Hawaiian patois, "Man, yo' in a *heavy* area."

Nearly every night the fishermen of Napoopoo arose in the morning dark, flaked their nets in canoe bottoms, loaded bags of papaya chum, and paddled swift as arrows out over rocky banks to where the *opelu* would rise. Before the night began to fade, they turned for shore with silvery mounds of these plump twelve-inch fish piled amidships. Then they snaked in between dark rocks and beached on a little sand patch. After unloading, the fishermen worked in the fading dark, cigarettes glowing, talking quietly as they butterflied and salted the fish, and then hung them up for drying in the rising sun. That ritual had gone on for a long time.

The jaws of encroaching tourism were closing just six miles down the coast, but another modern change, the hippie revolution, had already hit. Because one can pick food off the papaya and avocado trees almost for the asking, and *lilikoi* vines drop their pungent yellow fruit all over the roadways, it is no trick at all to live off the land at Kealakekua. Sandal- and loin-cloth-clad escapees from industrial America walked the roads everywhere, seeking a simpler way of being. Some of these newcomers brought with them that other accoutrement of their culture, drugs. The Hawaiians responded with bands of young toughs who went under the name of Primo

Warriors, and who badgered and bullied the defenseless hippies, but some joined forces with them too, attracted by the easy money of the drug traffic.

Hawaii is prime country for marijuana culture. Some say the economic value of the crop is greater than the major legal industry, tourism. The warm maritime winds seldom cease, the rains predictably wet things down, and, most important, the rough revetments of lava make the landscape all but impenetrable for those who would seek out the hidden plots. As a result Maui Wowie and Kona Gold are established brand names in the illicit trade.

Because this time I had no big boat at my beck and call on which we could follow the dolphins and on which we could live, it was impossible for us simply to sail into the bay and fish up a mooring buoy and then wait for the dolphins to come in under our bows. We had to plunk down in the midst of all the ferment, where we would have to solve several layers of human problems before we could settle back, human to dolphin.

By this time Tom had moved on to head up a big offshore marine mammal survey project, so I began to look for new field leadership. As a full-time professor in a big, pressure-filled university, I knew that I needed the best young professionals I could find, because there was no way I could run the day-to-day operation myself. I was, sadly, relegated to putting the larger pieces together, and throughout the project I would only descend on the field camp when my university duties let me.

I know at least some of my own limits and have long since learned to seek coworkers who excel where I am weakest. My forte is the visionary stuff, but to run a field camp such as I knew we needed, there had to be people with their feet on the ground, ones who would guard the always-meager budget, keepers and massagers of the precious data, ones comfortable with modern statistics, and somewhere in the team there had to be a wizard who could make reluctant equipment work in the rain and salt spray. The older I get, the more mechanisms of any kind tend to decay and disintegrate when I fumble with them.

Also, I wanted at least partial images of myself in my younger days. My team had to include young, resilient field scientists who could take an idea or task and run with it when I wasn't around. They had to have the doggedness to overcome all the natural and human obstacles that seem to be the fate of every scientific field camp I've ever visited. Then, once camp was established and we had achieved détente with both the locals and the resident bureaucrats, when the moorings for boats were down and holding, and when a source of beer had been found and we knew how to keep it cool, we could all turn our eyes to the dolphins.

I hoped to surround this leadership with the brightest, most imaginative bunch of fresh-caught students I could find. Young minds unrestrained by traditional wisdom always jog their elders, and always shake out new thoughts and directions that give field work verve and excitement. The trick, once one finds some good prospects, is to nurture them instead of pounding them into this or that preformed mold and thus removing all their lovely individuality.

A lecture tour happened to take me to the State University of New York at Stony Brook, out on Long Island, where an old friend from graduate school days, Dr. George Williams, was a luminary in evolutionary biology. George asked if I would like to sit in on the final Ph.D. exam of a young student of dolphins, Bernd Würsig. I sniffed a possible field leader and went off to pose a few conundrums for his exam. He passed with flying colors, and later I signed him on as the first member of the new spinner dolphin team.

Bernd, son of a German master woodworker, carried much of his father's precision with him. As he sat before us trying to answer our questions, he and his wife Melany were almost alone in doing what the study of dolphins then needed most. They were providing *proof* for the observations they made, lifting the science from the level of anecdote to that of testable ideas. With almost overwhelming industry and integrity they had watched, counted, measured, and verified every little detail of the things they saw. In their studies, hundreds of hours of field work were frequently distilled down to a short prose paragraph or two followed by the numbers they had wrested from nature. These were quantifications of everything they had observed, telling the reader exactly what had taken place. Their work was peppered with statements of how many, how far away, how deep, and then, routinely, a probability figure followed, telling

Bernd and Melany Würsig on board our vessel *Nai'a*. Bernd was in charge of our field program and Mel, among many other contributions, ran the theodolite station. *R. S. Wells*

the reader how much one should trust the statement they had just made. I very much wanted that stamp on my next effort.

Such intensity implies much personal discipline and Bernd has plenty of that. Sometimes it can also imply a difficult field companion, and that can happen with Bernd too when his colleagues are sloppy about this or that measurement or schedule. Bernd simply cares too much to allow sloppiness to go unchallenged, and that, in my mind, is a tradeoff I was eager to accept.

Bernd also has a miraculous affinity for any of man's metal creations, anything with moving parts or that is actuated by wires and electricity. They lie there on his table waiting to be fixed, and since they are in a master's hands they do not explode into odd-shaped bits of metal and vibrating springs as they do in mine, but stay composed while he runs his fingers over them seeking out the place that hurts. He then makes them go again with a part of a beer can or a piece of wire.

Later in our camp this soothing instrumental presence rejuvenated everything from an ancient pickup truck we named Winifred—already comfortable with the idea of rusting in the weeds behind Jim Simmond's garage—to complex listening gear.

Bernd filled in another gap in my scientific armament. He is a master statistician, and often uses these numerical methods as a detective might. He sorts statistically through the piles of hard-won data, looking for meaning. I've never been able to do that very well, because my method of seeing comes at nature the other way around. I go out in nature, floating in a skiff on some bay, watch for a while to take in the entire ambiance, and then after I *feel* that I understand a little I begin to formulate ideas, and from them come pointed questions. I then ask my question. For example, I might think I saw the schools of dolphins tighten as they came into Kealakekua to rest.

"Do the schools tighten?" I ask. Nature says to me as I check again with her,

"Well, there's some truth in what you say, but that's not all you can see if you just look harder."

Then I think some more and go back to nature with a refined new question. This time I ask if the little clots of animals we call subgroups begin to disappear when the dolphins near the resting grounds. Usually by this time nature says, "You're getting there, but that's still not all there is; try again."

Then I hone the idea a little, form a new question, and ask nature again. As with a pocket knife being sharpened, my questions become sharper and sharper with each iteration. Pretty soon I can ask penetrating questions that no one thought of at the outset. I propose to nature that the school members coming into the bay suppress their individuality, tighten, and in effect their schools come to be structured much like those of schooling fish. Now, isn't that interesting? Why should dolphins entering the rest period begin to act like fish? Next round. Sometimes it takes moments, and sometimes years, to play out such questions and answers.

Once I'm pretty sure I know what is going on, I can gather specific kinds of data, and then apply my few old-but-trusty statistical tests so someone else will believe me, and move on to the next round. "Spinning the observational wheel," I call it.

The exciting thing about working from these two divergent methods, Bernd's and mine, is that they frequently uncover wholly different sorts of information. A research effort such as I was planning is enriched by having both approaches.

I'd heard a little about Bernd's wife Melany, but I had no idea what the other half of "Bernd and Mel" was really like. Mel proved to be a tiny bundle of strength, energy, warmth, and perception, and by the time I met her she had become the best tracker of wild dolphins anywhere.

Indefatigable, she had already perched for hundreds of hours on various remote cliffs in the cold wind or the sun, talking dip angles and azimuths into a tape recorder as she followed schools of dolphins through the telescope of a surveyor's instrument. Later she entered the resultant figures into a special computer program that compensated for the height of her observation post above the sea, the curvature of the earth, and the tides. Then, miraculously (for a pre-computer biologist like me), the machine printed out a drawing of the exact paths the animals had followed. Because Mel had talked about other things to her tape recorder while all this was going on, her road map of dolphin travels became a story of how often they breathed, how far they went under water, and how they milled about this or that underwater obstacle. Mel was to perform this and other kinds of magic for us even while she tended their kinetic young daughter, Kim, in our field camp.

Soon after Bernd and Mel joined me, my first lieutenant materialized. Randy Wells had already begun to establish an enviable research record before he joined me as a doctoral student at the University of California Santa Cruz. With great perseverance, he and his colleagues Blair Irvine and Michael Scott had set out to understand the life patterns of a population of bottlenose dolphins living near Sarasota, Florida. The work still goes on today in those shallow bays, and each iteration fills in more about the richness of dolphin life. Like Jane Goodall with her chimpanzee troop, Randy knows essentially every animal personally, more than a hundred in all, and most of the dolphins have been caught, marked, measured, aged, had their chromosome patterns uncovered, and then been released again to live out their life patterns under Randy's benign eye.

For Randy the chance to work with the very different spinner dolphin was a chance to gain perspective. Just as working with both captive and wild animals of the same species gives precious perspective, so does comparing the life patterns of two different species.

Randy possesses many of Bernd's tal-

Randy Wells, my lieutenant at *Hana Nai'a*. Here, on the platform in front of our field headquarters, he records a "scan series"—all the comings and goings of the dolphins in Kealakekua Bay. *Bernd Würsig*

ents: a quiet force, humor, an orderly mind, dedication, absolute intellectual honesty, and the ability to handle himself at
sea. Like all good seamen everywhere, Randy carries with him
a knowledge that the placid sea can switch quickly into a storm-
tossed maelstrom. This causes him to put extra fanbelts, rolls
of duct tape, and little bundles of toothpicks down somewhere
in the bowels of his boats where he can find them. "One," he
says, "never knows."

Both Randy and Bernd were skilled wildlife photographers,
and my early attempts to draw spinner dolphin scarring patterns received little acknowledgment from them. Once the
project was under way, no school passed unphotographed. Soon
stacks of neatly annotated and filed boxes of slides began to
pile up, recording all the intricacies of dolphin interaction and
association.

With these three I had the nuclear spinner dolphin team.
With a crew like that, I not infrequently thought afterward, it's
all down hill. To be sure, as with any complex foray into a
culture with imperatives different from our own, it was often
not easy, but the problems were never about the integrity of
our science. Instead they were about money, social ferment in
Hawaii, used-car dealers, bureaucrats, and small planes that
always flew with the stall indicator light glowing red.

Beyond this research core came the students, and they were
quite as wonderful in their individual ways as my central team.
They shook us out of our preconceptions and each added
much to what we ultimately accomplished. Best of all,
our Hawaiian field camp was to be, as I had hoped,
full of life and excitement and discovery, and in
no small degree it was because the place crawled
with students.

We decided to name our project, and with
this came our first exposure to the Hawaiian
love of the double entendre. I can't

remember exactly who suggested it but some local resident at Kealakekua said we should call the project "Dolphin Work," or *Hana Nai'a*. We bought the idea immediately, and after we'd printed it on our T-shirts along with a leaping spinner dolphin, the locals snickered at us, saying: "Do you really KNOW what *Hana Nai'a* means?" We didn't, but soon enough we found that it was a shorthand description of the graphic non-Victorian caressing the fishermen could see when they looked down at dolphins traveling below their outrigger canoes.

Delighted instead of shocked, our reaction was something like, "Gosh, a double entendre of our own! That's lots better than having a dog for a mascot. No feeding, no messes on the rug, and it's always there when we need it. And it has a nice racy ring to it." So our effort became *Hana Nai'a* and we wore then, and still wear, our T-shirts proudly.

Together my team and I rustled up support for our project through the National Science Foundation, and the National Marine Fisheries Service, who, fortunately for us, felt that there was still much of importance that needed to be learned about spinner dolphins. Though far from the actual battleground, we were still trying to solve the dolphin's dilemma on the tuna grounds. Though our minds were tightly focused on our local dolphin friends, we could never truly forget their beleaguered relatives living just two days' run to the southeast by tuna seiner. Always, always, and not very far below the surface, that situation was there, troubling us even as we watched the Hawaiian animals, as we celebrated the day's new discovery around our dinner table, and as we listened and watched, trying as hard as we could to be unobtrusive observers.

When Tom and I had gone to Hawaii much of our time was spent on boats anchored in the bay, or up on the cliff near the pig traps, and only a little in the rented house in town. We were visitors who touched down, and then left, and we scarcely knew Kealakekua. This time was different. This time we would, willy-nilly, become members of the Kealakekua community. It took three different tries before we finally were able to settle down, push the world back a little, and begin our work: just us and the dolphins.

Field work with dolphins, or any other animal I guess, has more than one lure. The animals are central, of course. Contriving how to "penetrate nature's veil" to learn true things from an unknown living thing is fascinating and often difficult business. It's like following a detective story. If you have enough wit and persistence, the story will begin to unfold. Dolphins are more difficult than most, even if they do come into populated bays. Nearly everything of importance that they do is hidden away from us below the sea surface, and they usually edge away out of view when you come near.

But there is another lure too, and that had everything to do with what we faced at Kealakekua. It's the sheer human adventure of going out to some unknown place in the world, amidst unknown people with values certain to be different from your own, setting up a research camp and making it function. The animals, wherever they may be found, provide the *raison d'être* to go in the first place. But they drop one in the darndest places, without regard for the weather, the language, the bugs, the things that itch, the differences in culture, the local bureaucrats, or, especially these days, the political situation. One has to be "up for solving such equations" because they are part of just about every field biologist's work. Another thing I like about these field ventures is learning the history of the area in which you work: the different tracks back in time that have made the locals who they are. At Kealakekua events were measured against the coming of Captain Cook, and the time of the first Hawaiian king, Kamehameha I.

I have never worked at a more exotic

place than Kealakekua Bay, or one so filled with the human conflicts and crosscurrents of our times. It took all our wit and tolerance to settle in and finally to learn about the *nai'a* who lived there. But we came armed with the field scientist's persistence, and in the end we prevailed, bundled up our precious data, and went back to the University of California to digest it all. But not infrequently we had to bite our tongues, step back, and say to ourselves, "We *will* do this thing somehow."

Especially we had to try to cross the cultural barrier ourselves, to understand the world we had invaded so that we could know how to act with subtlety and consideration.

What protected us most, I suspect, was the experienced field biologist's almost mystical sense that, yes, everything will surely go wrong at times, and despair will not infrequently be at hand, but with persistence the opposite will also come. Winds, and torrential rains, will very likely sink your boat and drive fleets of toads, huge spiders, and centipedes into your field shelter, the forestry commission (of whom you have never heard) will rise to deny your permit to use state land for your camp, but maybe next week you will find the key government person who will say, "Oh, no problem. Just put your camp on that lava flat and promise us in writing that you will leave no traces when you are gone."

All these things and more happened. For example, our viewing vehicle sank on us. We had named her *Maka Ala,* or Hawaiian for "watchful one," at the suggestion of a local fisherman, and this proved to be the second of those lovely Hawaiian double entendres we became entangled with. In an utter deluge the *Maka Ala* filled to the scuppers with rainwater, heeled over, and settled to the bottom forty feet below, in a trail of bubbles. But next day she was miraculously resurrected by my team, who dove down to her and attached inner tubes to her rails. Then they inflated the tubes with a scuba bottle. Up she came. Only then did we learn that *Maka Ala* really meant, "Watch her carefully or she will sink on you."

I COULD see that camp at Kealakekua! In my mind's eye, it was set under the big spreading *kiawe* trees and palms alongside the ancient and now abandoned village of Kaawaloa, on the north limb of the bay where there were no people. We would build ourselves a field shelter and every day we would walk a few yards down to the bay's edge, right over the stones where Captain Cook had met his demise, paddle out to our boat moored in the stillest part of the bay, and there we would find the *nai'a* diving daintily in the emerald depths. Nothing but us, the trade winds in the palms, the flashing Keawekaheka light, and the dolphins. A twice-weekly run a mile across the bay and a four-mile drive to the Captain Cook store would keep us in supplies. That was my private Swiss Family Robinson dream.

So we set to work in my California backyard, building the necessary parts of the dream. The first item was a forty-foot-long collapsible field headquarters. My version of a tree house.

First we built a floor of heavy plywood, laid it on big timbers, and bolted these in place, every bolt hole numbered and logged into an instruction manual: a sort of gigantic version of the swing set or barbecue that you might be given on Christmas and then have to assemble using an incomprehensible set of instructions: "Insert the stacking swivel screw in the upper of the two smaller holes . . ."

Amazingly enough it worked, and we were able to assemble the building in about a day from an eight-foot stack of plywood, bolts, tar paper, and timbers. The compact shelter had a darkroom, a projection space, a little kitchen and dining nook, and a bunkroom that in a pinch could keep six people dry during tropical downpours. I could see us in there, just my crew and I, talking over our latest discovery, while *huli huli* chicken cooked on the propane stove.

In distant California I conjured up all the parts of this castle at night and then during the day I drew them on the plan or went shopping to find parts. I rigged up a solar shower where five gallons of water hoisted to the roof could douse off the day's grime. And we built big, open screened windows all around to let the breezes blow through and keep the mosquitoes out. With this building we could promise officialdom that we would occupy this state land and leave without a trace when we were done. A delicious scenario it was, too. My rich dreams of that camp propelled the early stages of *Hana Nai'a,* but, alas, they were not to be.

I sent Bernd and Randy out to scout out the exact place for our headquarters building, and after a couple of days my home phone rang:

"Ken, how long since you were at Kaawaloa?"

"Oh, it's been about three years since I actually set foot there. Why?"

"Well, we hate to tell you but the place is a zoo. A shanty town. Randy and I landed and walked back into the trees and the place is full of little huts, and most of 'em seem to keep pet rats in cages hanging from the palm trees."

"Wow," I said, my heart sinking. "Now what?" My dreams of dolphins playing in crystal water a few yards from camp were fading fast.

"Well, we certainly don't think we can put up a camp there. Rumors have it that it is a drug center. None of our gear would be safe out there."

"What do you think we should do?" I asked.

"Well, we've scouted that out and we might be able to set up at Manini Point, across the bay. There's a beautiful palm grove there and a good place to launch our boats, if we can get permission. We think it's state land."

We did obtain permission, and while I finished the Expedition Building, the team constructed four platform tents at the new site, built atop timbers and heavy sheets of plywood. Manini Point, we found, became a marsh in the frequent heavy rains. Bernd, compact and powerful, soon learned how to scale the sheltering palms to cut green drinking coconuts for everyone. Our inflatable boat was pulled up in a little channel amidst the palms. It took only moments to launch her, and a few minutes to reach our larger boats moored offshore.

The grove proved to be alive with life. Big toads hopped out in the dusk or during the rains, and we loved them for their beautiful eyes and flutelike double-noted trills. But the giant venomous centipedes snaking among the pebbles were another thing, and I felt no different about the swift, flat spiders, half as broad as your hand, that infested the outhouse walls. I don't think they spent much time biting people, but their swift scuttles out there in the dark were enough to make me shine my flashlight in all the crevices before entering.

A daily scan for dolphins entering the bay was begun. This involved climbing atop a lava pile on the nearby shore and keeping watch for dolphin schools. Many details of the dolphins' arrival, their numbers, their behavior, how and where they rested, began to accumulate in log books. This "scan series" was to go on, once every daylight half-hour, throughout the many months we worked in the bay, and from it many subtleties about dolphins visiting Kealakekua began to emerge. Most came via Bernd's statistical sleuthing method.

For instance, after the log books were all finished and the data crunching began, we learned that the dolphins' time in the bay varied throughout the year, with the fewest hours in the winter. It began to seem that the time needed for a dolphin to sleep was one thing, and waiting for sunset to set out into the dark sea to feed was another. In the winter the short days scrunched these essential patterns together, while in summer the longer days spread them out.

On the last scan of the day we sometimes lingered on the shore in the warm twilight, watching the sun set. As darkness crept in and the palms became inky black silhouettes, we sometimes saw lights come on across the bay at Kaawaloa. Truck lights jolted down the lava trail from the bluff above, and we could see little winking running lights round Keawekaheka Point and stop off Cook Monument, where once we had hoped to camp in peace, just us and the dolphins.

About this time a saturnine local took to bursting out of the *hale koa* bushes by our camp with all manner of demands and propositions for us, in what ultimately was an attempt to dislodge us from the bay. On days when he wasn't confronting us, he spent much time harassing visiting yachtsmen who came to anchor in Kealakekua. He was, we found, a self-appointed protector of the bay.

Gradually the reasons for his harassment emerged. Rumor had it that we were in Kealakekua to find a site for a huge new dolphin exhibit in which the local *nai'a* would be the attraction. I unearthed the basis of this rumor after our project was over and I was searching out references to earlier work at Kealakekua. I found one in a survey of the marine life of the bay that mentioned the proposed exhibit, but I never did learn who was behind it.

With this ominous obbligato in the background, we assembled the newly arrived field building on a baking lava flat next to Manini Point. After many vicissitudes, permissions had all been extracted from the officials in Hilo, far away on the other side of the island. A long power line was laid over the lava flat to the nearby house of an accommodating biologist friend, Bill Walsh, and we moved in. Bernd, Mel, and Randy dismantled the tent platforms and stacked the plywood alongside the palms.

By this time Randy had arranged for monthly flights around the island to look for dolphin schools. We hoped to compile a record of which coves the dolphins occupied throughout the year, where they moved, and how many there were. A couple of weeks after dismantling the tent platforms, the two of us swooped in over Kealakekua in our rented Cessna spotter plane. Looking out one window toward Manini Point, Randy said, "Oh oh, I don't see the plywood."

I, looking out the other window, said, "Well, I can see it. Isn't it piled in that backyard?"

Sure enough, we circled again and concluded that either someone had a giant pile of plywood very much like our own and ours had disappeared to a destination unknown, or there it was down there behind the little house.

What to do? In the last analysis the wood belonged to the government, and we felt responsible for it. We thought we knew the house and also knew that it was not infrequently occupied by a bronze statue of a man, a giant stern-visaged Hawaiian who visited Napoopoo when he had leave from the U.S. Marine Corps. So, a few days later, screwing up our courage, Bernd and I knocked on the door of the house where we thought the plywood was stacked.

Instead of a marine we were greeted by a bright-eyed old lady who immediately chirped, "Hello, I'm Mrs. Prim, but some of my friends call me Mrs. Primo,[1] but I don't drink. Who are you?"

Bernd and I launched into a long elliptical description of our arrival at the bay, the establishment of the palm grove camp, and our recent move to the collapsible field shelter.

She listened patiently, and finally said, "*Oh,* you want to know about the *plywood.* It's all stacked in the backyard, except for three sheets uppa my bedroom where the termites are eatin' the wall. The 'boys' watched it for a

1. Primo is a popular local beer.

long time down at the palm grove and finally thought the hippies must have left it. We were worried that the boys over at Honaunau would cock-a-roach it."

She was right. It had been stacked there a long time, two weeks at least, and the boys from Honaunau very likely did plan to cock-a-roach it. Cock-a-roaching, as I understand the activity, isn't to be classed with thievery so much as it is liberation of things that don't seem to be working, in an actively competitive environment. It cleans up the environment and keeps understanding of boundaries and ownership current.

"Well, Mrs. Prim," I said, "I think we will have to take it back because we are responsible for it, but I'll tell you what. I wouldn't think of taking those three sheets up where the termites are eating your bedroom wall."

Mrs. Prim seemed to regard this shift in ownership as a normal part of the cock-a-roaching process, and she said calmly, "You boys have to come meet my sister. She's next door and she would like to hear about the *nai'a*."

That took care of the plywood, but the story about me planning an exhibit using the spinners of Kealakekua just hung there, unresolved. I thought that the seeds of a real attempt to drive us out of the bay could well spring from such vague beginnings. What to do, what to do? I thought.

Finally it dawned on me that I should call my old friend Roger Coryell, who would know exactly what to do.

Roger, born on the islands, is a sage and subtle student of the Hawaiian psyche. A blithe spirit, Roger had been a newspaper man, Hilo's first disk jockey, and for many years a successful publicist in Honolulu.

"Give a *luau* and invite everyone in town over to see what you are doing," was his suggestion.

Then he laid out a complete plan for me. There would be *leis* and *pupus* (snacks) all around. Roger would come and bring a few of our many *kamaaina* (native born) friends from Oahu, including our mutual friend, the Hawaiian dancer Cissy Lucy, who might help convince people we were just a bunch of harmless, even friendly, biologists.

I drew up a sign which we duplicated and tacked to the Napoopoo telephone poles, inviting everyone to our collapsible field building for a slide show about the *nai'a,* and for punch, and there would be spider lilies and vanda orchids for the women's hair. We would see if Leon Stirling would come over from his Baptist church in Kailua-Kona and give a little welcoming speech.

Then Bernd and I decided to invite everyone in Napoopoo personally. We walked every winding dirt street in the village, knocking on doors and issuing personal invitations to come to our plywood home, a structure that thankfully was not capable of creating envy in anyone in Napoopoo for its lush appointments.

On *luau* day a continual stream of visitors came down the rutted road to our little green building. They were greeted by Mel and our three new student members, among them Shannon Brownlee. Shannon is a *kamaaina,* born and raised on the islands. She had instructed us on how a good Hawaiian *luau* ought to be run. She was dressed in her floor-length white Hawaiian party dress with lace collar, while the others had bright new muumuus, and little Kim was resplendent in a new flowered dress the women had sewed for her.

Then Leon Stirling sauntered in. A tall hulking *hapahaoli* (half-Hawaiian), he looked at the world through knowing eyes. He had dabbled in politics and served on the Honolulu police force before going off to California to become a lay minister. He was a remarkable amalgam of a man, who knew all about human foibles and now spent much of his life steering young native Hawaiians into productive paths.

He taught them that there was more to their future than simple physical reaction to the injustices they had suffered.

Later, when the house was full, with the leaves of fragrant *maile* dangling around his neck, Leon rose before us and said something like this: "I am just a man. I can't do anything special for you but I can ask that you be a friend to the *nai'a*. Don't do anything to harm them, for they were here long before any of us, even the Hawaiian people. What you visitors to Hawaii take from the islands try to give back to her in full measure."

He then noted the passing of the whirlwind, a puff of breeze, through the open shutters of our little laboratory, which signified that good fortune lay ahead. Indeed it did. The *luau* had dispelled some of our strangeness. Many of the townspeople now greeted us with smiles of recognition, and we too felt more at home.

8

Monogrammed Dolphins

I KNEW I was watching old pros when I first went to sea at Kealakekua with Bernd, Mel, and Randy. A school of dolphins was soon sighted and then approached with a delicacy that comes only from long experience. Randy and Bernd clambered onto the bow, steadying themselves against railings in readiness. Mel stayed in the cockpit, filling out data sheets, while I took the helm. Then the *hatcha hatcha hatcha* of powerwinders was heard as film raced through the two cameras. We circled and circled in and around the school. It made my budgetary head ache as they kept at it, making sure that every animal had been photographed enough times that usable films of both sides of its dorsal fin were "in the can." They used high-speed color film, powerwinders, exposures of a thousandth of a second, a 200 mm. telephoto, and lots and lots of film.

You may recall that in my first spinner study I began a catalogue of spinner dolphins by drawing their scars and marks, and that Tom Dohl, whose drawing talents caused all his dolphins to look like cigars, had tried to steer me toward photography. I simply doubted that photographs were the way to go. The light on the sea surface produces about as difficult a photographic situation as you can find. It's all flashes of brilliant sunlight and dark water, black as ink. The sun is mirrored from wet bodies, and most photographs I had seen seemed to mask rather than reveal the body patterns or scars of dolphins. Besides that, I liked to draw.

However, I now knew we could learn all sorts of things with the help of photography. Before Bernd, Mel, and Randy were done we were able to identify about 30 percent of the individual dolphins along the Kona coast (many had no distinguishing features on their fins), and we could say who swam with whom, the time of day they had been seen, where they went, and what dolphins made up the subgroups of the school. We were doing at sea what behaviorists Stuart and Jeanne Altmann had long before shown to be so important in their studies of African mammals. We were carrying out a slow frame-by-frame version of their *focal animal sampling,* a method in which the observer follows a single animal through its activities in the midst of the confusion of the larger group.

If the observer tries to record all the animals in a group at a given time, there is usually no hope of success. In the case of dolphins we were able to piece together the very broadest of interactions, slide by slide. More intimate analysis, however, proved very hard to come by. It seemed to depend either upon observations of captives, or upon piling up little seconds-long events from the *Maka Ala*'s windows.

When all our slides were in, they revealed a remarkable number of things about Kealakekua's spinners. We found that some animals were photographed much more frequently than others; these dolphins seemed to hang out where we did. But other dolphins showed up just now and then. When we traveled away from Kealakekua, some of these missing dolphins were found spending most of their time in coves miles away.

It slowly emerged that the schools we saw were not monolithic family units, but instead pickup assemblages forged for reasons we didn't at first understand.

Mel, who had been through these filming sessions before, took over the utterly essential function of keeping all the piles of slides straight. Each exposure was logged, keyed to detailed field notes without which all would have been utterly lost and the entire effort made useless. It is indeed marvelous to have organized colleagues. A field camp can stand just one or two artists.

Then Bernd, Mel, and Randy and various volunteers crouched in a darkened lab for weeks and weeks, looking at every slide, arguing about identifications until everyone agreed, deciding what was a real scar and what was an artifact of the light. They checked the side from which the photograph had been taken. Most markings are visible from only one side, and even some fin-edge scars look different from each side. In all they waded through an estimated twenty thousand slides in order to bring into soft-focus the still-incomplete picture we now have of spinner societies and their movements.

Some decisions were easy. Old Finger Dorsal, for example, with his deformed fin, was unmistakable from any angle. His distinctive profile showed up forty-nine times in the eleven years I had been looking at spinners, and he was one of the few that bridged the gap between my drawings and that pile of slides.

There were a great many other unexpected things. For instance, a dolphin we came to call Old Four-Nip was usually found amongst the juveniles. One day Four-Nip jumped right in front of Randy's lens, and was caught in mid-leap. That thousandth-of-a-second frame showed that he was an adult male, and we knew then that spinner dolphins sometimes have babysitting old boys in their social

schemes. This view has since been strengthened by the work of Professor Nobuyuki Miyazaki of Japan. He examined whole schools of a close relative of the spinner dolphin taken for the Japanese market and found a cadre of adult males (but almost no females) accompanying the pure juvenile schools. I wonder if these males are also teachers, helping to pass the cultural elements of dolphin society along.

Through accumulated stacks of slides, trunks full of slides, small mountains of slides, we were able to watch Four-Nip's scars change over the months. When we first saw him, his fin had four tatters on its rear margin, probably pieces of his tissue left after an attacking shark took a swipe at him.

Later, one by one, the tatters pinched off, but because our record was continuous, and we had totted up sixty-nine good slides of Four-Nip, we were always able to identify him.

In the end Bernd, Mel, and Randy produced a series of tables that showed when and where a given dolphin first appeared on the coast of Hawaii, and then when, where, and with whom it was seen through the rest of the study. The results of this accumulating data pile were surprising to all of us.

For one thing, they seemed to show no such thing as a permanent school with a history and a regular membership. Not only did the size of the bay-dwelling schools change drastically from day to day, through a range from four to about eighty-five dolphins, but school membership seemed almost entirely fluid. One day Finger Dorsal, Four-Nip, and E-Fin would all be in a bay, all in the same forty-dolphin school. Next day E-Fin was gone and the school had grown by twenty dolphins. The day following that, Four-Nip and Finger Dorsal disappeared and the school was down to thirty. Then, for the next week, no dolphins came into K-Bay at all. It wasn't easy to give up my preconceived notion of a family school, but the slides convinced me that view was incorrect. How the deck was being shuffled, and perhaps why spinners moved from cove to cove, seemed to lie out of sight in nighttime events we couldn't see.

Just a few small recognizable groups of dolphins were seen over and over. Even their associations seemed to be something that happened only now and then. It was like old friends meeting for a gab session before each went his way. Broad "friendship," at least, seemed a constant value. The dolphins seemed to accept the shuffling with equanimity; apparently anywhere along the coast of the Island of Hawaii a dolphin could find comrades.

Our three photographers kept logging in dolphins we had never seen before. The rate at which these new animals appeared never seemed to slacken. Where, we wondered, was their society centered, if not in these daytime schools that rested in the bays of Hawaii? Was it offshore as they were diving and feeding? Why should their bay schools fluctuate so? How could they maintain a society if the members changed all the time? Puzzles on puzzles filtered through our minds as we tried to make sense of it all.

If our Hawaii spinners represented a closed population, one of finite numbers, there should have come a time when animals new to us became fewer and fewer as we came to know all the players. Only newborns or occasional migrants should provide new animals. But that never happened. Either there were an awful lot of players and we hadn't dented the supply, or there was a leak somewhere.

We wondered if these new dolphins came from Maui, across the Alenuihaha Channel, or perhaps even from the open sea. Neither of these ideas could explain all our observations. Some of our animals, such as Four-Nip and Old Finger Dorsal, were obviously residents. Perhaps dolphins at sea waited until there was a vacancy along the Hawaiian shores. That's what I would do if I lived out at sea with no decent place to rest.

After contemplations like these, I

urged my team to widen their activities beyond Kealakekua. We needed to go up and down the coast to see what dolphins we would find. We went clear around the island to Hilo, and there, lo and behold, we found one of our dolphins, Twin Peaks, swimming in an otherwise totally foreign school. Twin Peaks had lost the entire center of its dorsal fin, leaving two triangles of tissue fore and aft, an animal unlikely to be mistaken from any angle. This distinctive dolphin had appeared five times north of Kailua Kona, about a dozen miles from Kealakekua, and then had disappeared for six months before Bernd and Randy found it again, clear around the island.

When we considered Twin Peaks' hundred-mile-long journey, we wondered anew: What did those schools we studied at Kealakekua really mean to spinners?

It was obvious that we needed to go to sea at night to track spinners. To track a dolphin we needed to capture it, affix a little waterproof radio to its dorsal fin, and then quickly return it to its school before its schoolmates were gone. We also had to be ready to follow where the dolphins led. Because that could be straight out to sea in the black of night, the *Nai'a's* gas tanks had to be full, life jackets stowed, and her galley stocked.

Radiotracking dolphins is full of pitfalls. Before we began to radiotrack, I found Bernd sitting at his electronics bench peering at the expensive little dorsal fin radios we had bought.

"What are you doing, Bernd?" I asked.

"Oh, I've learned the hard way that these radios that come from the factory don't all work the way they're supposed to. Look at this one. It seems OK, doesn't it? But when I wet it with salt water, it blocks out and doesn't send any signal at all."

He then added, "But, never fear, Oh Great Budget-driven Leader, wipe the terror from your eyes, I think I've found it."

He drew me over to his desk lamp and showed me a tiny

pinhole in the radio's rubber insulation. He dabbed it with a rubber compound, tested it again, and the radio worked perfectly. As he set the radio aside and began checking the next one, I reflected on what Bernd's care had saved us: a useless dolphin capture, a failed effort of tagging, and a fruitless tracking effort had all been averted.

There is another major problem for dolphin trackers who follow animals by boat. Lying over the sea surface most of the time is a vapor layer that all but blocks lateral transmission of the dolphin's tiny radio signal. If the ship is big enough or has a good mast, one may be able to extend the antenna high enough to overcome this. But the twenty-five-foot *Nai'a* had us right down in the vapor with no way out, so our tracks were long quests after a wraithlike signal. The little beeps came and went, and even changed positions from bow to stern. Our primitive radio-direction finder could not resolve the "ambiguity problem." Newer direction finders do better.

We could hear the conversations of taxi dispatchers and drivers up on the slopes of the nearby volcano, who seemed to share a frequency with us, but sometimes we couldn't seem to hear our dolphin when it was just a quarter of a mile away. We wondered if the taxi drivers heard beeps from our dolphin.

I accompanied the team on one of the tracks. A dolphin was caught off Hoona Bay, near the Kailua airport. The capture was quickly done with a device that grabs the dolphin's tail with padded jaws as it rises to breathe at a vessel's bow. In minutes the dolphin was drawn aboard, a lovely docile animal, painted with dark and light gray and immaculate white. It lay nearly still on a foam mattress while it was very quickly measured, sexed, and the tiny radio affixed to it, a little whip antenna angling up above the fin so that when the dolphin surfaced this tip would break first into the air. The radio's attachment was of magnesium, so that shortly after a track had been completed the bolt would erode (magnesium is very soluble in sea water) and the radio would fall away, leaving the dolphin free of any encumbrance.

In less than ten minutes the tagged dolphin was lifted over the rail and slid back into the sea. It bolted into instant and powerful swimming, disappeared in a dive, and then reappeared within the school, a hundred yards away.

Bernd began to track the dolphin by plotting our position on a nautical chart, while Mel called in compass bearings of nearby landmarks read from a hand-held bearing circle. Mel said, "I can see the Keahole Light. It bears 190 degrees. We're 2.6 nautical miles north of Keahole Point."

Randy entered the fix in our running log.

"Now let's see if the dolphin is giving us a signal," Bernd said. He turned up the volume on the radio receiver and waited. Nothing came at first. "I think he's down," Bernd mumbled to himself.

Then we heard a faint *beep beep* for a few seconds, and then it stopped.

"There he is. He surfaced and dove again," Bernd said in quiet triumph. "We're in business."

The dolphin and its school skirted down the coast in the fading light. Our little vessel moved easily in the glassy swell, its engines burbling gently. Keahole Light winked its coded signal to us, as we headed south after the dolphins. Lights appeared along the shore, a jeweled necklace of glittering white, red, and green stars just at waterline, and above them, up on the great shoulders of Hualalai, a tracery of lights marked the circum-island highway. A hundred little windows scattered across the dark mountain now glowed yellow. Then, when the last light faded behind the mountain, we lost palpable contact with the shore except for the lights. Even the water disappeared unless we illuminated it with our big hand-held spotlight. The disembodied *beep beep beep* led us on, now strong and then almost too faint for us to hear. Sometimes it did disappear if we let the signal fade too long. Then we circled this way and that, retraced our path, lost in the ambiguity of our direction finder.

Then we would hear it again, clinging to its faint sound, our hearts lifting as it grew stronger along a new course. Like a blind person with a cane tapping this way and that, we found our animal again and again, but only the dolphins knew where we were going.

Keahole Light dipped into the water and was gone, but by that time Kailua Light had risen ahead and winked its telltale pattern. On and on down the unseen coast we went in the nearly calm blackness. I felt very, very alone in our insubstantial craft, out in the black, even though the dolphins swam nearby. It was their world, not ours. Little traces of fear raised by our aloneness sharpened my perceptions. The gasoline gauge, the manifold temperature, the small life raft affixed atop the cabin, all received a hundred glances as we zigged and zagged back and forth along the unseen shore. In the black predawn we made a long zigzagging traverse down past the populated parts of Kona toward Kauhako Bay, where massive lava flows of Mauna Loa descend without a break to the abyssal sea floor.

Now and then our radio signal grew very loud and insistent and we found ourselves in the midst of the school. Thankfully, the dolphins seemed to be leading us along the shore, and not out of the sheltering bulk of Hualalai and Mauna Loa, not out to where the swells would grow and the winds rise, and we could venture no further. The dolphin's path was not straight but composed of short traverses followed by abrupt reversals of course. We zigged our way along, usually just a couple of miles from shore.

The searchlight beam occasionally revealed dolphins swirling about our bow, looking up at us as they maneuvered in the lighted water. Once our beam picked out our tagged dolphin's radio, and we moved away.

The hazy light of dawn brightened toward day as we closed on the black lava fin of Lepeamoa Rock. But the dolphins kept moving south, almost to remote Hoku Point, three-quarters of the way to the southern tip of the United States, before they turned north again. They had traversed almost the entire length of the Kona Coast in a single night, moving continuously, diving for three or four minutes and then surfacing, zigging and zagging! My former vision of local dolphin schools going out at night to favorite nearby feeding spots evaporated. These dolphins were doing something very different from anything we had conceived.

When we looked at all our radio tracks it was clear that their last traverse might or might not bring the school back near Kealake'akua by dawn, the time when they usually began to edge in toward a rest cove. Thus it was not too surprising that individual dolphins in a bay changed from day to day. We also had a possible explanation why none at all might show up for a couple of weeks at a time. Presumably, their nighttime zigzags simply ended near some other cove. But we knew there was more. The day-by-day mixing implied that the nighttime trek mixed the animals into new associations.

Sometimes we received hints that the offshore school was very large, much larger than the ones that frequented Kealakekua. Sometimes when we snapped on the mast-light, we could see wave after wave of dolphins, and we might travel through them for several minutes before we left them behind.

We theorized that these feeding schools represented the coalescence of schools that had rested in several bays along the island during the day. The bay schools might simply be parts of the larger nighttime school, and it might be first-come, first-served for daytime resting space at Kealakekua. That view began to make sense when we observed that when Kealakekua had its full complement of about eighty-five dolphins, newly arrived schools passed it by without entering.

So the radio tracks told us much, and raised questions that required us to go aloft again. For example, our new view of dolphin society said there should be big schools offshore and little ones in the coves, adjusted to the size of the resting area. So Randy cobbled together a new flight series that took him clear around the big island, cataloguing and counting spinner schools from two hundred feet above. He found a flying club over in Hilo that was willing to work with us at modest cost. Once or twice a month he and a flight team piled into Winifred-the-Pickup-Truck in the dark and arrived at Hilo in the early morning, just in time to stop at the local fast food joint for a breakfast before climbing aboard the little four-seater aircraft. Its high wing let Randy see and photograph down upon the schools as the little plane banked and circled in tight vertiginous turns. Urp-City it sometimes became for the more susceptible observers, and soon the aerial spotting team was winnowed down to the very hardy.

On every successive flight Randy had the pilot go the opposite direction around the island. This let him average out the effects of time of day in his records. If schools normally left a cove before he arrived going one way, he would get them in the opposite direction.

Some constant patterns were soon obvious. Dolphins were always scarce on the rough Hamakua Coast where the trade wind seas almost constantly piled against a rugged cliffed shore. Did this mean that spinner dolphins avoid rough water? How odd in a species whose oceanic populations had to take anything the wind gods offered.

Down on the south coast, where Kilauea volcano sometimes sluiced its bright red lava rivers into the sea as we flew overhead, dolphin schools were in some of the coves and not in others, and up on the calm lee shore, beginning two dozen miles north of Kealakekua, spinner dolphin schools were almost nonexistent. A long stretch of calm waters and inviting sandbottomed coves seemed to go begging.

I fished out a hydrographic chart one night and plotted the schools we had seen on it, noting abundances and absences.

"Randy, it looks to me as if spinner dolphins aren't commuters," I said.

I meant that the depth and width of the offshore shelf near a rest cove seemed to determine whether or not it would be occupied by dolphins. If the ocean was shallow for a long way before the island drop-off was reached, dolphins were not likely to use it. It looked very much as if they wouldn't go far to reach deep water. One of those energetic relationships, I thought. If it took too much energy commuting to a rest cove, the cove would go begging, no matter how nice its sandy spots might be.

As Randy's records piled up we could see that every cove did indeed have its number. That number seemed to be related to the area of white sand: a large sand area, a lot of dolphins; a small sand area, a few dolphins.

When all the data were assembled into neat bar graphs for all the island's coves, it became obvious that there were times when Kona's dolphins left Kona, and then almost the whole population seemed to appear on the opposite coast, way around by Hilo. Factoring in the weather data, Randy had gathered it was obvious that when the wind blew hard at Kona the spinner population all but disappeared. When it blew at Hilo they came back to Kona.

We came to suspect that when storms roiled the waters in

rest coves, the dolphins would leave for quieter, clearer waters where they could see their predators. Back and forth, back and forth, a hundred miles or more they seemed to go in search of vital clear water. That clear water, of course, was never absent at sea, even in a tropical storm. And now, as I write, one of my doctoral students, Michael Poole, has confirmed the pattern on the much smaller South Pacific island of Moorea, where spinner schools perform the same back-and-forth pattern in relation to storms.

While Randy flew his circuits around the island, Bernd and Mel puzzled about where to put the theodolite station. This instrument, a very precise surveyor's transit, would allow us to make very precise tracks of dolphins in Kealakekua Bay. My tongue-in-cheek grand scheme for hanging a rope ladder a third of the way down the cliff to a ledge was disposed of as impractical. Instead they found a similar ledge of lava that with spirit one could climb to. It was about a third of the way up the cliff ridge, but still no easy matter to reach.

So the theodolite and its tripod and materials for protecting it from the frequent rains were all hauled up that nearly vertical ridge of mud and rock to Bernd's little flat place and tied to the tree trunk.

Bernd surveyed in the location. He picked landmarks in opposite directions—Cook Monument at one end of the bay and Palemano Light the other way—and then he put a stake in the beach down almost directly below his perch and surveyed in mean high tide level. Then he was ready to go. Volunteers for theodolite duty were instructed on how to work everything, and a watch was set.

Climbing up to the theodolite meant starting in the dark before the dolphins arrived in the bay, and then waiting in the cool gloom for the sun to rise. That part was wonderful in the balmy Hawaiian air, but unfortunately each night spiders by the hundreds spun their webs across the "trail." One had to break almost continuously through strong webs, and, brushing away the displaced architects with a spare hand, move upward.

There were two kinds of spiders up there—big lovely green, gold, and black mommas, and little spiky gray-with-red-spots folks. All had incredible persistence, and each morning their webs were back. You'd have thought they would have run out of web juice, but they never did.

It was no easy matter to scale the cliff, either. It involved crashing through the thick brush, grabbing little trees and

Kealakekua Bay, Hawaii. Our field headquarters is blocked out by the strut of the airplane in the lower left corner. The dolphins rested just to the right of the moored boats, and the theodolite station is hidden in the trees part way up the cliff. You can see Captain Cook's Monument at the upper edge of the bay on the Kaawaloa Peninsula. He met his death just to the left of the monument. *Bernd Würsig*

swinging up, and up, never letting go because it was simply too steep. Then a call was made by walkie-talkie down to camp to log in. With this two-way communication operating, we had almost palpable contact with our observer up there hidden in the vegetation.

"How's it up there, Chris? Can you see signs of a weather front?"

"Yeah, it looks pretty black down off Honaunau. Do you think I'd better come down before it hits?"

"Your choice. You're the one who has to come down that mudslide."

"OK, I'll be down for lunch."

The tracks of spinners were talked into a cassette recorder taped to the tripod, leaving the observer's hands free to manipulate the surveying instrument, and to hang on.

It's zero nine fifteen, October 10, 1980, I'm Mel, the weather is clear and flat calm and an estimated twenty-five spinners have just passed Manini Point, heading right for the rest area. Bearing 273 degrees true, dip angle 13 degrees. They are in spread school formation. Zero nine eighteen: all dolphins down in a synchronous dive.

When finally all the accumulated tracks were reduced to tracklines drawn on a chart, we could see when the dolphins took long traverses at the surface, when they dove and surfaced, and when they entered the rest area and began their tight little traverses back and forth, back and forth, during rest.

We could even see when they woke up. Abruptly the dolphins began long swims uninterrupted by diving, and then followed what we called zigzag swimming. Our interpretation was that the dolphins were coordinating their school for the night's work.

A small school of spinners swims lazily near the shore of Hookena Bay, south of Kealakekua Bay. The beaks sticking above the water and the spin probably mean they are waking up. *Bernd Würsig*

So piece by piece we formed new ideas and reshaped old ones about spinner lives. That slow coming-into-focus is what carries much of the fascination of learning about a wild animal on its home grounds.

While these broad patterns were being sketched in, my students and I were watching and listening below water to formulate our conceptions of how dolphin societies worked on a more intimate level. We knew that dolphins never left their schools, and that these formations changed their structure markedly when dolphins rested, when they traveled, and when they were attacked. It took my entire two decades with spinners to formulate a theory for how they worked.

9

The Magic Envelope

OCEANIC animals and their predators are thrown together in a cat-and-mouse game that begins when they are born and ends only with death. It is easy to imagine how that might go. An old spinner dolphin, having somehow lived out forty years in this equilibrium, at last falters, and, unable to rise to take its half-second sip of air, inhales the sea, quivers, and rolls onto its side, sinking stiffly away from the still-moving school. Nearby schoolmates, seeing its trouble, swim around the stricken dolphin, lifting it with their beaks, but it is dead and they soon leave, pulled back into the departing school, the only safe haven they have ever known.

For a few moments the dead dolphin sinks like a falling leaf, now outside the shield of the school. In moments, attending sharks slice in out of nowhere and the corpse begins to jerk under the impact of their rushes.

These sleek fish, perhaps capable of swimming faster than the dolphins, have traveled for their lifetime too, nearly always beyond the dolphin school's boundaries. There they have made much of their livelihood by scavenging. For them, it is no break in life's patterns to eat the dead dolphin. But they had to wait until the school disgorged its dead, closed again, and moved on.

The open tropical sea provides few protections other than the school for the dolphins that live there. Instead they live suspended in a world of glass. Aside from darkness, and the clouds of living things, it's mostly three physical features of the sea that provide a place to hide. These are: ocean swells, which form parading inverted canyons of water up into which they can swim and not be detected; the opaque clouds of bubbles driven into the water by breaking waves; and the junctions between one water mass and another. These wavering undersea blankets of water formed where warm water floats on cold can deflect and garble the sonar beams of mammalian predators.

Night must be a blessing for dolphins. Their unique sense, echolocation, then comes fully into play, giving them a crucial advantage over attending sharks. The dolphins emit long trains of snapping clicks and listen to their faint echoes from distant objects, and from such information learn much about things far beyond the limits of sight.

The dolphin's echolocation shield is its own special defense. With it these mammals buy an advantage in the costs of predation over their silent antagonists. Because dolphins can search the environment around them for hundreds of yards, they are made too expensive to catch. Given that seemingly insignificant advantage, they can then afford to express all the complexity and individuality of their mammalian heritage. They know where the predators are better than the predators know where they are, and therefore they can let down the school's shield long enough to afford nurture, instruction, tradition, and even culture. But should the predator swim close, they then must again revert to the fish's strategy, the school, in which they become faceless ciphers, obeying without question a group strategy. Otherwise the illusion by which schools work will fail. No adult can take a young animal into its care during danger and help it survive. Instead each member, old adults and infants included, must become mechanical reactants operating with such speed that fractions of a second determine the outcome.

Even then there is no escape from the insistent clicks of other echolocating cetaceans, especially the fearsome false and pygmy killer whales, who are known to kill and probably eat the smaller dolphins.

Some intrepid divers who have swum in the open sea report that sharks and schools of dolphins may not swim alone but instead can be parts of much larger retinues that include many kinds and sizes of animals, both below and above the water. Lacking a landscape of forests and mountains to spread them out and to provide refuges, the dynamics of their collective lives can clump them in cadres, according to the speed at which the members habitually swim or fly. This clumping happens even though in doing so each animal takes its place in the hierarchy of predation and scavenging.

Dr. William Perrin and his colleagues have called these remarkable assemblages "multispecies aggregations." We see a parallel to them on land in the traveling herds of African antelopes, attended by their predatory lions and leopards, and, circling all of them, the scavenging hyenas and vultures. The lion's table scraps provide for the birds and mammals who clean the landscape of carrion.

It is certainly no mistake that both these aggregations occur in open space where the elements of the equilibrium can play themselves out with somber, almost mathematical elegance.

I think that when we seined for dolphins

and yellowfin tuna out in the tropical current system, we dipped into these aggregations, and many of their members came up in the net, or flew above it. Not only did we raise sharks and dolphins along with the parading schools of tuna, but flights of little flying fish filtered through the net mesh, launched themselves, and glided away. In the water, portunid crabs did the same—darted down into the blue and were gone. Now and then a big bill fish came up.

Above these water animals were the birds who dove upon the smaller fish that both predators and the net drove to the surface. From the air-half of the aggregation, boobies plunged like arrows into the sea to catch fish down deep in the water, while the frigate birds hovered above everything, batlike, to harass the boobies until they disgorged their catch in midair. Kleptoparasites, the biologists picturesquely call them.

But steal is not all these sepulchral birds do. They also swoop down in magnificent aerobatic flight to pluck up flying fish when these are flushed into the air by the predators below. The frigates marked the path of the aggregation for us because they circled high in the air where we could see them for long distances. They moved with it, as it zigzagged within the swells faster than a person can run. And just as Georges Gilbert had said, the number of frigate birds was a rough measure of the size of the ocean aggregation that swam below.

Ponder for a moment the enigmatic forces that let such a retinue form, and then lets its members live long enough to reproduce themselves. Somehow, a high-order mammal has found a way of carrying out its complicated life's patterns in such a system. It has found a way to live out its long life, to nurture and instruct its young in a world in which there is no lagging behind, not even for a minute. The school has some-how kept these antagonists apart so perfectly that a dolphin's long life is possible. What magic is there that allows this? Why does the effect so quickly disappear with death? The answer, I think, rests mostly on two things: the first is an illusion, and the other is a communications net made of individual school members instead of nerves.

The *magic envelope* is what I call the dolphin's school, because, as with other animals that form schools, flocks, or herds, its operation provides subtle, almost instantaneous communication to its members. A predator attacking such a group of animals finds them reacting just ahead of its rush, parting a fraction of a second before it can snap its jaws upon one of them. Only when predators join together, or when the school is maneuvered against a rock formation or a floating object, or when a school member for some reason stands out from the others, do the predator's attacks succeed. How the school provides its protection is what I want to describe here. It is far from simple, playing as it does upon the ancient history of both the sense organs and the brain that must interpret their signals.

The illusion is the property of the schooling animals in the multispecies aggregation. Tuna, flying fish, dolphins, and even some of the birds that fly above them all use it to find their place in the fluid equilibrium of death and survival.

How can it be that by banding together both the fish and the dolphins can find protection in that transparent world? The parts of the puzzle have taken decades to unlock, but now at least the basic elements of the illusion seem clear. These elements have been discovered by students of fish schools and insect swarms, by fighter pilots and those who taught them how to survive an aerial dogfight, by close observers of chorus lines, and by naturalists who watched and wondered at the lightning-fast maneuvers of shore birds when hawks swooped in to attack. My colleague Carl Schilt and I have thought long and hard about how it all might work, he from the standpoint of a student of anchovy schools, and I from the dolphin's perspective.

The game at its most elemental seems to be based on anonymity. If a fish or a dolphin is among enough others that look
very much like it, if all face the same general direction and
move in generally the same way, and if there is no point of
reference for a predator to fix upon, the cat-and-mouse game
will be close to equal.

One causal element, Carl and I postulate, seems to lie deep
in the way all vertebrate eyes work. In an attack sequence the
predator's eyes track the prey, but if the prey is moving fast
across the visual field, the predator's eyes may not do so smoothly
but progress in a series of jumps called *saccades*. When each
jerk of such saccadic motion stops, the predator uses this fixed
frame to make an automatic mental calculation of the course
and speed of the prey it sees before it. Remarkably, in between
jumps the predator's consciousness shuts off and it knows
nothing at all about its own jumping eye movements.

Such a visual system can be fooled by a faceless rank of
identical-appearing prey. If, as the predator's consciousness
returns after a saccade, it settles on the wrong prey animal from
the many passing in front of it, the calculation of course and
speed needed for the next point in its attack sequence will be
incorrect and the attack will fail. The predator will wallow in
indecision, and will have spent precious energy in fruitless attack.

The prey animals have taken measures of their own to speed
their group reactions. Their group reactions have become faster
than a single predator can follow. One part of this has to do
with school coordination. Under attack, the prey school tight-
ens its ranks, I think to a distance between school members
that lets them see all the signs of incipient turns and dives by
their neighbors, without having to move their eyes. Such eye
movement is too slow to be acceptable in these split-second
reactions.

The onrushing predator faces a school that outmaneuvers it
in the last instant before any of its members can be engulfed.

The game is so close a one that a prey species swimming within the school four or five ranks away from an attacking predator, and remarkably close to its rush, may hardly react at all. Instead, events such as the moment of attempted engulfment are the real parts of the survival equation. The predator must, at the last instant, open its jaws to snap, thus biting not only at its prey but also opening its mouth into the passing water column, which instantly slows it a little, so that if the attack fails an entire new approach must be made. In the statistics of a predator's life, only so many aborted attempts can be tolerated before the energy balance sheet shows a crucial deficit. The predator must succeed to survive, just as the prey must escape.

I have watched this drama from the window of an oceanarium into which the silvery ranks of an anchovy school had been introduced. Already present were several big predatory striped bass, who immediately rushed to the attack. The school flowed in front of their rushes. When the bass bolted up from below, the anchovies formed a circular mill around the big fish, who stopped dead in the water, pectorals fanning, one mill of anchovies above it and another below, circling slowly. Soon the balance sheet of success and failure separated the two species a little, and the bass ceased to attack and began a watchful waiting game, waiting for the slightest hint of relaxation of the anchovy's magic envelope. The bass had receded into the role of waiting until some school member violated the shield, for whatever reason, and could then be caught.

It's probably not much different between dolphins and their predators, except that with echolocation providing an early warning system, all the complexities of mammalian society become possible when no predators threaten.

Being a member of such an envelope

seems to involve a psychic price to its members. Because when under attack, whether they be spinner dolphins or anchovies, each member must conform to iron rules, individuality is reduced close to zero. Such conformism, I think, spills over into the other times of their lives.

The hallmarks of the dolphins that play this group survival game are several. They all tend to swim continuously in the same general direction at the same general speed. Their members all look much alike. The differences between males and females are muted, and some such differences are movement patterns such as the serious swimming of male spinner dolphin coalitions: patterns that may be overt when they are appropriate, and otherwise hidden. Schooling dolphins are also cooperators, utterly alone outside their schools. That, I think, is why they are docile, almost beyond belief, upon capture, and in captivity.

The tightening of the threatened school that I mentioned earlier is a sign of a much deeper organization of a dolphin school, which I will describe further in the next chapter. My colleague Carl Schilt and I call it the school's *sensory integration system,* or SIS. Because every animal in a school can send messages to all others through movements or sounds, and because these can flash across a school from any direction mediating its maneuvers, the school becomes a reactive unit that can respond adaptively in three dimensions.

Some experiments show that, using the SIS, information of various sorts may pass across a school much more rapidly than a predator can react. The passage is achieved by body movements, by changes in the position of pattern components in the visual fields of adjacent schoolers, or it may travel by sound or by simple mechanical disturbance of the water, such as when one fish "feels" the turbulence generated by the swimming of an adjacent animal. A dolphin beginning to dive will automatically signal its neighbor and the ranks beyond, because it will begin to show more and more of its white belly as it rolls and makes its turn downward. The sharp edges of the dolphin's pattern will give even more precise information, especially to a schoolmate that has moved in close where little movements are, in effect, magnified. There are special receptors in the vertebrate eye, called edge detectors, that amplify the passage of such edges across the retina and consequently register especially strongly in the brain of the recipient.

I well remember the first time I saw a dolphin school tighten its ranks in the face of a predator. The predator was a wild, curly-headed giant—a fisherman called "Big Bear" by others on the fish docks. Big Bear had become the collector for an oceanarium where I worked, and we were cruising along the Baja California coast at the tag end of a storm, looking for dolphins. Big Bear brought his fifty-foot vessel in perilously close to the pounding surf, so close that the humping swells heaved the vessel up and broke in white foam not seventy-five feet from our inboard rail. Big Bear had seen dolphins skirting along the wave crests, and, good predator that he was, went after them with only momentary consideration for the danger we faced. The dolphins leapt ahead of us, pouring from the water in ragged ranks. Suddenly Big Bear, steering with one hand, reached inside the cabin door for a rifle and began pumping shells in the water behind the dolphins to see, he said, if he could "drive them." The impact of those shells in the water near the dolphins must have been concussive, for they leapt from the water as one, so tight to one another that you could not see between them. Soon the dolphins ducked into the combing white water and appeared again in the foamy apron inside the breakers, where, thankfully, we could not go. Big Bear cursed, shook his fist at the sky, and turned offshore. At the time I felt only the relief of the somehow spared, but later when I thought about the experience I knew that those dolphins were true schooling animals and that they, like the anchovies, possess a sensory integration system.

The faceless ranks of a true school have been experimented with by two clever behaviorists, Laurie Landeau and John Terborgh, giving us a sharp insight into how crucial it is for all school members to appear alike. They performed the simple test of temporarily dyeing a few silvery schooling fish blue and introducing them, one by one, back into a school faced with a predator. The blue fishes stood out, of course, and were attacked far more frequently than the normal fish in the school. But, interestingly enough, the silvery fish that swam next to the blue fish were nearly as vulnerable as the blue fish itself. The colored fish had become a landmark, allowing the predator to fixate upon both it and its nearby neighbors.

The experiment shows clearly how disruptive and dangerous it can be for a schooling animal to lose its anonymity, and why it was no accident that we had so much trouble telling male from female in our spinner dolphins.

These same two scientists put the first numbers upon how many fish, or dolphins, or flocking birds, it takes to produce a minimal sensory integration system, though they didn't talk about such a system. They found that a single schooling fish alone is a dead duck to an attacking predator, and that two such fishes somewhat delay the average time of capture, and so on up to eight fish, when the little school becomes essentially invulnerable to attack from a single predatory fish. The predator simply ceases to attack, having been utterly defeated by the now complete magic envelope.

I suspect that also deeply involved in this effect is a mental characteristic of all vertebrates, namely that in terms of events taking place in the fractions of a second it takes for an attack, we cannot track more than six or eight other objects in our field of view. Even then we do so only approximately, guessing within quite large sectors where the prey individuals actually are. This results in what behaviorists have called the *confusion effect,* in which a predator fails in its attack upon a school and falls into confusion.

How fast the sensory integration system can transmit information was tested by the ornithologist W. K. Potts, who wondered how little flocking shorebirds named dunlins could escape from attacking hawks. When a hawk stooped on these birds, he could watch and time the waves of reaction that swept across their maneuvering flock. When he tested the reaction times of individual hawks and compared the two figures, he found that in the intact maneuvering flock of shorebirds, information was passing about 2.6 times as fast as an individual hawk could react. This may make it seem as though there is real magic in the envelope, but Potts went on to explain it by what he called the "chorus line effect."

He was referring to the Radio City Music Hall Rockettes, whose precision leg kicks pass with remarkable rapidity down the whole line of dancers. Upon inquiry he found that the dancers watched not just their neighbors, but a way down the line, and were able to initiate kicks before the "wave of influence" actually reached them. Hence they could exceed their own individual reaction times by as much as Potts's dunlins.

There seems to be one further defense that schooling animals throw in front of their would-be predators, and that is the illusion I mentioned earlier. Under the right circumstances it can not only leave a predator befuddled but can induce a sense of false motion in it. It is a circumstance well known to fighter pilots in World Wars I and II, and it is based on the peculiar way in which we and most other

animals determine our position in space. As everyone knows, when we walk through a room our sensation is that we move and the room stands still. Yet if you think about the cues we are given to make such a foray, every one of them is a measure of relative motion between us and the objects in space around us. Our brains somehow convert these relative measures into our sense that the world stands still while we move.

Scientists have concluded that the *gaze stabilization system* involves two kinds of information, which may sometimes work at odds with each other. The first kind of information is derived from the eyes and the second from the labyrinth, or the organ of equilibrium inside our inner ears. The labyrinth directly senses the motion of an organism, but is not equipped to make assessments of how these relate to other objects in the animal's environment. This makes the labyrinth easy enough to fool; we do it every time we climb into an airplane. As soon as the plane reaches a constant speed, as far as the labyrinth is concerned the world moves with us, even though we may be traveling over the ground at high speed. Our reference is the interior of the plane, and the little motion sensors inside the labyrinth have become quiet as we ceased to change speed.

The same thing happens to an attacking predatory fish. As the fish attacks, its labyrinth gives it information about how fast it changes speed. If the fish accelerates, decelerates, or changes direction, new information is provided, but if the predator swims at a constant speed and direction, the labyrinth quickly ceases to tell it anything at all. It says, instead, that it is sitting still in seat A-4.

It's not surprising, then, that through the course of evolution the eyes, whose job in this case is to detect relative motion, learned to compensate for the inability of the labyrinth, and let the animal know how fast it is moving relative to everything else in the immediate environment, and in what direction. The hitch is that the eyes require discrete points in the environment—rocks, jellyfish, the edges of tables—upon which they can fix to make such calculations. Lacking such points of reference, the eyes search and search and search, jumping from one inadequate fixed point to another, and the attack fails in a welter of indecision. That's where schools come in. They mask such fixation points, and provide the predator with inappropriate information to make its attack.

I mentioned the fighter pilots of the Second World War. Their debriefing reports showed that if the sky was cloudy and the ground hard to see when a dogfight began, sometimes they would lose all sense of their own speed or direction of movement. Sometimes, as they closed on an enemy plane, the pilot would feel that his plane was actually flying backward. The problem was the old bugaboo that there were no solid stationary points for his eyes to fix upon. In the absence of such a "ground truth" point, the labyrinth began to assail the pilot with its inappropriate information.

Such problems must trouble predators in the open ocean, especially when they are some distance below the surface where no patterns of passing waves or trash floating on the surface can stabilize their eyes for them. When the experimenters put the blue fish in a school, this provided an anchor for the predator's eyes, and it suppressed the variable information the balance organ kept sending in. The blue fish itself was a fixation point that allowed the predator to focus on adjacent fish, even if they were silvery and identical to the rest of the school.

At night all bets are off. Fish generally cease to school in tight ranks, the birds roost, and only the dolphins continue oriented schooling, perhaps, as I mentioned, because in the dark they have not escaped the sonar beams of the false and pygmy killer whales. Perhaps some acoustically mediated simulacrum of a daytime sensory integration system exists in those nighttime schools that we have yet to understand.

Even without such extra nighttime protection, it seems clear that neither dolphins nor schooling fish could survive in the open sea without their magic envelope. It is implicit in the form and movement of their schools, and I believe that it is so crucial a feature that during the day no open-ocean dolphin can leave it for even a moment.

I suspect that the backdown channel of the tuna seine destroys the dolphin's magic envelope by crowding the individuals of its school so close together that their signal systems no longer function. Bereft of their protection, they sink in those pathetic ranks. This is another indication of how deeply they are schooling animals. Much of their place in nature is lost without their magic envelope functioning.

So when we think of releasing dolphins from a tuna seine, we must contrive not to destroy their magic envelope, and then, I predict, they will stream out of the net, their social arrangements and their psyches intact.

10

The Yugoslavian News Report

ALERT dolphin schools are typically noisy islands of sound traveling in a quiet sea. The long strings of little sharp clicks we call "click trains" generally cascade from them, whistles are often heard from every sector of the school, and a whole lexicon of enigmatic squawks, blats, and barks may pour forth. It was crucial, I thought, to see if we could learn a little about how they use these sounds in their societies at sea. Except for the clicks, we dolphin biologists know precious little about what most of these sounds mean, even after almost four decades of listening to various dolphin species. The clicks, like those of bats, allow dolphins to find their way around in the dark and to track prey, predators, and each other by listening to the tiny echoes the sounds produce. But the way spinners use their other sounds is a much more shadowy matter.

It had been that way for a long time. The problem is a knotty one. The dolphins live down there in the water, out of sight, and, at the time we worked, almost never had the two crucial opportunities occurred together: the opportunity to listen and the chance to see what went on in their lives.

Nearly everything we know about echolocation (which is quite a lot) and bits and pieces about the rest of their sounds have been learned from captives, but how all those other wild sounds were used was one of the great challenges and opportunities of *Hana Nai'a*. Such sounds represented the way wild dolphins did things, what sorts of information mattered to them, and when such events occurred. We were on our way to learning quite a lot about their wild lives, and if we could somehow learn what their babble meant we would find ourselves tinkering with the linchpin of dolphin society. That enticing vista was much on my mind when we settled in at Kealakekua.

All this was not something I wanted to do by myself. As I have noted earlier, people in the know shoo me away from their instruments. I can *think* about how dolphins use sounds just fine, and I can set up a plan for unraveling what they might mean, but I'm not the right guy to go to sea and come back with a lot of clean tape recordings and meticulously kept records over a couple of years' time. I knew I had to find people of the proper temperament and skills to do these things, and then we could talk and think together about dolphin communication.

A start came soon enough. When Bill Schevill and Bill Watkins brought their listening array to Kealakekua Bay, we were in the company of the best in the business. They had practically invented dolphin listening and recording.

In fact, Bill Schevill and Barbara Lawrence had made what I think may have been the first dolphin recordings ever taken. These first records were of white whales, or belukhas, made from a small boat in the Saguenay River, Quebec, Canada, in the late 1940s. Decades of listening by many people have followed, mostly devoted to finding out what sorts of sounds the various species of dolphins make. It has been painstaking work, and not nearly so simple as it sounds. First one has to get to sea and find the animals, then one has to wait for a nearly glassy calm so that the background noise of breaking swells, or of waves splashing against the recording boat, don't drown out the dolphin signals.

Then comes the toughest part. How do you know what species was making the sounds you have just recorded? The scientist is above water and the dolphins are below, mostly unseen. Sound travels so far and well underwater that it is easy to mix sounds from an animal swimming fifty yards away with those coming in from ten times that distance. To do it right one has to watch, listen, and burn up a lot of tape to be sure that the sounds of a single species are all that has been recorded.

Bill Schevill and Bill Watkins, both of Woods Hole Oceanographic Institution, asked so many irritating questions of would-be dolphin listeners that we dubbed them collectively "The Woods Hole Wet Blanket." But, demanding or not, they set the standards that were necessary to make sense of these simple-seeming questions, and most of us learned that anything those two said about cetacean sounds demanded the closest attention.

At Kealakekua I saw an opportunity to make an important step beyond the cataloguing of sounds. Our spinner studies had made us among the first scientists to understand the daily behavioral cycle of any wild dolphin species in real detail. We knew when and where the dolphins slept, where they fed, and a good deal about where they traveled. We even knew a fair amount about what they did underwater, and in that we were unique. With this knowledge base we could hope to record their sounds during each of their major activity patterns, and then, noting the behavior pattern underway, make conjectures about the functions these sounds served.

In the 1970s when we began, other scholars had begun to think in the same way. Dr. John Ford of Vancouver, British Columbia, had just begun an extensive study of killer-whale sounds in Canadian waters, and although he couldn't see very far underwater in the murky precincts frequented by killer whales, he knew a great deal about where his whales went to feed and play. Another was Dr. Peter Tyack, of Woods Hole Oceanographic Institution, who, as an undergraduate student at Harvard University, had studied bottlenose-dolphin sounds recorded in Argentine waters, and had then attempted to put these sounds into the context of their lives. As our three separate stories unfolded, it was fascinating to watch each of us struggle to understand our separate data piles and then come to remarkably similar conclusions.

All of us faced one problem: many cetacean sounds cannot be heard by humans at all (though John's killer whales graciously make most of their remarkable squeals down where we can hear them). High C is left far below by dolphin clicks that ascend ten or more times as high as we can hear, so special recorders are needed.

These expensive and sometimes balky machines are uncommonly sensitive to salt spray. A vagrant splash can reduce to junk a recorder costing more than the family car. At *Hana Nai'a* we carried ours in a special watertight case, handed it gingerly over the rail of the *Maka Ala,* wiped the case clean of any moisture, and opened it below in the relative safety of the viewing vault. We then hitched up a long, specially made cable designed to defeat the maddening tendency of underwater listening gear to pick up the firing noise of outboard motor sparkplugs and other stray electrical signals. This cable ran to a hydrophone, which some in the trade call a "pickle."

Pickles are highly evolved and expensive little rubber-jacketed blobs of technology, and you have to learn the tricks of each new model. Each can pick up a different range and directional pattern of sound. Some, especially those that receive high frequencies, are so insensitive that they require built-in sound boosters, or preamplifiers. These receive the tiny current patterns generated when the sounds of dolphins enter and vibrate special crystals inside the pickle. These molecular-level vibrations are amplified many times and sent up the cable to other electronic gadgets and finally to the recorder.

While we were assembling this equipment I began to search for a new *Hana Nai'a* member with the talent to carry out the planned recording study, and as it turned out she was right in front of my nose all the time.

Her name is Shannon Brownlee, and I had known her and her parents for a long time. As an undergraduate student, Shannon joined my annual university odyssey around wild California and then another expedition that I sponsored, to remote Cerralvo Island off southern Baja California, Mexico. On that trip she was listed as the artist but came back with an ingenious set of observations about why vultures stand for hours on tall branches with their wings spread. She built a device out of moistened sticks for measuring the relative humidity of the air (which she thought might be related to the wing-spreading behavior) and produced a tightly reasoned and beautifully written analysis that, while it didn't prove what was going on, pointed the way for future tests. Clearly she had two priceless assets for any scientist: the ability to see and state with dispassion what her tests had actually shown, and the imagination to spin the naturalist's wheel.

But Shannon's real joy for me was that even though she was young and untested and I a graybeard, we could argue with each other. Done this way, science looks like an ever-renewing process—with the older folks bringing perspective to an effort and the young scholars the new challenges, tools, and constructs.

Shannon Brownlee on board ship off the Kona Coast. *R. S. Wells*

Shannon and I had been arguing for quite a while with each other about this or that, rolling up our big guns to point at each other's ideas.

"*Dr.* Norris" she would say, laying special emphasis on the *Dr.*, "I find it hard to believe that!"

It was such fun, teetering there at the edge of irritation with each other's obtuseness. At any rate, when I suggested *Hana Nai'a* and the daunting sound project to Shannon, she jumped right in.

The overall task was simple enough. We would listen to spinner dolphins throughout the day and night, and we would attempt to typify the kinds of sounds they emitted in every behavioral state we had been able to recognize. We would somehow follow them at night, listening as they dove deep off the island shore. We would swing our recording boat in front of their zigzags, catching the sounds they made as they raced for the bay entrance. We would sneak up close to their sleep groups and quietly deploy our pickle without, we hoped, disturbing them.

I set up the task boundaries for Shannon by requesting that she obtain ten tapes of each behavioral state we had recognized (while remaining alert for new ones, too), so that we would have enough data over about a hundred listening episodes to apply statistical tests. These huge piles of tapes would lift our observations from the level of anecdote to that of reasonable proof.

Even such a vast sample would be modest, I knew, in providing statistical proof. Only if the patterns were very clear would we be able to understand the broad outlines of the sounds dolphins used during a given activity. And, conversely, only if our categorization of their lives was correct could we expect such clarity.

Shannon would have to make endless traverses between our red house and the boat, protecting the vital recorder. She could not, at all costs, drop it in the bay. Somehow she, Randy, and Bernd, and occasionally the old professor, contrived to bring it off. The requested tapes began to accumulate.

One major feature of spinner dolphin sounds particularly intrigued me. It was a remarkable and incomprehensible babble that we sometimes heard toward the end of the day just as the dolphins began their dash out to sea.

The *Hana Nai'a* team and I had first recorded these sounds off the tip of Palemano Point, at the south limb of Kealakekua Bay. A school of about forty spinners swept along the coast, moving fairly quickly, and we expected them to turn toward the open sea at any moment. Glassy swells reflected the darkening sky just as dusk edged into dark.

Randy brought our vessel nearer and nearer the school, watching with practiced eyes for hints of fear or retreat from the dolphins. He delicately hooked the vessel in front of the school, two hundred yards between them and our boat. Then he shut down the engines. The boat slowed while Shannon looped the cable over her arm, ready to drop the hydrophone. Once the *Nai'a* lay still Shannon slid the hydrophone into the water, noting that there was still an almost imperceptible drift to the boat because the cable stood at an angle down into the water. Soon it came vertical and we could begin to listen. Even a slight current can produce a rumble on a tape as the water flows past the pickle.

Shannon whispered down the companionway to Bernd, who lay belly-down on the bunk, his feet in the air, ready to press the recorder into action. I heard a click and a whir as the recorder came on and revved up to speed. I put on a set of earphones and could soon hear the approaching dolphins. It was an amazing din. Cascades of clicks, seeming to come in showers like meteorites, preceded the school. They came right at us. I heard weaving clusters of whistles, clear notes nearly as high as I could hear, each a rising call somehow entwined with the others. The whistles came in thickets, with quiet times in between, as if the animals were calling and responding to one another and then lapsing into quiet.

As the school began to swim abeam of our hydrophone, I could hear these whistles, loud from the nearest animals, then growing fainter and fading, as if the dolphins nearest me had begun to whistle and those next in echelon had picked it up in a traveling chorus that raced down their rank and faded toward the distant edge of the school.

Then, as the traveling chorus of whistles subsided, there came the damndest cacophony you ever heard. There were sounds like barking dogs, banjos being plucked, and a reasonable facsimile of cows mooing. We imagined that a Yugoslavian radio station might sound like this to those who did not speak one of their languages, so we began to refer to these thickets of dolphin sounds as "the Yugoslavian news report."

Very soon after the school had passed us, it bolted for the open sea and was lost in the gathering darkness. On the way back to our mooring I thought about those thickets of whistles and the moos and twangs, and wondered if there might be an association with this particular time of day, when the dolphins usually dashed out to sea.

We had to wait more than a year before Shannon's sound sample was complete. Ahead lay the most difficult part. We (mostly Shannon) had to extract from that accumulation of tapes regularities about when the noises were made. Our question to her remained: What kind of sounds do spinner dolphins make, in what amount, at what time of day, and what was the behavioral state of the dolphins?

Before Shannon started recording I had thought ahead to this data reduction period. I realized that for us to successfully sketch in a picture of changes in sound emission, we would have to know two important things. First, we needed to know approximately how many dolphins were in the phonating group, and, second, we had to make repeated assessments of how many of these generally faced the hydrophone. The first measure allowed us to say how often, on average, a single dolphin emitted a given sound in our records. For example, after all the data were in we could say that overall squawks were given more frequently at night than during the day.

The second caution arose because many dolphin sounds are emitted as directional beams, and without some estimate of whether or not the school as a whole swam toward or away from us, we might well be fooled. We might, for example, think that all the dolphins had gone silent when they had merely swum away from us. So during every recording Shannon talked constantly into a little hand-held recorder, time-keyed to the main recorder. She spoke in her estimates of the number of dolphins in the school, and each time they turned toward or away from the recording vessel she noted it.

When the sea work was all over, we took our tapes to the Navy sound lab at Oahu and used their very sophisticated (and expensive) equipment to sort out what we had recorded. There, Shannon first rough-graded the tapes, making imperious decisions about which recording met her standards. Hours and hours of field efforts were cast aside with scarcely a backward look. Not infrequently the weather had kicked up during a recording session and the noise of cascading whitecaps dug into what we could hear from the dolphins. Sometimes human and instrumental error intervened.

Shannon reduced the tape pile to about one third. Then she began to print out the good tapes on a curious artifact of technology called a "waterfall display machine." This machine gulped down huge expensive rolls of photosensitive paper that looked like stiff, oversized toilet paper rolls, and then spat the paper out while a wiggling light beam drew a trace of the dolphins sounds on it. Then Shannon sat down for days and days and counted the various signals printed on those rolls. Because clicks were tiny blips of sound much too fast for this machine to catch, she had to analyze the tapes all over again on another machine to learn about them.

When the data reduction was complete, Shannon found that resting dolphins simply "went visual," as we had suspected. As they cruised over their patch of white sand deep in Kealakekua Bay, very few sounds issued even from large schools: only an occasional desultory burst of echolocation clicks, or now and then a whistle, was recorded. But mostly there was simply silence. If a water skier or a motorboat happened to pass near the school, an animal or two might stir itself and jump part way out of the water. We would hear a few sounds, then silence would set in again. In that way we came to understand the dolphins' dependence upon vision during rest.

We also began to understand why resting schools swam so close together. The dolphins had to be close enough to see each other. When a storm had roiled bay waters and the dolphins moved on, bypassing the bay, they were simply going to a place where they could see one another.

As the dolphins awakened, and began to caress and spin, sounds in Shannon's records abruptly increased; clicks came in cascades, whistles punctuated the record, and those squawks, twangs, and moos began to be heard.

As the dolphins began to zigzag, their sounds rose and fell with the level of school activity. And as they began their dash for the ocean, the noise level rose still further, soon reaching true Yugoslavian levels.

Sounds from the dolphins proved to be abundant all night long. The night seemed to be a time of social interaction as well as feeding, judging from the abundance of social sounds. That made sense too, because at night dolphins have a good advantage over the sharks because of their sonar capability, and they can afford to be noisy.

Not infrequently we were present when one dolphin school encountered another. Sometimes these groups of dolphins merged into a single school and sometimes they seemed to thread through each other's ranks and go their separate ways. I thought it was especially important to record such events. Perhaps we could learn if dolphins greeted one another at sea. Perhaps we would hear special calls. But no such calls appeared in our records. The dolphins simply met with a "business as usual" lack of change and went their own ways. I wonder now if such greetings might be given at considerably greater distance than we expected, considering how well sound travels at sea. Perhaps our human preconceptions had led us to assume *when* in the course of a meeting greetings should be given. We are, after all, visual, landbound creatures, and we usually wait until we can see each other's facial signals before we greet each other. Resolution of that question awaits the time when we will record approaching schools that are as far away as we can detect them. Maybe dolphins greet each other at fifteen hundred yards. This difference in human and dolphin viewpoints was underscored for me one day when we lay listening with our hydrophone two miles offshore, well outside of Kealakekua Bay, and could hear a dolphin school making all sorts of noise while it was swimming right under the Kealakekua cliffs.

THE constant sounds emitted by spinner schools traveling over the island slope at night were another subject of interest to us. Such schools almost had to be mediated by sound, since even at the surface the water was so black a dolphin could hardly see the one swimming next to it. What kinds of sounds did they make in the dark, and what might they be used for?

Click trains were constantly recorded in those nighttime schools, and that was not hard to understand. Clearly, dolphins need to find food or locate predators, but reasons for the constant whistling seemed less obvious. These high-pitched but audible sounds (a young person can generally hear them well) are not so strongly beamed as clicks, and we came to suppose that they made good "contact calls." A contact call is one that announces the position and state of one animal to others.

It was quite clear that the dolphins of a school kept track of each other even though the school might be spread over a mile of dark sea. Whenever we encountered them, they swam in well-formed schools that obviously required a means of communication between animals. We suspected that more than the click trains were required to achieve such nighttime synchrony, since clicks were emitted in directional beams, hardly suitable for keeping an entire school informed. The animals at the rear of the school might travel without clues to where the others were swimming if clicks were all they used to keep track of one another.

Could such organization be accomplished by the ubiquitous whistles? The more we thought, watched, and asked, the more sense the idea made. First, whistles were about as nondirectional as any dolphin sound, and hence dolphins at many places in the school could listen in when one school member whistled.

In a very revealing study of captive common dolphins made before we began our work, Melba and David Caldwell had shown that each dolphin develops its own distinctive whistle as it grows up. Whistles of mother and calf have similarities, but are still distinctive. Thus if a dolphin whistled it would be transmitting information about its location, and simultaneously about its identity.

The Caldwells called these sounds "signature whistles" and found that they could be modified, or "modulated" as the acousticians say, to carry further meaning. For instance, a whistle that is warbled, or broken into steplike segments, is known to be given by distressed dolphins, such as those being captured. So, to anthropomorphize for a bit, a single warbled whistle could carry a complex message such as, "I'm So-and-so. I'm over here, and I'm in trouble."

Dr. Peter Tyack of Woods Hole Oceanographic has revealed in recent years another refinement for this proposed contact call system. He devised little lights that he could stick to the top of a captive dolphin's forehead with a suction cup that would light up when the bearer made a sound. He calls these gadgets *vocalights*. With them he was able to unravel communication exchanges to a level no one else had achieved, and he discovered something remarkable about whistles.

The dolphins did call back and forth

with the whistles, as we supposed they would, but—what was more revealing—the partners in such an exchange, even though they both had distinctive calls, tended to mimic each other. The first dolphin emitted a call, and the second animal gave its impression of that call with, I suspect, enough of its own identifier to be recognized. This then expands the precision and content of the message further. It now, at its most complicated, could say, "I'm So-and-so, I hear you, I'm over here, and I'm frightened."

The precise channel of an exchange could thus be specified by the participants while others in the school listened in, staying silent if they wished but nonetheless privy to the information involved. The information that could be carried by whistle exchanges became richer and richer the more we thought about it.

We began to think of whistles as the basic stuff of what one linguistics scholar named Jakobsen has called a *phatic communication system*. That bit of jargon identifies an important concept, namely that in social animals, some sounds provide a communication matrix, a set of party lines running among all animals, over which the basic state of the school can be assessed by any animal listening in. With our spinners the whistles might be the wires of the party line, and the ways they were modulated carried the messages, whatever they might be. Thus, it seems to me, dolphins in their schools can know the state and identity of each member in the dark, or at considerable distance, and the school as a whole can react appropriately.

Shannon and I then puzzled over the oscillating choruses of whistles we had encountered as the dolphins prepared to go to sea. As the dolphins zigzagged back and forth across Kealakekua Bay, why should they whistle with those weaving choruses one minute and then subside the next, just as their schools speeded and slowed?

Once again the Caldwells provided a clue. They had listened

to a small captive group of newly acquired common dolphins. The Caldwells' dolphins each turned out to have a distinctive whistle, as was widely found to be the case throughout the dolphin family. These dolphins traded whistles back and forth. Then the Caldwells noted that what was happening was more than two animals trading whistles. If one dolphin whistled and the second dolphin responded with a whistle near or at the end of the first dolphin's whistle, a chorus would ensue. But if the second animal responded too soon or too late, both would fall silent. And when two dolphins started to reply together, one deferred to the other much more frequently than did the other. There seemed to be a social hierarchy, just as Gregory Bateson had found, and one dolphin seemed to have the privilege of interrupting or overriding the other.

This tendency to chorus is common in social mammals and birds. African wild dogs twitter at each other prior to going out on the hunt, coyotes and wolves sing their beautiful music, parrots, jays, and ravens all hype each other with call choruses.

The general context seems to be assurance of social cohesion prior to carrying out some group act. The animals in a flock or school seem to test each other's alertness or motivation for the next activity this way. So it seems to be with spinner dolphins. When they arouse from rest they begin to call insistently to each other, and then after a while the chorus subsides, probably because synchrony between dolphins is still lacking. Some are not yet "awake."

The Caldwells' experiment suggests that dolphins test each other by measuring each other's timing. If a responding dolphin chimes in at the wrong point it must be clear that not all school members are ready to go out to sea. And if acceptable synchronicity is reached, even we, above the surface, could detect something like joie de vivre in the animals as they speeded up and began to leap. Beneath the water the Yugo-slavian News Report broke out.

Parenthetically, the use of precise timing as a means of car-rying messages is a feature especially appropriate to dolphins. The ocean is sometimes layered in a complex way by different temperatures and densities of sea water, and this can distort sound in unpredictable ways. What it does not distort nearly so severely is the timing within a series of sounds given close together. So we find dolphins timing each other's reactions when sounds come from a distance, rather than interpreting the var-iations in pitch.

Just as is true in the choruses of other animals, the events of the Yugoslavian News Report seem to be metaphors of the cir-cumstances of dolphin life at the moment they are given. By this I mean that each school member can detect the emotional level and alertness of others, just as the wolf can tell by the pitch and tension in another's call where it is in the chase. Near the kill, a wolf's voice will be high. Under the greatest excite-ment, tension on its vocal cords may cause its voice to break just as our own voices break in heightened circumstances.

Note that the state of the voice and the events of the moment happen together; they are metaphors of each other, and thus the communication is precise. But unlike our human language, this communication is good only for the immediate present in which it occurs. It doesn't store events in abstract symbols (words) as our language does. Instead, it requires animals to act things out, which, depending upon the event in progress, can be swift as lightning or very slow. No orders flash by sound across a school with a message such as, "Wake up, the rest of us are ready to go to sea." Instead the dolphins must play the message over and over until all the dolphins are alert and all go off to sea.

Zigzag swimming also began to seem a perfect example of a variant of metaphoric communication. As the dolphins alter-nately raced along and then slowed, went silent and then again sprayed the environment with sound, they were acting out their own group indecision about whether or not they could go to sea. By testing each other they first found that not every animal was alert, so they slowed and waited, then they tried again, and finally their communication showed them that every dolphin was ready for the night's fishing.

Only then did the Yugoslavian News Report break out, and they were off to sea in a joyous rush. Well might they be joyous, I thought. It had taken them hours to communicate that need for synchrony to every school member. It was, in fact, the democratic process at its most tedious.

I've just used the word "joyous" to describe swimming during the height of the Yugoslavian News Report. I did that because I think that beyond these rather simple structural rules for vocal exchanges, there must be the emotional glue that gives richness and nuance to a metaphoric communication system. Just as our spirits rise when the tempo of a symphony increases, or fall when the French horns or cellos enter a slow passage, so might something like emotion be transmitted throughout a school. It could be a highly unifying and coordinating aspect of dolphin communication.

That dolphins use such metaphor as a central element in their communication is an indication that they do not also use a sophisticated symbolic language like our own, contrary to popular folklore. To be sure, we retain layers of metaphor in our own communication. We carry metaphoric messages in words, tempos, and the pitch of what we say, but we can also say things in a sentence that seem to take dolphins three hours to get across.

We routinely talk about future events when we say something simple like, "Let's go to the store." But the dolphin school, it seems, must match event and action while it acts out an emotionally based metaphor of what is going on. Dolphin communication, like that of other social mammals and birds, and unlike ourselves, seems to be a process of acting out the group perceptions of a given individual state at a given moment, of achieving some kind of group consensus, and not, so far as I can perceive, of relying heavily upon symbols to indicate things in the past or future.

Can they store culture in any way beyond the overlapping memories and actions of their membership? Can they ruminate over past events and embroider them the way we do? I see no evidence that they do.

And there is little evidence in them of a mechanism called *time binding,* upon which much of the richness of our culture is based. Time binding implies that we store our collective experiences in the written word, or in the storytelling of a culture, the oral tradition.

In this way humans have built a rich pool of collective experience. Nothing I've yet been able to perceive in dolphin society suggests that they exceed the metaphor of other higher social mammals, but we shall keep looking, because nature says the votes aren't all in. As in many other higher mammals, isolated signals may be symbolic: a given sound indicating a given circumstance. That's about halfway to being a word. Some of Shannon's banjo twangs and barks may fall in such a class.

Shannon was ultimately able to typify the general acoustic trends within the dolphin's day. They were generally much more vocal at night than during the day, and she even found special nighttime sounds, *screams* she called them, which we do not yet understand. But in her data gathering, and in our long discussions back in camp, we had laid out a plausible scenario for how their whistle systems can mediate dolphin lives at sea. Together we had formed a theory for what all that

Yugoslavian sound was about, and it matched what was known from other social mammals and birds.

All the refined use of signals remains to be understood. We cannot say why they moo, or why some of them twang on banjos, but they do.

11

Maka Ala

I CRAWLED down in the belly of the *Maka Ala* and lay looking out into the blue water racing by. We had just launched her for the first time at Keauhou Harbor and were driving her around to Kealakekua. Now and then, as we skirted close to a headland, I could see the blue shapes of coral-encrusted boulders come into view. Where the water shallowed further, clouds of fish resolved out of the murk, hovering over the pale rock formations. The craft heeled a little as we doubled Cook Light and came in under the cliffs of Kealakekua. We crossed over a field of yellow-green coral castles and onto the gleaming bluish-white sandy plain at the shallowest part of the bay. I looked up to see the glowering cliff only a hundred yards away.

Then, below me, I saw the shadowy forms of a school of spinners come into focus, moving slowly like a carpet over the clean sand. Now and then I could see a dolphin dip down below the others, roll, and flick its flukes into the sugary coral sand, stirring up a little cloud before it returned languidly to its sedate brethren swimming above. At last, I thought, we are where we belong. At last it is just us and the dolphins.

I secured the *Maka Ala* to a mooring, and the bowline plopped in the water. On that day in 1980, underwater adventures that stretched before us for many months began.

By that time, we had disassembled the last of my Swiss Family Robinson dreams in favor of much more practical and gracious arrangements. We had unbolted and stacked our collapsible field shelter, closed the outhouse door on the spiders in favor of a much larger, bathroom-equipped, tin-roofed house by the bay. There we had a big space for dealing with all the photographs, and a dining room and *lanai* where we could argue about dolphins after the day's fieldwork was done, and right off the front porch was a little beach tucked between lava headlands, where we could launch our rubber boat for trips out to our two moored vessels. It was a ten-minute swim out to them for most of the crew.

I had to admit that civilization had its advantages, especially because the house provided space for a larger team, which in time spilled over into the garage and onto the lawn.

One of the newest members was Chris Johnson, who claimed a portion of the garage as her domain. I'd first met her when she came into my university office asking to do a project on dolphins. During that work I had seen a person capable of looking beyond the immediate scene to understand how things work in a deeper sense, especially the minds of animals.

Chris is nocturnal. We could see the garage light on at 2:00 A.M. while she read new papers about animal cognition and tried to fit the Kealakekua dolphins into the conceptual frameworks built by others. I like this approach too, and so the discussions ranged widely between us.

I remember the first time Chris went out in the *Maka Ala*. We had loaded our gear into the raft at the beach and rowed out toward the ungainly viewing craft bobbing slowly at anchor. We tied up alongside and gingerly handed the gear across to be stowed. I

Chris Johnson, before going below in the *Maka Ala* for an observation session. *R. S. Wells*

told Chris to go below into the observation vault while I drove the *Maka Ala*.

I could see a tight little school of about twenty spinners, milling slowly over the sand patch. I cut the engine down to idle, and the *Maka Ala* slowed and crept forward toward them. The school dove as one, twenty yards off the bow. Then from down below I could hear Chris's excited voice.

"I see them, I see them! They're right below us swimming over the sand. There's a baby with its mom. I can see those echelons you told me about. Nobody's touching, they're all separated by about a foot."

"Hey Chris," I said. "I know it's exciting but don't forget to use the video!"

I heard the whirring of the video camera as she began to record. I knew that she was looking at a *rest formation,* in which the dolphins swam with none of the buoyant social interaction we would see later when they "woke up." I put the "woke up" in quotes here because dolphin sleep is so different from our own. We really are on our way, I thought to myself gratefully. All the trials of settling in to Kealakekua did, in fact, seem to be behind us.

Randy and Bernd had solved the problem of shelter on the

Maka Ala by building a little house over the vault. It featured big plywood flaps that could be propped open, letting the delicious maritime breeze waft through over the observer tucked below. Equally important, the house allowed observers to watch out into the blue water from a darkened vault.

None of this construction added in the least to the grace of the *Maka Ala*. In fact she became just about the oddest-looking creation that had taken to sea since the coracle was invented. But grace was the last thing I required. She was our "low sticker price" ticket to the undersea world where dolphins truly live. Most of us who have tried to learn about dolphins have dreamed of a submarine that would cruise amongst them. Like Captain Nemo sitting before his underwater picture window, we could then look out on their lives from the comfort of our air capsule. But submarines are vessels from the high-rent district, and few of them, except for ones in which you look through a transparent plastic hemisphere, have windows of any size. I didn't like those hemispheres, because they act as reducing lenses, making everything you see very small. I preferred the old cheap, flat, plastic bow of the *Maka Ala* for what we dolphin biologists try to do.

Before settling on the *Maka Ala* we'd tried or thought about as many ways of observing underwater as we could imagine. We'd attempted scuba diving with dolphins, but I'd discarded that idea. Dolphins usually give divers a wide berth, probably because releasing bubbles is a signal dolphins direct at each other when they are frustrated or angry. There are electrolung rebreathers that produce no bubbles and might solve this problem, but we did not obtain one to test. I think it is likely that the dolphins would regard a bubbleless human swimmer as something close to a shark, and perhaps avoid him too.

For me, the crucial problem with these

The *Maka Ala* enters a dolphin school.

free diving methods is that no human swimmer can keep up with a dolphin school for long. The dolphins simply flirt in toward a swimmer, peer at him from this angle or that, and cruise off into the murk. Swimmers are, I thought, just too slow, though a student who joined us later would challenge that notion.

It works pretty well to insinuate a snorkel-equipped swimmer amongst the dolphins from a small boat. We tied a foot-rope to the bow of our rubber boat and Randy or Bernd inserted one foot into it and rode under the craft. These agile and self-assured swimmers obtained some excellent film sequences this way. They let the boat move them slowly into a school, then they cast off and swam amongst the dolphins for a few moments, expending their film. But the method made me grit my teeth for the swimmers' safety. The boat's propeller churned a few feet astern of their flippers. One slip and they could slide back into the slicing screw. Moreover, the method served only to capture random images on film, mostly images of dolphins reacting to the presence of a swimmer in their midst.

I suppose a diving sled might do better. They are underwater skateboards that can be towed into a dolphin school with a diver holding tight atop. The jockey of such a craft must steer very carefully in order to avoid spiraling off into the blue, where there is the possibility of ruptured eardrums, or, worse, gas bubbles forced into the bloodstream. Death can follow swiftly from such an accident, so much care must be devoted to maneuvering the craft. And the attention of the observer is certainly diluted. I know only a few scientists who can do these two things at once: observe and keep from dying.

Finally, such ways of seeing do not allow all of the crucial elements of my field observation method to occur. I require time for the first vacant contemplation of nature's events, and then time to formulate questions, to look and ask, again and again.

So I have returned over and over to cumbersome craft that let me travel as fast as the dolphins while I look through this or that window. Uncomfortable and ungainly though all of these craft have been, the *Maka Ala* included, I am able to forget myself completely in total contemplation of the dolphins.

As we talked and looked at the "D's," as Chris called the dolphins, I was struck again by how men and women tend to see nature in a slightly different way. Chris had a special empathy for the subtle relationships between one dolphin and another, the way they signaled each other, the processes of nurture and instruction, while I, assuming I am representative of my sex, tended to look for the patterns of their society: how they deployed themselves, how they kept their school organized when out of sight in the dark water, how they protected themselves and dealt with the world of water, pressure, cold, and light.

As fellow humans, however, Chris and I faced nature in similar ways. She was no better than I, I thought, at escaping from herself. We all tend to look at the world from our human viewpoint. Behaviorists especially, I think, have had to struggle to escape viewpoints based on their own lives rather than the lives and environment of the animals under observation.

IT didn't take long to fall into a routine with the *Maka Ala*. After rowing the gear out from the beach, we unlocked the deckhouse and arranged everything on the shelf above the viewing vault. Then we washed the viewing windows. The growth of fouling organisms such as little calcareous tube worms, films of algae, or clumps of hydroids is amazingly rapid in the tropics. If the windows weren't washed every day using strong chlorine bleach, the growth would get ahead of us and the grit of the animals' skeletons would then scratch the plastic windows and ruin our viewing capability.

Then we cast off the mooring and headed almost at an idle toward the dolphins, trying to leave their rest area alone most of the time. The observer down in the vault talked the scene into a hand-held recorder. Once dolphins were sighted, we watched ever so carefully to see if we were frightening them. That first contact is a touchy time. If the dolphins had not settled into the bay, if they hadn't yet made some sort of group decision to sleep, they would sometimes continue on their way out around Keawekaheka Point. But if we let them descend toward rest, they would stay and tolerate us quite well. In a kind of interspecific empathy we came to recognize small signs of unrest that told us to break off contact and leave the dolphins for a while.

Chris became very good at this as she played the balance between her desire to see and her hope that if she showed herself to be an unthreatening presence they might learn to know her, letting her a little way into their life patterns. To a modest extent, this did happen. But it was a slow and halting process. The problem was simply that the inhabitants of the bay changed from day to day. There were usually some "old friends" there to remember us, but there was also a sizable percentage of new dolphins, cycling into the bay from unseen hundreds of dolphins that made up the entire Hawaii spinner population.

A first order of business after *Maka Ala* was launched and safely moored at Kealakekua was to see what *Hana Nai'a* was all about.

From our underwater viewing windows there was no way to escape *Hana Nai'a*. It was often the first thing that hit you looking at an active school of wild spinners, and we found it went on all year long. Chris and I estimated that at any one time about 30 percent of the dolphins in such schools were typically engaged in some sort of caressing, much of it apparently sexual, at least to the untutored human eye. One of a pair of dolphins trailed its pectoral fins, flukes, and fin tips over the other. Another pair caressed the sensitive area between the pectoral fins of its partner, one dolphin rolling toward the first while both swam along. Other pairs whetted their pectoral fins like butchers sharpening two knives at once (Gregory's pat-a-cake). Sometimes two dolphins rode along, a lower animal with its dorsal fin tip in the genital slit of the upper; they rubbed bellies, mock-mated, and when they were moving slowly we not infrequently saw a curious pattern we named "beak-genital propulsion." One animal swam sedately over another while the lower animal inserted the tip of its rostrum in the genital slit of the second, pushing it along.

Beak-genital propulsion between two female spinners, at Bateson's Bay, Oceanic Institute. *K. S. Norris*

With her earphones on Chris reported bursts of soft clicks while all this was going on. She called this a "tickle buzz," assuming that the pushing animal was stimulating the other with these clicks, though she remained unsure where the sounds came from. It is an intriguing idea that one dolphin could stimulate another using its echolocation sounds, and Chris might be right.

Something about all this overt behavior raised my naturalist's caution, but it took a while to say why. Anything, I thought, that happens for 30 percent of your waking hours has to be utterly central to your life. *Hana Nai'a* was too continuous and too stereotyped for it to be entirely sexual.

As we watched, we began to see complicated rituals of interaction in *Hana Nai'a*. One dolphin caressed a neighbor for a short time, switched partners, and started over with a new partner. There were subtle signals of affirmation, acceptance, or rejection in those caresses. The entire process, though at first appearing very sexual, did not seem to involve actual mating.

There were two things I had known perfectly well all along. First, dolphins are oestrus animals, coming into reproductive readiness only once or twice a year. I knew that oestrus cycles typically involved profound changes in the reproductive physiology and sexual readiness of dolphins. Hormones that had been at low levels during the fallow nonreproductive times rose and readied both males and females for reproduction, and only when these hormonal levels peaked did true reproductive behavior typically appear.

There was a second consideration. Because dolphins have had such a long evolution in the sea, they are often considered without reference to other mammals. But the more we understand them, the more it is obvious that dolphin society has deep parallels with mammalian societies ashore, especially with the patterns of higher social animals such as baboons and the monkeys of the treetops.

The dolphins, I realized, were using sexual patterns to play out the very glue of their fluid societies, the reaffirmation of relationships in an extended society that involved numerous animals, many not relatives.

I shared these thoughts with Chris. "You know, Chris, dolphins aren't well equipped to express their feelings and cement their relationships," I said. "They're locked up inside a hydrodynamic shape. There are no eyebrows to wiggle, no hair to raise. They're a long way from us, with our incredibly expressive faces and our postures that can signal all sorts of things. I bet these quasi-sexual patterns of *Hana Nai'a* are like the grooming of primates. They cement a very fluid culture."

Mating, when we finally saw it, was nothing like *Hana Nai'a*. In the late spring, just when Randy's captive school showed that oestrus was imminent, we began to see dolphin couples swimming rapidly along, fast-moving bluish-white blobs at the edge of our vision. As we neared, we could see that they were stacked over one another, often with the male beneath, upside down, and sometimes we could see the penis dart into the female. The pair swooped along, twisting this way and that like fighter planes in close formation, to break away a few seconds later and go in different directions.

The very brevity of the male's erections was a hint of the dolphin's hoofed-animal ancestry. Like a ram in a flock of sheep, male dolphins can produce an erection by simple muscular means. Such conscious rather than hormonal control is needed when an entire flock or a school comes into sexual readiness at the same time. The males of this group of mammals can "cover" a dozen or more females in a remarkably short time when the hormonal signals indicate that the females are ready and when the males have also reached a full reproductive capability.

The testes of the male dolphins swell until at the time of mating they are among the largest relative to their body weight of any mammal. As a result, dolphins produce enough sperm and fluid to inseminate a small school in quick order, or to compete sexually with other males bent on the same thing.

Actual mating seems not always so simple or so brief. Sometimes a dozen animals or more race in a wild tangle. Bill Schevill, who was with us when we first saw these twisting, twining, jostling masses of animals, gave them a name that stuck.

"Looks like a wuzzle to me," he said laconically.

And wuzzles they became. Wuzzles could be seen as far away as any behavior we observed, and I'm sure the dolphins can also detect them a long way off. I wouldn't be surprised if such a distant signal of a shimmying, twisting mass of dolphins was an invitation to join in. A closer view revealed that there didn't seem to be much, if any, mate choice going on. Things happened so fast, and partners were so many, that that hardly seemed possible.

In other mammals, females in group mating situations sometimes exert mate choice by intrauterine rejection or acceptance of sperm. In the case of spinners the votes are not all in, and we are not even sure if mating is successful in wuzzles.

It also seems curious that in spinner dolphins we should see two very different kinds of mating behavior, if in fact wuzzles are mating assemblages. The first are the discrete mating pairs rocketing along as part of a traveling school, and the second these twining masses of dolphins. One of my young colleagues, Richard Connor, has reported that in the Australian bottlenose dolphin, a shore and bay-dwelling species, coalitions of half a dozen or more males cut out sexually ready females and run off with them for a time, presumably to mate away from the gen-

Rachel Smolker
recording
observations.
R. S. Wells

eral competition of their larger school. We don't know if wuzzles represent something like this for spinners, since we never saw wuzzles taking place away from the main school.

ABOUT this time Chris was visited by a student friend, Rachel Smolker, a skilled young animal behaviorist. Rachel staked out a tent on the front lawn and stayed for months, swimming out every morning to the *Maka Ala*.

One day, I heard the two women talking about "Temple Baby and Mom." I asked for a translation and was told that a mother spinner and her baby had entered the bay as part of a large school. The name "Temple Baby" referred to the little dolphin's habit of swimming up high alongside its mother, just back of her temple. Needless to say, I had to see them, so next morning we took the *Maka Ala* out, once the D's had arrived for their daily rest.

Temple Baby and Mom weren't at all shy of the *Maka Ala*, much to my surprise. The school swirled in close to us, the mother and young closest of all. Just as the women had described, the baby dolphin hung there alongside its mother's head. Mom, a big sleek spinner, came over to check us out, cruising effortlessly along within about fifteen feet of the viewing chamber. She craned her neck at me, gave a couple of pumps of her powerful tail, and the pair rocketed off back into the school. The baby, as sleek and beautiful as a little plump tuna, stuck right next to her side.

The "temple position" was one I had long been familiar with. Years before I had published a paper with John Prescott (now director of the New England Aquarium in Boston) that described how baby dolphins manage to keep up with their mothers on the first days of their lives. Most dolphin schools travel forty or more miles a day, and it seemed a puzzle how a newborn could manage such a feat. It was also clear that the mother could not leave her school, which was her vital protective shield against the seagoing predators of the ocean world. So the baby had to keep up somehow.

I had noticed that newborn dolphins hitch a free ride on their mothers by positioning themselves up near her head, in front of the widest diameter of her body. Then I realized that the baby sometimes could ride there without even moving its tail; it just hung there without moving a muscle while mom did all the work. I discussed this with a hydrodynamicist friend, Howard Kelly, who promptly came up with a physical explanation, and later put it all into mathematical terms. In effect, the water racing over the mother dolphin's body becomes funneled between her side and the positioned baby. A Bernoulli effect: the same effect that causes lift on an airplane's wing pulls mother and baby together as the water rushes between them, pressing the baby's inside pectoral fin against the swell of the mother's body, allowing the mother's swimming to pull the baby along.

Little dolphins such as Temple Baby seem to use this handy way of hitchhiking only when mother swims fast, or perhaps when they get tired. Most of the time, as their school lollygags along at three to five miles an hour, the baby zips around rambunctiously, getting into dolphin trouble and being reprimanded by the watchful mother. I watched Temple Baby get in such trouble. He began to race in circles around his mother, juking in sharp turns way out away from her. Mother, probably wary of letting her very young baby travel so far away, whacked him smartly with her flukes as he circled to check her out. Startled and chastened, he pulled close alongside her for a brief period of good behavior.

Temple Baby was as cute as they come. Many of those "baby features" we recognize in our own children are present in baby dolphins too, and they make them just as "babylike" to our eyes. I marvel that this should be so in mammals as distantly related as our two species are, even though scientists since Darwin have commented on it. Those signals have come through the long course of our separate evolutions unalloyed, and we can see them in young animals as widely separate as birds, mice, humans, and dolphins.

Baby dolphins are sleek and pudgy, their snouts are short, and they have a beguiling innocent look about them. Some species even have little folds of blubber called *fetal folds,* which persist a few days after birth and then fade. These seem only faintly present in spinners, though.

The most striking marks of youth in little dolphins such as Temple Baby are evident in their behavior. They zip this way and that, they exaggerate adult movements in such a way that a baby can be recognized as far away as the bluish-white flash of its moving body can be seen. The *metasignals of youth,* an animal behaviorist might call them.

Though we watched carefully we seldom saw nursing. Temple Baby spent much time swimming down under Mom's tail, alongside her genital area, and we thought we could see him prod his little beak into one of the two mammary slits located near there. Mother dolphins seem to be able to supply their babies with milk in just a few seconds. It is thought the mothers do this by contraction of muscular sheaths, just beneath the blubber, that cover the buried mammary glands, squirting milk into the positioned baby's beak.

The long, slim spinner beak might seem to be poorly designed for nursing, but it is not. Even in those slim jaws the tongue extends right to the jaw tip, with little lappets that seal the spaces between the teeth, and it can move sharply back and forth in a pistonlike motion. My guess is that when the baby prods its beak into the mother's mammary slit, she gives a contraction just as the baby retracts its tongue, pulling the gulp of milk into its mouth. I've seen nursing dolphin babies miss a bit, and then a little cloud of milk may escape into the water. Dolphin milk is lots richer than cow's milk, too: in some species more than 40 percent butterfat (compared to cow's milk at about 3.7 percent, depending upon the breed), so a gulp may go a long way. At any rate, in the short time Temple Baby and Mom were with us we thought we could detect that the baby had grown noticeably.

You might think Temple Baby could

escape his mother's watchful eye down there behind her, but Randy and I later measured the visual field of a spinner and found that they had excellent vision to the rear. When you think about it, this is close to essential for a seagoing mammal that must defend against predators coming up from behind. Parenthetically this behavior placed the baby under its mother's major weapon, her flukes, and thus close to both discipline and protection.

Then mother and calf were gone. Some nighttime shift in the composition of dolphin schools that entered Kealakekua had taken the two elsewhere. We wished them bon voyage.

One day, after they had gone, I was able to show Chris young dolphins swimming in a group amidst the larger school. Included were a couple of very small calves. I had noted this kind of separation of juveniles during our earlier study, and Bernd had seen it in Argentina, but the behavior was new to Chris.

"Look at that," I said. "There's a calf being escorted by a juvenile so small it's surely not weaned yet. And mom is nowhere in sight."

After that we frequently saw these juvenile groups, and observed that they had adult babysitters. Old Four-Nip among others, often swam with them, probably keeping a watchful eye on the young. In a spinner school, there is evidence of a time not long after birth when the newborn calf is introduced into a subschool of other young, where they gambol with one another while most of the adults swim nearby. We later learned that a Japanese dolphin biologist, Nobuyuki Miyazaki, had recorded the same pattern in captured dolphin schools of a closely related species (the striped dolphin, *Stenella coeruleoalba*), taken by a drive fishery off the Japanese island of Honshu. One captured school contained almost a thousand juveniles, a modest cadre of adult males, and a handful of adult females.

Over the years our view of the dolphin school had begun to

change from being a simple cluster of dolphins into a structured fluid society that contained the necessary parts of life for a high-order seagoing mammal.

One essential part was slow in coming for us at Kealakekua. At first we had an awful time telling adult males and females apart except by the roles they played. I think this is related to the absolute needs of the magic envelope. Spinner dolphin males and females cannot afford to look very different in the clear Hawaiian waters, but they can *act* different if they do so when predators are at a safe distance.

This was a serious deficit for our work, because one of the first things a behaviorist must try to do when learning about a wild animal species is to describe the subtler relations between males and females. Are they monogamous, or does the male gather harems of females about him? Who tends the young? Do the sexes fulfill other roles in society? Do they trade duties back and forth? How is the effort of all this apportioned between males and females? We'd been able to see some of these things when actual matings took place, when we could tell the sexes of the partners, but much remained cryptic for us.

At first, the only way we could be sure if a given animal was male or female was to get close enough to look up from beneath at the genitalia and the mammary slits. That only happened now and then, especially because the *Maka Ala*'s slanting transparent bow directed our gaze downward.

Then our own experience began to solve the problem, as it often does in field observation. Out on the tuna grounds two of the spinner subspecies that lived in waters cloudy with life had obvious differences between the males and females. The males had muscular tails with an almost grotesque ventral hump, and very tall dorsal fins, some even canted slightly forward. I thought that the emphasis of sexual characteristics was related to that murky water—it simply took such emphasis for schoolmembers to identify the opposite sex.

After this, we began to see these same differences in Hawaiian dolphins, only in much more subtle form. That made sense, since the Hawaiian animals lived in clear water, where even a slight difference was easy to see. Associated with these sexual differences in form were behavioral differences that we learned to appreciate.

The adult males often swam together in coalitions, and they seemed to take themselves much more "seriously" than the females did. Frequently when we first approached a dolphin school we were greeted by one of these male cadres, patroling, checking us out. Many of our photographs show these coalitions in place, the other school members arrayed behind them.

Karen Pryor and Ingrid Kang had seen similar coalitions in spotted dolphin schools during their swims in the tuna nets. Karen, in her own graphic way, had described them as looking like street gangs coming at you swinging their chains. At any rate, when the old males came between us and their school, it also seemed to us that the guards were out.

I wondered about that dome of tissue that the old males carried behind the anus. Did it house special anatomy, or was it just a swelling? I examined one of these domes in a dead dolphin and found it to be composed solely of fibrous tissue. This dome, I finally came to believe was a *signing structure,* a bit of tissue that enhances the transmission of a visual signal. I now believe that the dome, or *post-anal hump,* visually enhances the threat posture of the dolphin as the male dolphin swings its tail down in the S-curve of threat. The threatening dolphin thereby signals aggressive intent and capability.

I became very curious about this threat posture, and how it might function, and why other dolphins seemed to regard it as menacing. I began to look in more detail at both the structures and the behavioral sequences involved.

I found that at the same time as the threatening male bends

his tail down and toward you, his upper body is also bent, perforce, in a sharp but opposite arc. The tall black dorsal fin, set on the apex of the back, seems even taller and straighter when the back is arched, and the very boldness with which these features are paraded before you gives them a kind of "High Noon" seriousness.

I also started to think that adult male spinner dolphins might mimic sharks. The idea began when Chris and I made a frame-by-frame analysis of an underwater film sequence Randy had made south of Kealakekua. While most of the dolphins in his film moved resolutely along, one interposed himself between Randy and the rest. This dolphin swam in wide, rapid figure-eights, and as it did so it rolled so rapidly that the frames blurred its tail movements. But we could see that these movements were partly to the side, not all in the up-down motion of the normal dolphin tail beat. As it rolled, the dolphin lowered its head, arched its back, and threw its radar dome tail forward toward Randy, in a swift-moving version of dolphin threat.

As I watched, I recalled a scientific paper by the shark biologists R. H. Johnson and D. R. Nelson, who had shown that most attacks from the fearsome gray reef shark of the tropical ocean apparently happen because a swimmer invades a shark's reef territory, and not because the shark is seeking food. Such a shark first displayed in a stereotyped rolling figure-eight swim, and if a swimmer ignored the warnings, it attacked. The divers were not eaten but instead left with their grievous wounds as the shark swam off on its rounds.

When I found the paper and compared it with what Chris and I had seen, it was obvious that the shark's swimming pattern and the behavior of the dolphin that had threatened Randy were nearly identical in several respects. It was especially interesting that Randy's dolphin beat its tail partly side-to-side in a direction 90 degrees from that

The threat posture of an adult male spinner dolphin. He arches his back, bends his head, and chatters his teeth just as the gray reef shark does. The male shark's claspers swell his body outline just where the post-anal hump of the male spinner is located. Although not shown in this drawing, the swimming behavior of a threatening shark or spinner dolphin is remarkably similar.

normally used by dolphins as they swim. The dolphins seemed clearly to be mimicking the shark, and not the other way around.

If this story proves to be true, and others need to see it to convince me utterly, the post-anal radar dome of adult male dolphins may symbolize the claspers, or male intromittant

organs, of adult male sharks. These swell the shark's body outlines at the same place as the post-anal hump of spinner dolphins.

My security that these observations were correct was
strengthened when I looked at pictures of the post-anal hump
of the open-ocean roughtooth dolphin, a species that swims
with the spinner and spotter dolphins out on the tuna grounds.
Its post-anal hump is grooved longitudinally into a pair of lon-
gitudinal swellings, a much more obvious mimic of claspers
than the hump of spinners.

If our male dolphins were mimicking sharks, how might
they use such threats: against members of their own schools,
or against threats from outside the school, such as from the
sharks themselves? My best evidence is that we have seen dolphins threaten each other with these patterns in the tuna nets,
and two of the *Hana Nai'a* research team were similarly threatened by dolphins off Hawaii. It looks as though the threats can
be directed toward schoolmates *and* to danger outside.

I began to thumb through books that described sharks from
the parts of the ocean where spinners live. Generally shark and
dolphin forms are similar enough to fool most of us. But my
eyes really lit up when I found pictures of the black-tipped
shark that lives in the same reef passes frequented by resting
spinners over much of the tropical world. In a moment of attack
I'm quite sure I wouldn't know the difference between the body
patterns of the dolphin and this shark. I certainly didn't when
I swam on a reef in French Polynesia and was circled by a
black-tipped shark. My first impression was that a spinner
dolphin was out there, and only minutes later did my
composure evaporate when I realized that a shark
was circling me.

Is there, then, a "circle of deceit" out there
in the ocean, until now hidden from us? Do
marine mammals such as dolphins find it

valuable to mimic their predators? During these musings I recalled that the strange oceanic dwarf sperm whale has a pattern of lunate light marks that look for all the world like gills, right where a shark's gills are located. The strange little whale also has a notably underslung, very sharklike lower jaw. Maybe. We need more observations before I'm willing to cast all my votes for these ideas, but my tentative guess is that I am right.

12

Of Dolphin Breaths and Fender Guards

*E*ACH creature on earth has a sharply bounded time window through which it sees the world. There are things that move too fast for it to perceive, and others so slow that they go by unnoticed. We humans do poorly, for instance, in perceiving such events as mouse courtship or starfish sociality. Mouse affairs take place in a blur that our eyes cannot resolve, but when a high-speed film is slowed to our time window we can see that there is richness there, gesture and signaling. Conversely, to our eyes starfish are inert bits of geometry, hardly possessed of the fire of life. They just seem to lie there in their tide pools; but when a friend of mine photographed them in stop motion, one frame every minute or so, and then made a film of the accumulated frames, that view was blasted away. The starfish danced about each other, they delicately touched arms, wiggled tube feet in the water, and gave every evidence of tide pool social concourse.

So too is it when we watch dolphins. Some very important behavior goes faster than we can see; for example, many of the details of their breathing and swimming are attuned to opportunities lasting only fractions of a second. As Chris and I scanned our *Maka Ala* films, I began to see things I had never understood before, simply because we began to look frame by frame, dividing those rapid events into little frozen segments of time.

We used a cheap, hand-actuated film editor. With one hand we could crank a film through, a frame at a time, watching events on its little screen. It was magic to slow down reality that way, to back up and look again, to time events, to pause to think about what had gone on, but at the same time to know that there wasn't much intervening between us and the dolphins.

We searched out a breath sequence.

"There it is, Chris, the first blob of air coming out of the blowhole. Run it over again. I think the air is sliding out *forward* over the dolphin's melon. What's THAT all about?" I asked.

In time, after running the films over and over, I began to perceive that the things we were seeing were rooted in the ancient history of toothed whales and dolphins, a group called the suborder *Odontoceti*.

Years before, I had investigated a central adaptation that defined the toothed-whale lineage, which was the development of the single blowhole and the sac system that lay beneath it. These structures were developed over the paired nostrils of ancient whales. You can see the ancient paired nostrils in every dolphin skull.

The function of all this new structure, I said, was that it allowed the diving dolphin to use its lungful of air over and over again, permitting it to make train after train of echolocation clicks for as long as it could hold its breath, without coming back to the surface for air. This in turn freed the dolphin ancestor to live its life as a truly aquatic animal, to dive, explore, feed, and evolve its societies with reference to water, not air.

Now I began to wonder if I was looking at another unexplored part of that complex adaptation: the way a dolphin dealt with breathing at the sea surface, an uncertain boundary at best when the wind came up.

The film editor also let us look, frame by frame, at a still more ancient pattern: the way dolphins swim, which has its roots in events five times as old as the entire dolphin lineage, back when mammals split away from the reptilian line in the middle of the Age of Reptiles, on the order of 200 million years ago. The very definition of "mammal" is involved, a part of which says that unlike most reptiles, mammals pull their legs under them, a feature that allows the rapid and sustained loco- motion of a warm-blooded mammal. To do this, mammals undulate their spines up and down, rather than sideways, as they run. Flukes move like that.

As the frames of film flickered by showing a dolphin swim- ming next to *Maka Ala*'s capsule, I mused that these ancient events had constrained some of the subtler aspects of how dol- phins came to swim. What I saw from the films was that having flukes both solved some problems and posed others.

Before I describe what we saw in the films, it is worthwhile to digress a little to sketch in the evolutionary history of ceta- ceans, as paleontologists have pieced it together. This will give us some extra tools to think with.

The bones and teeth of the most likely ancestors of ceta- ceans, curious carnivorous relatives of early hoofed mammals called *mesonychids,* have been found in rocks deposited in what is now Pakistan. They seem to have frequented muddy estu- aries to chase schooling fish and to stab at them with spe- cially adapted daggerlike teeth.

The shallows they entered were at the margins of the now-fragmented Tethys Sea, a winding cor- ridor of water that girdled the globe during the Eocene epoch, for most of its length wander- ing not far north of the equator. It passed westward from Pakistan, through the present-day Mediterranean, across northern Africa and Spain in separate shallow-water channels—epicontinental seas, the paleontologists call them. It crossed the then rather narrow Atlantic, pierced Central America, and wound its way across the Pacific to Asia and back to the Mediterranean again. Then, as now, the continents were jockeying for position, swirling about on the surface of the slowly moving earth's mantle like blobs of foam. India, a detached subcontinental island at the time, had been rafted up from the southern Indian Ocean, and as it approached Asia it began to define the southern margin of the Tethys near where cetaceans first appeared.

India's hegira ended thirty million years later as it collided with the Asian continent. It closed the Tethys right where the cetaceans had their genesis. The unimaginable force of India's northward motion, driven by unseen vortices in the plastic mantle below, then rumpled and wrinkled the land it hit, raising the Himalayas and shaping the course of the great rivers of Asia, whose waters now run in the new mountain folds: the Yang'tse, the Mekong, and, against the Himalayan base, the Brahmaputra, which flows onto the newly attached subcontinent and there takes a new name, the Ganges.

Because the Tethys never wandered far from the tropics, it became very warm. It may have been that this warmth had much to do with allowing those cetacean ancestors to enter the sea in the first place. Much time may have been required before subdermal fat stores spread into the complete blubber coat. Then heat conservation physiology and anatomy had to unfold, allowing modern cetaceans to penetrate even the coldest waters.

Students of ancient ocean history measure the warming of currents like that in the Tethys by what they call *dwell time,* or how long a water mass stays in a given general latitude. If a current dwells briefly in the tropics and then turns toward a pole, or misses tropical latitudes altogether, it will be cool, and its influence on world climate will also be to cool. But if it is like the Tethys, it can become very warm and everything that lives in it will be shaped by heat, not cold. So it was with the ancient cetaceans. Fossils from the Tethys reveal that many of them lived associated with coral reefs, and at first all of them seemed to have stayed close to shore. Only later did they escape the Tethys, and in a single brief event (from the paleontological standpoint, which means it may have required a few million years) spread throughout the oceans of the world.

So the warm Tethyan waters eased the chill of swimming, and thereby nudged the evolutionary balance sheet a little, making it easier to go to sea, lending time to prepare for colder climes.

Warm water notwithstanding, it seems likely that the process of weaning cetacean ancestors from the land was slow. At first, these creatures must have simply made forays into the water, like children racing across the beach to play in the waves. Just as for the children, many things were wrong at the start. They couldn't swim very well, their eyes stung with salt water, their voices—normally directed to each other through the air— fell mute, and they could hardly hear underwater. But the warm waters teemed with fish for the taking, and, in the evolutionary sense, the balance was tipped toward the sea.

I think that even today that process of being weaned from the land may not be wholly complete for many cetaceans. The spinners may be giving testimony to this when they retreat from the open sea and come to island margins to rest. Perhaps the spinners of Kealakekua still reach out with encased fingertips toward the shore, no longer able to leave the water, but still needing the land.

I NOTICED that we had captured entire breathing sequences from the *Maka Ala*'s window. We could see the dolphins arc up toward the shimmering silver mirror of the surface, pierce it, exhale, take incredibly brief sips of air, and dive again, and over and over we caught long sequences of spinner dolphins undulating past our capsule, sometimes with rapid wide-amplitude strokes of their flukes, and at other times just gliding along, slipping without obvious effort through the water.

"Have you ever wondered, Chris, how a dolphin can breathe at sea?" I asked rhetorically, not waiting for a reply.

It must, I thought, be something for a dolphin to breathe when the storms come. I've been out in enough bad weather to know that the sea surface can lose its meaning at such times. Walls of bubbles are driven down dozens of feet into the water, making the surface water an insubstantial greenish froth. And conversely, just above the old surface what passes for air becomes laden with spray.

I talked on. "How do you suppose a dolphin, who cannot support its own weight in bubbly water, can get to the surface to breathe, and how does it deal with spray?" And I added, "The dolphins have somehow solved these problems or they could never have gone to sea. Let's see if our films have any clues."

We saw that if a dolphin was moving along briskly, those shining sheets of exhaled air moved *forward* over the surfacing dolphin's head, right into its direction of travel. Then we sought out sequences of fast-moving dolphins rising to breathe. We could see that the path of a dolphin about to breathe began half a dozen feet below the surface when it broke away from its schoolmates, arched its head 40 degrees or so upward, and pumped toward the surface. *Almost exactly* as the dolphin's beak tip hit the surface we could also see a tiny shining blob of air at its blowhole lip. I began to think that the beak tip was a fender guard, a contact point that could tell the dolphin when to start its breathing sequence. I withhold endorsement of this idea until somebody shows that a dolphin can sense that air-water interface with enough precision, but somehow their timing is precise.

Dolphins, of course, breathe through a single arcuate blowhole opening atop their heads, set about midway between their eyes, and not through two nostrils such as we use. When closed, the blowhole is a hard, half-moon–shaped shelf, with its cusps directed forward. A soft blowhole plug or lip lies swung up underneath, sealing it closed. When the animal breathes, this lip is pulled downward and forward away from the hard shelf, opening the single orifice a crack. When wide open, the blowhole reveals a round, nearly vertical passage. Sometimes one can even look down on a captive dolphin when it breathes and see that deep in the forehead the single passage divides into two nostrils, like those of land mammals.

We continued our inspection of the surfacing sequence.

"Look at that air! It's a sheet over the entire forehead now." We could see that the dolphin's beak was pretty much out of the water, and the leading edge of the air sheet had broken the surface. Then, frame by frame, the air sheet got thicker and more vertical the closer the dolphin's head came to the surface.

"That's probably due to the blowhole valve pulling forward and more air from exhalation escaping"; and I cranked back the editor for another look.

Just as the dolphin's melon hit the surface, the air blast cleared away a wedge of water in front if its head and the dolphin arced forward, right into the cleared space. It swam right into its own exhalate!

I was surprised about that and later began to watch rising dolphins from the deck of the *Maka Ala*. Indeed, I could see them slide up into their own exhaled air, and I could also see that the force of the air blast blew water droplets out from the surface in a radial spray that sprinkled down for as much as three feet around the rising dolphin. The dolphin had in effect cleared the way around its own rising head by blowing into the water just before it broke the surface. The exhaled air, known to travel as rapidly as 200 miles per hour in some cetacean exhalations, had literally been used to scour out a space within which the animal began its inhalation sequence.

I felt that an important mechanism had been revealed to us, by which dolphins could breathe when the afternoon chop filled the air with spray. They could clear the water over their blowholes for the fraction of a second it takes for the speeding droplets of sea water to race away, and if they could exhale fast enough, they could breathe in again before the sea collapsed over them. Bernd tells me that they change strategies again when a real storm turns the entire sea surface to foam. He described watching dolphins in a sixty-knot wind, as they leapt up through the froth at the surface to breathe during mid-leap.

Was there time enough for my scenario to work? Chris and I began to put times on the events we were watching, since we knew the frame rate of the camera. It turned out there was time, and that briskly moving spinner dolphins routinely exhaled in about three-tenths of a second. Unlike us, dolphins are known to exchange their entire lungful of air with each breath. The explosive propulsion of those droplets therefore became easier to understand. They were radiating out like thousands of watery bullets, cleansing the air of sea spray before them.

At the time spinner exhalation was complete, the dolphin was just about at the top of its roll into the atmosphere. In the instant left before it submerged, it had to inhale. We timed many inhalations and found that they lasted twice or more as long as the explosive exhalation, even though the dolphin had about half its time at the surface left. How did that work? We wondered. It didn't seem to add up.

Asking the question focused our eyes for us. We noticed that with each reentry the dolphin beat its head downward, and this, together with its arcing trajectory, excavated a transient cavity in the sea surface, right over its blowhole. Inside this temporary cavern the dolphin finished taking in the last of its breath, quite freed of any surface spray.

That part was familiar enough. Thirty years before, when I first began my career with dolphins off the southern California coast, I had noticed Dall porpoises literally beating such a breathing cavern in the surface sea, producing a little splash of water as they dove. I have a picture of that movement engraved in my mind. I was on the collecting vessel *Geronimo,* with a Dall porpoise running at the bow, and I was able to look down into the cavity the porpoise had just made. Then I could see the animal close its blowhole an instant before the water collapsed over it.

There are two final pieces to this story of dolphin breath. The first is, dolphins don't mind if a little water runs into their noses. That was shown years before when Bill and Barbara Schevill filmed respiration in a captive dolphin during their studies of how dolphin upper narial passages work. Their dolphin lay still at the surface so they did not see it beat a hole in the water, nor did it spray them with water bullets. But their high-speed films not infrequently showed a trickle of sea water running into the corner of the dolphin's blowhole just before it closed, presumably to be held in the little sacs located just below and then exhaled on the next breath. Perhaps this explains part of the dolphin's supply of water bullets, the remainder coming from the surface water they blow away.

As I thought about these breathing mechanisms, I was struck by the profile of the dolphin's upper nasal passages. The single upper airway narrowed markedly at the blowhole from a much wider conduit beneath. This would speed the exhaled air as it was blown free. Such locally restricted tubes, or venturis, are used widely by animals and engineers to speed fluids, whether they are of air or liquid.

I wondered if the reverse flow might also be

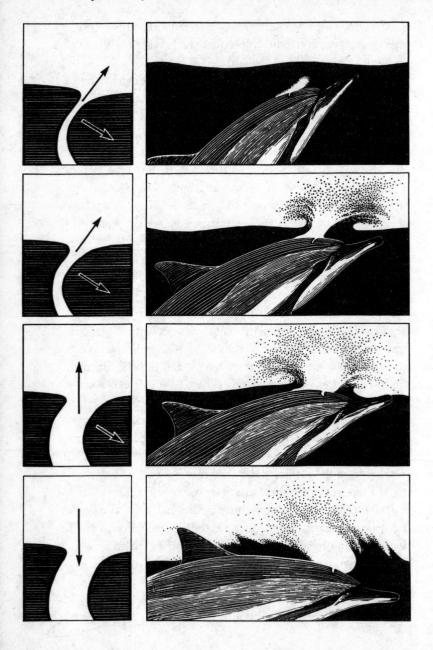

The breathing sequence of a surfacing spinner dolphin. TOP TO BOTTOM: The dolphin's blowhole begins to open as the valve moves forward. Air escapes at high speed through this slit, forward over the dolphin's head. Sometimes, when dolphins are going very slowly, the air is released more slowly and will slip back over the head. Just as the dolphin's snout touches the surface it blasts out air and blows away the surface water. Then, as the blowhole opens, the blast becomes more vertical, continuing to blast the water away as the dolphin starts to inhale. At bottom, the dolphin beats its head against the surface as it submerges, excavating a cavity in the water, inside which it finishes its inhalation.

important. Upon inhalation, the venturi arrangement would *slow* air as it came into the respiratory system to the same degree that it had speeded it going the other way. I wondered what the cumulative impact of sharp pressures of inhaled air might be for an animal that breathes so rapidly, every minute or so, all its life. I wondered if I was looking at an elegant engineering design that both allowed the dolphin to breathe in rough seas and at the same time protected its delicate lungs from the cumulative battering of inhalation. My respected respiratory physiologist colleague, Dr. Gerry Kooyman of Scripps Institution of Oceanography, says the inspired air of a dolphin breath is slowed almost to a standstill by all the branchings of the respiratory tree before it ever reaches the delicate lung membranes, and that he doubts my scenario. But, tenacious colleague that I am, I hang onto my idea, wondering if the repeated sharp pressure changes upon the delicate cellular layers that make up lungs might not be damaging over time. Maybe the fact that exhalation in dolphins is twice (or more) as fast as inhalation means something besides providing time to inhale.

DOLPHIN breathing and swimming are inextricably intermeshed. When those Tethyan

cetacean ancestors entered the sea, they had to rearrange the way they accomplished both breathing and swimming so that these vital processes would not interfere with each other.

The basic pattern of the swimming motion was clearly evolved long before cetaceans returned to the sea. The ancient up-and-down undulation of the spine that we see in all present-day mammals seems to have appeared well back in the time of the giant reptiles. Perhaps it arose from the need of tiny mouselike protomammals to jump during escape, a means used by a good many modern descendants.

When the early cetaceans took to sea, a series of new loco-motory and respiratory problems was posed. These newly aquatic animals needed swim fins and diving planes, and they needed to smooth out the hitch in their swimming stroke caused by inhaling air through the tip of their typical mammalian snouts.

Not only was there the problem of being limited by how far they could go on a single lungful of air, but the single breath competed with and limited use of the air for underwater sound production. Over perhaps fifteen million years after their original sea entry, blowholes, upper air storage spaces, and new ways of phonating out of their foreheads came into being, as did a whole series of subtle adaptations that increased the capacity of a cetacean to swim and dive.

Chris and I began to look at what wild dolphins actually did when they swam. We saw something neither of us had seen before. The dolphin's tail and its flukes didn't just trail out behind like a snake. Instead, when a dolphin glided by our viewing vault, not beating its flukes, the plane of its flukes cut along just at the level of its belly.

Then we looked at what happened to the flukes when a dolphin raced by. Back and forth we cranked our films, watching these events. These swimming dolphins now and then did give heroic pumps of their powerful tails, their flukes hinging up and down as they were pressed against the water on both up and down strokes. And such power they could exert! The terete dolphins could race forward like bullets when they wanted to.

Something else caught our attention. Even during its most powerful strokes, no dolphin ever lifted its flukes up to the plane of its dorsal fin tip, or beat them below the tips of its trailing pectoral fins. The dolphin had fender guards! If the dolphin had folded its pectoral fins up tight against its body as it swam, it could never be sure that it wouldn't hit its flukes on an object it passed. The tips of a dolphin's pectoral fins and dorsal fin, then, define a space through which the dolphin can pass safely without catching the flukes working behind.

Neat! Just like a cat's whiskers. My guess is that this fine-tuning took place in ancestral cetaceans who swam in the shallow, coral-crowded Tethys. Our next question was, why should a dolphin's swimming stroke oscillate about a midpoint at its belly line? Then I recalled some tests the hydrodynamicist Tom Lang and I had once run on how fast a little trained dolphin named Keiki could swim. We had induced the dolphin to swim down a lagoon racecourse, rewarding it royally each time it beat its old record. Soon we had the dolphin clipping seconds off its world record day after day, until its performance leveled out at about 17.1 knots (20.5 miles per hour).

What I recalled about these tests was that as Keiki began to swim near his peak performance, he turned on his side and swam the entire racetrack underwater. His flukes then beat from side to side and he did not breathe until the race was over. He became, for the time being, a fish.

In his normal orientation, the faster Keiki swam the harder his flukes pressed upward against the compliant sea surface. There the sea surface humped up and formed great boils of water, or dolphin *footprints,* as Bill Schevill calls them. These boils represent a great deal of lost energy for the dolphin, a thing that no animal that swims constantly can easily afford. When Keiki turned on his side, the symmetry of his swimming stroke returned, and he pressed equally hard on much less compliant water that could not hump up into the air.

When we put together the way Keiki had swum when pressed to his limit, and what the fluke stroke of swimming spinners was like, it all made sense. Dolphins spend most of their life near the surface, as they undulate up for their breaths of air. By having their flukes beat as deep as possible, this energy loss on the upstroke is minimized, and their fender guards let them orient to both the surface and the bottom as they race along, without fear that they will hit anything.

It's probable that these swimming arrangements also had their genesis back in those ancient Tethyan estuaries, when the earliest cetaceans settled on the way they would swim for the next fifty million years. It certainly must have been an early order of business.

"Remarkable what you can see through a film editor," Chris said.

13

Jody

I THINK of myself as half-teacher, half-scientist. I find myself involved with a flood of undergraduates who enter my office for one reason or another, spilling out their difficulties and aspirations. I hear them out, watching for the crucial signs of promise, integrity, excitement with ideas, concern for the world, the artist's eye, or the mathematician's logic. They take many paths, both in and out of science. I'm delighted that these intellectual children are all over the place.

The teaching process for me is not so much standing up in front of a class and giving out what I know as it is providing students chances and places to excel and then directing such skills through exposure to good science, example, and opportunity. That is why *Hana Nai'a* was a schizophrenic place, led by the clear and obvious professionals who didn't have to be told what to do, like Bernd, Mel, and Randy, but at the same time heavily populated with lively younger scholars not quite out of the chrysalis. These young students, if let, bring a crucial iconoclasm to a project such as ours. New and often uncomfortable views come to jostle with older wisdom. *Hana Nai'a* evolved into just such a place.

You may have noticed that most of the young scholars at *Hana Nai'a* were adventurous women. That happened because a quite remarkable change has swept over the science of animal behavior in the last three decades (when I entered field science in the late 1940s nearly all field work was dominated by males; women, it was assumed, didn't do rugged field work). Women scientists in unprecedented numbers have now moved into the tropical forests, onto the tundra, and everywhere else on earth along with the more traditional "field men." Meetings of the Animal Behavior Society are now delightful assemblies populated by men and women alike, tanned and lean from long periods away from creature comforts. I've joked that you can tell a member as far away as you can see one by their lion-proof khaki shorts.

It's not just that the numbers of women are so refreshing (I guessed it was about 50:50 at the last meeting I attended) but that the viewpoints brought by the women have forever changed the face of the science. They have helped to make it complete in a deep scientific sense.

Jane Goodall, with her remarkable work on chimpanzees, was certainly among those who led that vanguard. She showed that a very patient and undemanding person could break down the barrier between humans and animals and make friends. She let animal behaviorists move into the space discovered earlier by cultural anthropologists who found they could learn most by becoming Boswells within the society they chose to study. To an observant scribe living within a society—whether of humans or of some other animal—much of the texture and subtlety of that foreign life was available for the looking. Inter-individual relations, personalities, nurture and teaching, or growing up became the new stuff of the science.

Archetypical men, the hunters, the explorers, have tended to see other things. But whether this came significantly from our basic differences as men and women, or from the cultural roles we play, I don't know. I was once such an archetypical male, and even now some of the things learned in those earlier days hang on, hard to shake loose.

When I began we tended to record mostly the things we evoked: the defense, the conflicts, the territories, affairs of food, courtship, mating and provisioning, and the ecological boundaries between societies. In short, we saw most clearly the parts of animal societies where we lived most of our own lives.

And now the women are beginning to record the places where they have tended to live theirs. This division is not a wall, but seems to me a set of tendencies springing from deep within our collective beings and separate experiences.

The change, I think, is the splendid indication of both a science and a people coming of age. It now seems so obvious to me that in order to truly understand a wild animal society, or parenthetically our own, we need both these viewpoints in equal measure. One must not dominate the other. By evolving out of such domination, we observers have let the animals we study become whole.

None of this was much on my mind when the young women began to drift into the *Hana Nai'a* camp. Each of them simply seemed like somebody with a lot of ideas, a lot of energy and integrity.

One of these was Jody Solow. The task she chose was to see if it was possible to make friends with a wild dolphin school in its own environment.

There are, in fact, solid indications that one can make friends with wild dolphins. Now and then the dolphins have even turned this proposition over and come ashore to make friends with people. Many times throughout history, single dolphins (probably mostly bottlenose dolphins) have come into bays and along beaches to mingle with humans.

For example, in modern times a bottlenose dolphin named Opononi came regularly to a bay in northern New Zealand, and there children delighted in taking rides on her back. And the dolphin Beaky (or Donald, as others called him) appeared at the Isle of Man, where he began to associate with humans. He moved down the coast of Wales to Cornwall, accumulating injuries from gunshot and boat propellors but this seemed to make no difference in his tendency to associate with humans. Beaky may have been "different," perhaps a bit like someone's "Crazy Uncle Charlie," whose exploits became the stuff of family legend.

Nicholas Webb, who followed Beaky's activities for several months, describes the dolphin's interactions with a seven-ton masthead schooner *Aquarius of Arne,* which had been anchored with a $5/16$th-inch chain and a 35-pound anchor but nevertheless was towed in a 100-yard semicircle by the dolphin. More bizarre perhaps was the dolphin's behavior toward smaller vessels, whose anchors were lifted bodily from the bottom, the chain held in the dolphin's jaws and over its back, and then towed for hundreds of yards. For a time no small boat was safe at anchor in Coverack Cove because it would be towed, sometimes dangerously close to the breakwater's crashing waves. The resultant snarls of anchor chains and lines were sometimes monumental.

But in spite of this curious obsession, Beaky remained very sociable, inquisitive, and even playful with most swimmers. "Playful" is certainly too mild a word to describe the experience of two middle-aged women, both of whom swam daily in one of the ocean coves Beaky visited. Beaky made apparent "sexual" overtures to them, and perhaps they were just that. He mouthed legs and hands, and caressed them with his erect penis, and then bore them off, draped over his head.

He took them away from shore, swimming with great power. One of these women had to be rescued from the dolphin's bold attentions. Beaky also "possessed" a young boy for nearly two hours before a rescue was performed by the crew of a passing speedboat. Parenthetically, he also made "sexual advances" to male divers. As we now know from our work with spinners, such apparently sexual behavior in these oestrus mammals can sometimes be social rather than sexual.

Another report of a bottlenose dolphin seeking association with people was that of "Charlie" (who turned out to be a female). Charlie frequented the Scottish coast for a time, and, like Opononi, associated with swimmers.

Our own Georges Gilbert in Hawaii had learned that when he anchored in a certain Hawaiian cove, the bottlenose dolphins would swirl around his boat in the dark, swooping in to catch the fish that darted in under Georges' boom light. One night Georges, ever the experimenter, stored up a bucketful of Hawaiian flying fish that had flown on deck. These curious piscine airplanes are favorite dolphin food. Georges doled them out one by one to the dolphins. The dolphins were lured closer and closer, and finally Georges hesitated before throwing another fish. A dolphin reared up out of the water in anticipation. Before long Georges had these wild dolphins bursting from the water in front of him, begging for more flying fish. He'd trained an open-ocean dolphin show using wild animals!

To me, the most interesting interaction in recent times between dolphins and people is the case of the bottlenose dolphins of Shark Bay, West Australia. There at the little fishing port of Denham, and later at a nearby beach called Monkey Mia, fishermen tossed "trash fish" to the dolphins that swirled around their boats. Soon this feeding became a ritual, and then a tourist attraction at a beachside trailer park. I first heard about it from "Chi-uh" Gawain, who in her wanderings around the world had found the dolphins and become fascinated by them. She returned again and again to that remote beach at Shark Bay and finally assembled a graceful little book (*The Dolphin's Gift,* Whatever Press, 1981, Mill Valley, California) about the school.

Today the school is protected, and detailed scientific studies are underway. Two of my onetime undergraduate students, Richard Connor and Rachel Smolker, are there as I write, unraveling dolphin society at this place where cetaceans voluntarily come among humans at the sea's edge.

And come they do. Some of the dolphins swim amongst the visitors in water so shallow they are nearly stranded, and there they take fish from human hands. Mother dolphins have been seen to "stash" their calves with other adult dolphins hanging just offshore, and thus unencumbered to mingle with the humans for a time. My students tell me that there are times when these dolphins turn the process around and bring in fresh-caught fish to the visiting humans!

So when Jody first proposed a plan to do a senior thesis project swimming with dolphins, well before *Hana Nai'a* began, I knew that precedent existed. There was even a slight precedent for spinner dolphin-human interaction. My first informant about the Kealakekua spinners told of having them cluster around him as he swam over the sandy area off Napoopoo Beach, and Tom and I had been in their midst many times.

Jody hoped for an undisturbed school; just her team and the *nai'a*. I directed her to Manele Bay, on Lanai Island, Hawaii, where Georges Gilbert had long before captured some of Sea Life Park's little spinner school.

Now I should tell you that I was a bit appalled by Jody's proposal. Two major problems seemed obvious to me. First, I worried about Jody's safety. The outlines of what she had in mind involved swimming with wild dolphins somewhere out in open water. By that time I had begun to suspect that sharks might sometimes be near some dolphin schools, though this was still conjecture. I also wondered how she was going to assemble the considerable support she needed: the plane tickets, the food, the boats, the underwater cameras, and so on.

Jody was not to be stopped by such talk, although to some

degree she did act on the various safety precautions I insisted on. Ultimately she put a signaling mirror in her inflatable boat, and supplies of food and water. We designed a buddy system, a person in the water and an attendant in the raft, always on the alert to take her quickly from the water. Among other things I was afraid that she and her student friends would get out there in the bay, have their engine quit, and begin to drift to China without food or water.

She understood well enough. In the string of delightful letters she sent to me about their exploits, I would find sentences like this: "Sorry, Ken, I couldn't resist eating the M&Ms in the raft's food supplies. They were yummy."

Although I had extracted a promise that she confine her work to the nearshore bays, I always suspected Jody would stretch the concept of "bay" and go where the dolphins were, because that is what I would have done. She did, in fact, encounter sharks, and she was ready for them. The buddy system was in force, along with a set of prearranged hand signals. Within seconds she flipped over the gunwale into the tender's boat when the gray shape was seen flirting along outside the school.

I've learned over three decades of teaching not to restrict young scholars by what I think they can or cannot do. The educational value of an imaginative dream such as Jody presented lies more in the doing, and less in the totality of the project in scientific terms. It didn't seem central to me that she should be asked to revolutionize some piece of dolphin biology, but it mattered a great deal that she should have the opportunity to spread her own wings and try, under her own steam and with her own ingenuity and imagination, to do this daunting thing.

Now that I know Jody better I shouldn't have worried about the *doing*, but I was right in worrying about the safety aspects. Jody has proved to be one of the most daring, buoyant, physically courageous people I've ever worked with. Her exploits since *Hana Nai'a* include living among the camel tribes of Africa, cajoling and threatening her way to safety with the Ugandan military (who were bullying her), travels in the Aleutians, and now, under sponsorship from Cambridge University, England, work in the New Hebridean jungle. There are many wonderful stories she's sent me on the backs of postcards that I hope she will one day tell on her own.

But when we first met back in my university office, I saw only this graceful, intelligent young woman, full of resolve and humor, anxious to find out what she was made of.

What she did was assemble and lead a team of half a dozen student friends, talk a sporting goods company out of an inflatable boat, obtain underwater cameras, tape recorders, tents, and camp gear, also mostly for free, and then convince an airline to fly this vast pile to Maui Island, gratis. Jody can talk birds out of bushes.

At Maui, Jody called a colleague of mine, Jim Lucky. Jim lives in the little one-time whaling port of Lahaina, and has a considerable interest in marine mammals. He drove over to the airport, stuffed the team and their gear in his truck, and then somehow housed them all as they readied themselves for the final leg to Lanai Island, where the dolphin school swam. Then he saw to it that they landed safely on the white strand of Manele Bay.

Her postcard reports soon informed me that life was complete. Her team was established on the beach of a subtropical island, the soft trades rustled the coconut palms at night, the postman was providing plentiful ice cream on his daily runs, and best of all, the beautiful *nai'a* swam close offshore.

Jody's approach to the *nai'a* was subtle. She swam into their schools with great care, trying hard to understand how they would view her intrusion. When the dolphins approached her boat and began to pass close by, she took this as a signal to go swimming. She was ready in a wet suit, jacket, mask, fins, snorkel, and diver's flag, and a Nikonos III 35-mm. camera was slung over her shoulder.

To announce her presence she immediately began to utter a vocalization in her throat that to my ears was a good facsimile of a dolphin chirp. The dolphins, with their acute hearing and good vision, must have known immediately about her entry. Jody wanted to inform the *nai'a* that she was not trying to sneak up on them, but instead announcing herself as a friend. I think it worked, too, when the dolphins were not consumed by their own imperatives.

She then paddled slowly toward the lazily moving dolphins and hung at the surface vocalizing slowly, waiting for a response from the animals. Not infrequently they swirled near to her, sometimes only a body's length away. Her notes report schools numbering from about twenty to sixty animals approaching her in those clear waters. She saw the same variability in their schools that we had seen from our viewing boats, in such things as aerial activity, vocalization, and social interaction.

She noted that when two schools encountered one another, one school might be more closely packed than the other, and more synchronous in its movements, surfacing slower and with less vocalization and aerial activity than the other school. I at once recognized that she had been watching a resting and an active school in close juxtaposition.

She noted other hallmarks of these two states: the more active school was typically divided into smaller subgroups of three to about twenty animals, while the slower schools swam as a unit. Her description of rest was close to ours made from the *Maka Ala*:

Sometimes groups of dolphins were seen swimming in extremely synchronous formation. On one occasion a subgroup was noted surfacing with many animals in or close to pectoral contact. Just as they reached the surface they radiated outward like the petals of a flower. At other times I saw them swim in a line of three or four animals abreast, pectorals touching, like cut-out paper dolls, swimming slowly toward the surface.

With head immersed Jody could hear the din of sounds produced by the dolphin school. Like the rest of us she wasn't able to attach clear meaning to the sounds, especially because most of the phonating animals swam out of sight.

Sometimes I heard the dolphins mimic my vocalizations. The more active the dolphins were the more vocal they were. I heard chorusing whistles, various burst pulsed signals, and click trains. Some burst pulse signals were very distinct sounds. One sounded like the twanging of a banjo, another like a laughing chimpanzee and another like rubbing a finger across a balloon. When in the water I could usually hear the dolphins before I could see them.

She went on:

I sometimes was able to observe them from 2 to 4 meters away. Sometimes the more active groups consisted completely, or almost completely, of paired adults. At other times there was a mixture of animals, ranging from small calves to very large adults.

.   .   .

Caressing behavior was seen between adult pairs. Trios, too, were frequently engaged in caressing, and once I observed a calf rubbing against and rolling around a pair of adults engaged in caressing.

Jody once found herself too close for comfort to an aggressive exchange between two spinner dolphins:

Only once did I observe aggressive behavior off the island of Lanai. A trio was swimming together; one animal positioned itself belly-to-belly with a second animal and when a third animal tried to position itself between them, one of the original pair darted toward the newcomer and displayed in such a fashion as to frighten me and to cause me to climb out of the water into the attendant raft. The two dolphins moved in short quick movements and contorted their bodies into an S-shaped configuration, with their heads down and to one side, and their mouths open, exposing their rows of pointed teeth. They shook their heads and swished their tails sideways with jerky movements.

But of all the behavior Jody and her campmates noted, the observations on play were the most striking. In fact, Jody became part of one of their play groups.

It was not always clear to me what was or was not play behavior. I frequently observed one dolphin, whom I dubbed "Linus," possibly a male, who played catch with himself by carrying a piece of flotsam (the black polyethylene sheeting used in the nearby pineapple fields to suppress weeds) on his pectoral fin. He then let it go and returned to pick it up with the edge of his flukes or rostrum. He continued this routine for some time. Sometimes Linus let go of the plastic near me. The first time he did this I dove down to retrieve it, and just as I was about to grasp it he rapidly darted by and took it away on his pectoral fin. Later that day he let go of it near me again and I succeeded in grasping it. I swam with it for a time while he swam back and forth two meters in front of me making a strange sound (like loud echolocation, but sped up). Finally I let go of the "toy" and he immediately took it on his pectoral fin and swam away. Later that afternoon the sequence was repeated again.

These observations of Jody's resonated with some of my own. I remembered that we had frequently seen such play among the captives at Sea Life Park, so often in fact that we began providing them with playthings. At the time I was struck by the deftness with which this balancing of floating objects was carried out. One of the dolphins, Kehaulani, was an inveterate toy carrier. She took her seaweed everywhere and showed a juggler's sense when balancing the plaything as she swerved and maneuvered amongst her sometimes pushy poolmates.

At sea Jody noted the same sure balance as the dolphins traded their plastic toys back and forth:

> One afternoon Linus and the dolphin that frequently traveled with him (it had a pronounced white scar below its dorsal fin) were playing "catch" with bits of plastic. Linus was playing with a white garbage bag and his consort with a clear baggie. On another afternoon several dolphins appeared to be engaged in the game. They passed a piece of polyethylene from one animal to another. One animal swimming near the back of a group of 8 to 10 dolphins raced ahead amongst its schoolmates and took the plastic away on its pectoral fin, and the others followed after to attempt the same thing.

After Jody's Lanai Island adventures were over, and her thesis safely filed, she joined our Kealakekua team. There she spent weeks swimming back and forth near the dolphins. Most of the time the schools melted in front of her and she had difficulty entering their ranks. By this time I'd equipped her with a diver's flag to signal boaters that there was a person in the water. From shore we could see the flag bobbing behind her as she tirelessly called to the dolphins and edged toward their midst. But she was, I think, old hat to them. Other swimmers came toward them nearly every day from nearby Napoopoo Beach, and they had learned to edge away to find their own quiet space.

Soon Jody decided firmly that Kealakekua was not for her. She had to find a more remote place where there remained hope that just she and the dolphins could make friends. After considerable searching we located Makalawena Beach, twenty-seven miles north of our camp, down a rough road over the *pahoehoe* (smooth and ropy in form) lava.

Spinner dolphins came up the coast to Makalawena in considerable numbers. A school often numbering 250 dolphins
patrolled along that low cliffed coast, spreading out over narrow shallow sand flats, and then hugging lava bluffs where the
water comes deep and dark against the shore. The *nai'a* seldom
ventured north of the twin cinder cones of Puu Ohai, just north
of Makalawena, but instead turned there and moved slowly
down to a deep cove named Hoona Bay, then doubled the low
lava bluffs of Keahole Point to move past the little manmade
nook of Honokohau Harbor, and on to "the Pine Trees" where
they generally turned northward again for another circuit along
the shore.

This twelve-mile traverse may be repeated a couple of times
during the day. The attraction is the nearby deep water off
Keahole Point. There the lava shield of the island drops precip-
itously into the deep sea, and, because of a juxtaposition of
island bulk and deep ocean currents, nutrients and their associated life accumulate and rise to the surface. The water is often
roily there, streaked and murky with planktonic life. The birds
know the food is there. Shearwaters by the thousands swoop
and wheel between the swells, or raft upon the surface once
feeding is over. The fishermen come too. Nearly every day big
cruisers troll off the point for billfish and tuna. Arrangements
were made for Jody to establish a working camp there, and she
soon settled in under the big beach cedars and *kiawe* trees.

But even though vacant coves and bare lava headlands
stretched away on either side of her beach, she and her boat
attendant were not alone at Makalawena. A large herd of goats
roamed the grove, and there was a low, sprawling fisherman's
camp made of flotsam just down the beach. Two gnarled Fili-
pino fishermen, Kirin and Sam, occupied this camp much of
the time. On our first reconnaissance of Makalawena they graciously invited us in. We bent down under the heavy, whit-
ened driftwood log that served as a lintel, pushed aside the
canvas flap to enter the sand-floored shelter. Inside was a spa-

cious rambling space without definable rooms, all their fishing gear stowed on rude shelves. We sat for a time on benches by their "cooking place," which was a rectangle of sand and smouldering charcoal held in place by beach cobbles.

Kirin and Sam obtained their water, they said, in a lava-bounded pool back of the beach. There the rainwater percolated down in the porous lava to float on top of the salt water seeping in from the beach.

Jody's camp was located a hundred yards down the beach, and she soon found some freshwater pools of her own. One was a cold, crystal-clear grotto down among the rough lava cubes, and it, she decided, was for bathing: a place where she could wash off the salt from a day's swim. The other, a smaller one, and closer to camp, was the place she could dip up her cooking water.

Kirin and Sam's shelter, though open on most sides to the warm Hawaiian air, beat back the trade winds with a bulwark of driftwood and canvas on the sea side. They told me that on the highest tides and with a strong onshore wind, the waves sometimes threatened to sluice among the supporting poles. Jody, wisely I thought, built her thatched shelter above the reach of the waves, back among the trees.

Jody's unexpected arrival at Makalawena Beach must have seemed like a dream to those old fishermen. By the time we returned to bring supplies and to see how she was faring, she and the fishermen were fast friends, and she had made friends with the goats too, especially one inquisitive young kid who had become the camp pet, and who sometimes even went to sea on the tender's boat. Ears blowing in the breeze, it stood with hooves dented into the compliant rubber thwarts, watching Jody swim. As a present to Jody, just for being there, Kirin and Sam had cleared an area of forest floor near her camp for that most necessary of all camp accoutrements, a dancing ground.

And from time to time she shared meals with them. Kirin

Jody Solow, Kirin, and Jody's little kid at Makalawena. Soon the kid grew into a full-fledged goat that went to sea with her. *R. S. Wells*

showed her how to pick the tiny leaves off the *kiawe* branch tips to produce a vegetable dish much treasured by Kirin's friends, and then induced her to dip morsels of food into a jar filled with an odorous Philippine fish sauce. This delicacy usually takes some adjustment for the western palate, but true to her spirit Jody never hesitated to partake. The sauce was made, she told me, by immersing fish heads in a jar of sea water and then letting them steep in the sun until a ripe, rich, rotted smell issued forth.

EVEN though Makalawena is on the lee coast of Hawaii, it proved to be a place of wind and surf and strong currents, where for many days at a time Jody could not venture to sea. But in time she swam much of the coast. The *nai'a* too, for reasons known only to them, proved less willing to let her travel amongst them than they had been at Manele Bay. The members of those big

Keahole schools seemed never to reach the deep levels of rest seen at either Manele or Kealakekua. Perhaps this was due to the exposed coast, which lay closer to the deep sea than either of the other coves. Or perhaps their nervousness was because their larger school always contained some contingent of wide-awake animals who kept the others from descending into deep rest. Or perhaps most likely, the Hawaii spinners live along a coast much more densely populated by man than do the Lanai dolphins. Jody's log carries the following entry:

> Generally, while working at Makalawena Camp we left the dolphins to rest in peace in the early afternoon. By about 1300 they were usually in Hoona Bay. This is the place where they begin their swim out to sea later in the afternoon. Their swim along shore often brought dolphins close to the cliffs. In this location they tended to travel in rough files, more or less head-to-tail, and when they moved out to sea they traveled in a broad spread formation, in ranks.
>
> Dolphins seem to swim quickly around points of land such as those at Mahaiula and Puukala, and then slow down considerably after rounding them. Do points mean danger because deep water is nearby? In fact, the closer the dolphins are to shore the quieter they tend to be.

Did Jody's grand experiment succeed? In some ways it did. She showed that a lone swimmer could be accepted a little into a corner of the life of a wild dolphin school. Such acceptance seemed to come from the same sources that others have found with wild animals ashore: that is to say, by avoiding bluster and threat, and by reaching out into the sensitivities of the animals.

Jody was able to take some of the most intimate photographs we obtained, from within spinner dolphin schools, and if our budget had allowed us to equip her properly with a moving picture camera, I have no doubt that she would have returned with a valuable chronicle of dolphin life. Nonetheless, I was relieved when her effort ended, simply because my fears for her safety were never stilled.

My guess is that the gentle *nai'a* would indeed have tolerated the chirping Jody in their midst had she been able to keep up with their magic envelope. They are clearly uncommonly welcoming wild animals. Yet no welcome they might have extended, I suspect, would have transcended their absolute need to maintain the integrity of their protective school. They could not afford to wait for her very long.

14

Lioele and His Friends

As *Hana Nai'a* progressed it gave us new eyes. We began to ask questions about the Sea Life Park spinners that no one had thought to ask before. Some of the things we learned are scattered in the earlier chapters of this book. What did a spin consist of? What was the context in which the dolphins spun? Did a spin make noise? What was caressing all about? and a lot more.

To a remarkable degree the tiny captive school—there were still five spinners in Gregory's experimental pool—seemed to be living its life using the old patterns; over and over again, watching this school changed our conceptions about what was going on at Kealakekua. For example, as I described earlier, we knew that wild spinners liked to play with floating bits of flotsam, and so we tossed fronds of seaweed into the big pool. They were quickly spirited away by the dolphins, and we began to see that there were dolphin property rights that were respected by all the animals. One dolphin carried its own special frond all through the jostling time of feeding, delicately balancing it on a pectoral fin or the tip of its dorsal fin while it vied with its boisterous tankmates for fish. No other dolphin tried to take it away. The "owner" saved the seaweed to continue the game after the trainers and their food buckets went away, and then "offered" it to the others, who took it up and traded it around.

Even I, who had studied captive dolphins before, was surprised at what unfolded. Key to our observation was the fact that the dolphins were undisturbed except at feeding time, and that we were able to watch them for as long as we liked. We could follow ideas and let answers emerge over many observations.

In the last analysis that little school provided an important cross-check for several of the hard-won and usually incomplete ideas we had developed at Kealakekua. And, in the end, it pointed us toward some things we had never imagined from our studies at sea.

Having said this I must also note that we were wary observers, sure that most things we saw were modified by captivity. My expectation was that patterns requiring deep water, extended swimming, and high speeds would be most modified, and that we might have to look hard to see remnants of them, while others, such as the intimate patterns between individuals, might be less affected. And so it seemed to be. We had to imagine a good deal when a captive seemed to be providing the echolocation shield for the little school. But it took only very direct observation to observe the intricacies of a spin or a caress.

These captive dolphins taught us a good deal about spinner reproductive patterns. For cool-water dolphin species, reproduction is a seasonal thing. But tropical animals in general tend to have less well defined reproductive seasons, in part because tropical day lengths are much alike throughout the year. Such changes in day length seem to regulate most annual reproductive cycles.

Our spinners lived at 19° N. latitude. If we knew about the hormonal cycles of captive female spinners, and about spinner dolphin gestation time (10.6 months for oceanic forms), we should be able to predict when newborns should appear in the Kealakekua schools. Our scant records suggested that newborn dolphins were most abundant in late spring and summer, but we wondered if the pattern was simply a chance one, produced only because we hadn't looked long enough.

Reproductive patterns relate to nearly everything that takes place in a wild animal's year. Such understanding, I thought, would probably be the key to understanding all that caressing we saw. If we knew when females and males came into sexual readiness, we might be able to predict when caressing should include true courtship, instead of simply the "reaffirmation of relationships" that I had proposed.

So Randy scheduled two days a fortnight at Sea Life Park. During those two days he had essentially no sleep. He paced the tank edge around Bateson's Bay, day and night, tallying the many possible indicators of an approaching or declining period of sexual readiness. He watched how close the animals were when they swam together, and what patterns of caressing they used. He watched for true mating.

Finally, when the data were all in, Randy had described a clear annual pattern of changing interaction between males and females. Caressing in fact did change markedly throughout the year. Over the months it cycled between social caressing to obvious solicitation and mating patterns.

Randy made sure that he was present for the spinner's regular health checks. The veterinarian routinely took a small sample of blood from each of the dolphins, and he gave Randy a little of it for hormonal analysis. Point by point Randy built a record that showed these spinners coming into sexual readiness in the late spring and summer. The male hormone patterns were very different from those of the females. While the adult females cycled through very brief peaks of sexual readiness, lasting just days, the males were ready throughout much of the season. In promiscuous spinner dolphin society, this meant that a female who had ovulated briefly became the active center of attention of the attending males, and then interest faded out as others took her place.

I suspected that sexual behavior in these dolphins might be cued chemically, probably by taste. The behavior might depend upon the timed release of some chemical into the sea, perhaps the hormones themselves. In these schooling mammals I felt that such a mechanism could synchronize mating through an entire school, just as odor-based chemicals do in hoofed mammal herds. My hunch was based on a story from my days as curator of an oceanarium. The story had it that during the breeding season of male dolphins, ovulating women divers were sexually harassed, and sometimes literally driven from the water by them.

While Randy paced above, Chris Johnson occupied the underwater viewing vault of Bateson's Bay, attempting to find correlations between the behavior of wild schools and the same patterns in these captives. She and I began to observe two kinds of behavior as a place to start. Since we knew the dolphins did spins in captivity, I suggested that we take a close look at how they performed their aerial behavior. Then I suggested a more difficult task: to see if we could see any behavior patterns that changed throughout the dolphin's twenty-four-hour day. It became one of the most exciting observation sessions I had ever participated in.

We started our vigil by simply taking it all in. We built a *gestalt* of the dolphin society that swam in front of us: a wordless overview of what these dolphins typically did. This background allowed us to make informed hypotheses about what we expected to happen.

Working this way can save much time. Having a feel for the broader patterns of an animal's behavior allows one to ask pointed, accurate questions. Then, when something interesting is found, pinpointed observations are made over and over to

allow statistical testing, so that other people looking at the conclusions can make judgments about their validity.

The dolphins swirled by. We watched their formations. We
noted who swam with whom, and in what positions. When
did they sleep? We tried to see if nighttime behavior patterns
differed from those we saw in daytime. The dolphins leaped
and spun before us.

Finally, late one observation night, I began to see some patterns I had never seen before. Chris was napping in the car,
having been up observing for twenty-four hours. I looked some
more, and reformulated my questions, watching as hard as I
could, with a kind of "clench your fists and grit your teeth"
intensity. Soon the wonder to me was that no one seemed to
have noticed before what was now so obvious.

A bit bleary-eyed from the hours-long session, I walked up
out of the viewing vault and shook Chris awake.

"The dolphin's behavior is all in *bouts*," I said, by way of
returning her to the living. When Chris decides to sleep it is
total engagement.

"Bout? What's a bout?" asked Chris. Then, wiping her eyes,
she stumbled down the stairs into the viewing room.

"OK, you watch now," I said. "Kahe is in a spinning bout.
She is probably about half through it now, so I expect her to
spin again in just moments."

Down curved Kahe, as if on cue, vibrating back and forth
like a tuning fork, rubbing her belly on the tank bottom. Then
she rocketed up and out of the water in a spin.

"Wow," said Chris. "How'd you know that?"

"Bouts," I replied. "And Lioele (*Lye-o-ele*) and Kehaulani (*Ke-
ha-u-lani*) are in a caressing bout. But they're midway too, so I
expect things to be pretty intense for the next five to ten minutes."

We watched while the pair swam alongside one another,
Kehaulani resolutely trailing the tip of her pectoral fin in a long
back-to-front caress that started on Lioele's tail and ended up

alongside his cheek. He rolled toward her and she trailed her vibrating fin between his outstretched pectorals, rubbing back and forth on that especially sensitive spot.

"Now, you watch closely, Chris. There are beginning and ending oscillations to these behavioral bouts. They're quite elegant little sequences."

Chris watched with awakening interest as the two animals began to oscillate their swimming, in and out, toward and away from one another. At first, as they cruised along, they were in intimate contact, and then Kehaulani began to move slightly away from her partner, out until just the tip of her pectoral fin touched Lioele. Then she came in again, and then out, and this time they merely swam side by side without touching. Then they came in again for a brief bit of vigorous caressing.

"This bout won't last much longer, Chris," I said.

It didn't. Soon the pair was cruising along together with a body diameter between them. I whispered so the dolphins wouldn't hear, "I think it's about to end. Let's watch how they sign off a bout."

The dolphin pair swam close again, barely touching pectorals for a moment, and then swam around opposite sides of another dolphin, and then both surfaced to breathe, going in opposite directions.

Kehaulani turned away and descended at once to the tank bottom, where she began insistent echolocation of all the features of the tank floor, now completely ignoring her partner of moments before.

"Chris, she's entered an echolocation bout," I said.

Chris said, "Hey, I think those breaths are punctuation marks that signal some kind of behavioral change. Did you see that?"

"Yeah, I think you're right."

As we watched it became obvious that generally surfacing to breathe marked the end of some kind of social pattern. Often old partners would go their separate ways at that moment.

"Chris, let's watch Kehaulani," I said. "She'll probably stay in echolocation for fifteen minutes or so, and then move on to the next pattern. Let's time her."

Kehaulani was swimming under the other dolphins now, spraying out click trains, inspecting every part of the tank with a singular intensity. She gave special attention to the dark central drain box each time she circled, poking her snout into it and emitting train after train of loud clicks. She swam over a seam in the tank bottom, and followed it for forty feet before passing our window, spraying our dim figures with clicks.

Later we found that dolphins in this bout used what we came to call "echolocation manners." Kehaulani and her schoolmates never sprayed each other with loud sounds, but when they were in an echolocation bout they generally swam below the others, head angled down and away from their tank-mates.

Sometimes when an echolocating dolphin came up behind other dolphins engaged in other bouts, it shut its sound generation down, and then made an obvious turn away from the other dolphins before starting to click again. We checked this surmise, watching and counting the times we saw and heard the dolphin approach and shut off its sound.

In one hundred passes, our echolocating dolphins never once sprayed the other animals directly with their click trains. This jibed with our earlier observation that wild dolphin schools almost always are arranged in staggered three-dimensional echelons, like fighter planes in formation. There was for each dolphin, I had come to realize, a *sensory window* in their schools, opening out into the sea. The echelons provided that for dolphins, just as they did for fighter pilots. Probably the formations we saw were at least partly a consequence of a need for such a window.

The ease with which we could perceive intimate details of a dolphin school in this little group of captives struck me hard. The crossruff between what we could see in the tank and what we could perceive at sea was at work. Out in the ocean the larger patterns could be detected, but over and over one was left wondering about the fine-grained details in a dolphin's life. We could see many of these things in our captive school, and thus our overall view of spinner dolphin life was made much more complete than if we had had only one way to see.

There proved to be just three general patterns that our spinners organized as bouts: echolocation, aerial behavior—including spinning—and caressing. During midday a fourth pattern intervened and supplanted the others, that of *formation swimming,* which we immediately realized was the "rest" we had seen over the shining sand patch of Kealakekua Bay. The first three bouts were performed by vibrantly alert animals, while formation swimming was a stately pattern that happened just once a day. In Bateson's Bay each of the active bouts engaged a given dolphin for about fifteen to forty minutes before it cycled on to the next pattern.

We began to feel in an almost subliminal way that these bouts were a major missing piece of how we must think about spinner society. They seemed to represent a division of labor that perhaps all spinner dolphins might expect to perform. If this was understood in advance by all the spinners on a coast, it would allow the construction of protective schools from *any* dolphins of that larger society of friends. All a dolphin joining a new group needed to do was to perform a bout and move on to the next pattern.

The echolocation bout, played out down below the others, seemed likely to serve three purposes. First, it could help with the navigation of the school; second, it could help the school find food; and third, it could provide the sensory shield that protected against predators moving in out of the murk.

After puzzling what spins might be good for, I've already described how we finally concluded that they could be short-range omnidirectional markers that defined the dimensions of a school for all its members. Any dolphin could locate those splashes coming from any direction and in effect hear the local positions of the school members. These splashes, together with the other sounds the dolphins made, could explain the mysterious synchrony of widely spread spinner schools.

As for the other bouts, we came to think that caressing was the essential social glue of an extended society of "dolphin friends." It seemed to be both the normal thing dolphins did in their schools and a means of assurance for them that they were in that "society of friends." And we realized that the information that was being passed around could be much richer than anything we had yet imagined.

Now these constructs we evolved are not truths. They are simply ideas, constructs, theories, against which we could form more questions in the fitting process that lets us creep up on true things. The questions and nature's answers come to reinforce one another if you are on the right track, and before long many things fit together with an elegance that could not happen by chance. But this method of learning takes time and one must be patient.

So a first and essential check was to find out if these bouts, seen so clearly in our captive dolphins, occurred at sea. But let us not forget that we would never have asked if spinning, or echolocation, or caressing were episodic in nature without those hours in Bateson's vault. Two hands of cards are necessary for a crossruff to work.

Bernd assured us that the spins of wild spinners were arranged in episodes, and I was sure he was right. Our eyes thus sharpened, we watched wild spinning dolphins again, and it was at once obvious that a given dolphin swimming in a given general area of a school would spin over and over. We could soon see individual styles, and we could watch a given dolphin burst time and time again from the water over many minutes' time. It didn't take long to convince ourselves that spinning bouts were apparently not much different from the bouts of spinning we had seen at Sea Life Park.

Caressing bouts were tougher to document, because our observations of them at sea were generally so brief. But as Chris and I pored over our *Maka Ala* films, we could see that caressing bouts were prominent features: a given dolphin caressed a given partner for a time and then switched to another partner. We finally even discerned those quite elaborate beginnings and ends to such bouts. Caressing bouts were clearly *entities* and not just chance encounters.

There were differences, though, between the caressing patterns we had seen at Sea Life Park and events at sea. The complexity of a school at sea, with dozens of animals present, produced a kind of competitive tension that was missing in the little Sea Life Park school. Interactions and partner-switching were much more frequent at sea.

This tension might explain why wild-dolphin caressing bouts seemed to be short sequences of twenty or thirty seconds' duration, as compared to the sessions of many minutes we had seen in the captive school. The difference probably also occurred because we had so few dolphins in the captive school. It seemed likely that the durations of each kind of bout were not independent of one another. If one dolphin was slow in the little captive school, the others were likely to be slow too.

In some of our *Maka Ala* films of caressing dolphins we could almost feel the social forces involved. When one dolphin offered a caress, or withheld it, you could see a reaction from its partner. If it tipped its white belly toward an adjacent dolphin, the two moved together in a caress. If it rolled its back toward the other, the interaction ended, sometimes evoking an irritated reaction from the second animal.

We noted with satisfaction that within an active wild school, insofar as we could document it, caressing bouts seemed to be in progress for about 30 percent of the school, which is what you would expect if there were just three main bout types that these spinner dolphins perform at one time. I reserve final judgment on that measure, though. It needs a better analysis than we were able to provide with our little segments of film.

As for echolocation, we have not yet found a way of quantifying it, or of listening only to wild dolphins in such a bout. But we can say that *always* when one encounters wild spinners at sea, significant numbers of dolphins are echolocating in long insistent trains. I'll bet they avoid spraying each other just as our captives did, but that too awaits some lucky opportunity for proof.

If our speculations were correct, bouts could be the missing feature that let a dolphin, any dolphin, join with friends it hadn't swum with for months and still be an effective part of a protective school. The pickup school could function if it could seek out food and predators, and if the member dolphins could always be sure they were within its protective confines. Bouts might also explain why caressing was so important. If spinner schools were the pickup affairs they seemed to be, there was a constant need for checking in with new schoolmates and reestablishing trust. Then, with the magic envelope functioning smoothly, and the members comfortable with each other, all the other aspects of dolphin society could unfold.

Such a system should also define the least number of dolphins that could safely and effectively travel together at sea. Below a certain number there should not be enough animals to carry out these critical patterns. Checking our thousands of records, we had never seen fewer than four spinners in a wild school, and that only once. A more typical small school had ten or a dozen dolphins in it.

It is hard to imagine that this cycling is not learned by each dolphin. Dolphins, as high-order mammals, seem to achieve many such social patterns by cultural means—instruction and learning—rather than by relying principally upon direct information from their genes. Yet if these patterns are learned by young dolphins growing up in the school, what imposes the discipline necessary to maintain such a system? Why shouldn't some dolphins dog it while the others do all the work? In time that kind of cheating could destroy a social system, but that is clearly not the case in dolphin schools. Such schools work, and appear to work well.

Perhaps echolocation provides one answer. Could it be that rapping out those intense, insistent click trains is something a dolphin can sustain for only so long, and then the animal has to turn to one of the other patterns, just to rest its acoustic system? If this is true, then even on a statistical basis alone some dolphins should be in one or the other of the remaining bouts.

But even this does not explain things. Why should a cadre of dolphins echolocate at all? Could it be the sheer self-interest of survival that drives them to echolocate? Once again, why shouldn't some dolphins cheat, and let the others protect them? If such a tendency toward social parasitism was allowed to grow, the whole social system could soon fall apart like a house of cards.

My colleague Carl Schilt and I have proposed a possible explanation. We suggest that the design of dolphin schools springs from what population dynamicists call an *evolutionarily stable strategy*. Simply put, the structure of the dolphin school is so important an element in the survival of its members that no animal can afford to violate its rules. To do so is to stand out and hence to invite predation at a much higher rate than the rest of the school members face. Such a situation will lock a social system into a single strategy, in this case the school.

Being a member of such a society carries with it rigidities about what each school member can and cannot do, upon pain of death. Maybe one of the messages of caressing is conformity to the iron rules of the school. And doesn't this situation explain why dolphins are such uncommonly cooperative animals?

Spinner dolphins seem so defenseless. Unlike the heavier

coastal dolphin species, one cannot imagine them using their small, almost deciduous rows of teeth or their delicate beaks for protection. Only their tails are obvious weapons, but they can only deliver blows as a last resort. You have to be very close to an antagonist to hit him with your tail. I knew I wouldn't want to venture to sea with just a club.

And yet there had to be more to it than met the eye. Those serious squads of adult males were taking the role of protectors. They showed that when they interposed themselves between the *Maka Ala* and the rest of their school. By what right, one thought, did they thrust themselves forward into danger?

I thought that the missing "weapon" might be intense claps of sound. Bottlenose dolphins "jaw clapped" at one another in aggressive situations. To make these sounds, the dolphins snapped their jaws closed at the same time emitting loud blasts of sound, like very loud, long-duration echolocation clicks.

I recalled that the protection of our ears from overloading by intense sound is a rather late development in evolutionary terms: a thing of birds and mammals only. Such protection resides in the tiny ear bones inside our middle ears. Muscles pulling against this chain of bones can tug the chain out of synch in a thousandth of a second. Then, when a loud sound hits a bird or mammal, its hearing stops in that thousandth of a second, and returns when the middle-ear muscles relax. Fish and sharks don't have these little ear bones, nor do they have the protective reflex.

Perhaps jaw claps were real weapons against fish. I decided to see if spinners used them that way. One day when Shannon Brownlee and I were recording in the viewing vault at Bateson's Bay, I suggested that we see if we could induce Lioele, the adult male, to jaw clap at us.

"If we annoy Lioele a little," I said, "he might sound off for us." I asked Shannon to take a metal pencil, and when Lioele swam in close, facing us, to tap hard against the glass in a series of clicks. "He might not like to have so much noise in his face from close up," I said. "And, oh, Shannon, turn on the recorder."

Shannon put on a pair of earphones and checked out the hydrophone that hung inside the window. Waiting until Lioele circled near and then faced us, she tapped. Lioele reacted as if he had been poked by a cattle prod.

He swam rapidly toward our window, arched his back, lowered his head and let us have it. Or I should say he let Shannon have it, because she was the one with the earphones on. I could hear the double blast of sound right through the glass and tank wall, and I could see him leak a double bubble of air from his blowhole, so great was his effort.

I glanced over at Shannon and saw her, eyes rolled upward, take her earphones off and slap both ears with her open palms.

"DR. NORRIS! DON'T YOU EVER DO THAT AGAIN!"

"Shannon, that was Lioele, *not* me."

When Shannon calmed down a little and the ringing in her ears stopped, we discussed what we had seen. We had both noticed that just as Lioele went for us the other dolphins had clearly fled, moving away from Lioele and ending up with their snouts pointed up the sloping opposite wall of the tank, as if they were avoiding a sound blast they knew was coming.

Protection of a dolphin's delicate hearing, on which their capacity to echolocate rests, is surely crucial.

The arched posture Lioele assumed before he blasted us was much like that used by other spinners when they mimicked sharks. What would that loud sound seem like to a shark whose ears and lateral line receptors are both unprotected by middle-ear bones?

Wondering what such sounds might do to the spinner's prey, I asked Randy to help me set up a test at Bateson's Bay. The first thing we needed was a school of fish. At Kewalo Basin where the trap fishermen came in every morning, Randy bought a school of thirty-five live akule, a silvery schooling species

Lioele zaps Shannon with a blast of sound, right into the hydrophone through which she is listening.

considerably larger than most spinner food, but the most appropriate species he could find.

We divided them into two schools; one was put into the big fish tank at Sea Life Park as a control, and the other sluiced into the dolphin tank. The latter fish immediately dropped to the bottom and gathered in a tight unobtrusive school at the deepest part of the tank. But the spinners knew they were there.

Two of the female spinners, more or less taking turns, raced in toward the side of the fish school emitting whining click trains as they came. The fish school split as if by magic, with both halves arcing in toward the passing dolphin's tail. This happened several times, and never did a fish seem disturbed by the click trains, nor were any caught. By that time it was noon, so I suggested that we observers take a break for lunch and see what had happened in our absence. My conclusion of the moment, I half-facetiously said, was, "Dolphins can't catch fish."

Things were dramatically different, however, when we returned forty minutes later. The two dolphins were still making runs on the fish, but some of the fish were obviously disoriented. One we called "Little Nemo" couldn't find the school at all. It wandered right through the loose, wavering akule group and on across the tank, alone in the open water except for the dolphin behind it, showering it with clicks.

Poor Little Nemo finally changed color from silver to pale yellow, fluttered upward in the water, like a leaf blown in the wind, and was sucked down into the central drain. The other fish fared not much better.

Something had happened to those fish but we couldn't be sure what it was. Clearly they were disoriented by the bombardments and chases, but this effect could be simple fatigue (though I doubted it, because the fluttering and arcing courses of the fish looked more like a debility of their ears than tiredness). But I also knew that fish are particularly prone to fatigue because their inefficient gill respiration system reduces their blood flow much below that of mammals and restricts their ability to clear their bodies of the waste products of exercise.

The din of clicks seemed to be the source of their trouble. But if the clicks had produced the effect, what good did it do a dolphin to spend two hours debilitating a fish? The effect was much too slow to do a feeding dolphin any good.

Kehaulani zaps a school of akule with her click trains; Bateson's Bay, Oceanic Institute, Hawaii. *R. S. Wells*

We checked our control school, and although they had been attacked almost constantly by Jack Crevallys, big swift predatory fish in the Sea Life Park fish tank, they were alert and active. Some of them, however, bore scars of near misses, enhancing but not proving my view that the click trains were causal in the problems of Little Nemo and his schoolmates.

Later I joined a bioacoustician colleague, Dr. Bertel Møhl, in his laboratory at the University of Aarhus, in Denmark. Together we explored the possibility that dolphins and close allies such as the sperm whale might be able to capture prey by sound. We found much suggestive evidence but nothing ironclad.

Some cetaceans could make incredibly intense sounds. Some bottlenose dolphin clicks were found to be so loud they verged on what is called "the finite limit of sound," a range in which more energy applied to sound production simply turns to heat instead of making more sound. Such dolphin clicks were *five times as loud* as any other sounds that had ever been recorded from them.

These remarkable sounds had been recorded by our navy acoustician colleagues at Kaneohe, Drs. Au, Murchison, Floyd, Moore, and Snyder, when they ran an experiment to see how far away a dolphin could use its echolocation system to detect a target in the sea. They had built a long clothesline out over Kaneohe Bay, on which they could suspend a metal sphere about the size of a tangerine. They could run the sphere out different distances from the dolphin's open-sided tank, and they could dip it in and out of the water by pulling on another line. Then by standard training techniques they began to ask the animal to tell them if the target was in the water or not. The dolphin reported successfully when the target was as far as 370 feet away! That's quite a bit farther than the length of a football field.

And then they studied the sounds the dolphin had used to perform this improbable feat. They found hundreds of those incredibly intense clicks in the dolphin's echolocation.

Many questions arise from these observations. How does a dolphin make such sounds? How does it keep from harming itself in the process? Can it use such intense sounds as a weapon perhaps both for catching prey and for defense?

Bertel and I found that sperm whales, who make a similar

very loud sound, ate a bewildering array of food, including both big fish such as salmon and very tiny lantern fish (how can, and why should, a fifty-foot sperm whale bother to catch a two-inch lantern fish?). In fact, sperm whales seem to eat the widest range of sizes and kinds of prey of any animal. This seems to make sense only if the whale uses some general means of obtaining food: something that stops just about anything that swims. Regular teeth and jaws hardly seem adequate to that task, especially the sperm whale's long, narrow lower jaw studded with very large, widely spaced blunt teeth.

We found records of sperm whales heard making such bangs from an estimated fifteen miles away. There were reports in the Russian whaling literature of deformed sperm whales with jaws so grotesquely twisted that they would not close, and yet these whales had full stomachs when they came aboard the whaling vessel. How could such a deformed whale catch swift-swimming squid?

Two of these Russian authors had even suggested the same thing we began to believe was true, that somehow toothed whales and dolphins might use sound to catch prey.

There were other puzzling facts that suggested sound as a prey-catching medium. The males of a certain species of beaked whale, the strap-toothed whale of the southern hemisphere, possess but a single pair of teeth, which arch over the upper jaw and permanently hold the mouth almost closed, and yet this is a normal circumstance for these whales. They must have to suck in food through the three-inch-wide slit of their mouth, and how can they catch a squid or a fish in that condition?

I found evidence from observations of a little shallow-water shrimp. These animals had been observed blasting small fishes with intense clicks made by a special claw that snaps together, causing the prey to turn over, inert. Then the shrimp emerged from its burrow and ate the fish. We wrote an article about these observations that stirred up a minor controversy.

Since then the accumulation of evidence about acoustic prey debilitation has gone on, and we are considerably surer of our ground. Several new recordings of dolphin schools made during feeding include fusillades of rifle-shot-like blasts of very loud sound. The new sounds were low in average frequency, unlike Kehaulani and Kahe's clicks, most of which were higher than a fish can hear. And the new sounds were enormously long compared to the usual dolphin click. A dolphin's echolocation click is about a thousandth of a second long, and these new sounds were between seventy and seven hundred times longer. They reminded me very much of the sound Lioele used to blast Shannon when she tapped the pencil in his face.

We now have records of schooling fish being killed by very similar artificial sounds. My colleague Dr. Ken Marten and I think that when the fish receives such a loud and long sound within its hearing range, its unprotected ear goes into overload, recovers, is overloaded again, and so on, as many as seven hundred times before the sound ceases. The fish simply turns over in psychophysical overload. Very likely the vital hair cells of its inner ears, which allow hearing to occur, are destroyed, as they would be in ours if they sustained such repeated assault.

What about the two female dolphins who insisted on buzzing away for hours at the akule school? I shrug at that one. They never produced a big bang like Lioele did when he zapped Shannon. Maybe only male spinners blast out the killing sounds. If so, is using such sound for school defense a role of those male coalitions we kept seeing between us and the rest of the school? We don't yet have a decent clue.

Not long after we made our observations in Bateson's Bay, the last of the captive spinners was released, and I was pleased they could go back into the larger dolphin society. But I was also glad they had been at Sea Life Park where we could learn from them. Lioele, Kahe, and Kehaulani had taught us a great deal. In fact, the large majority of what we know about the intricacies of dolphin behavior generally, and about their physiology, cognition, and sensory capability, has been learned from such captive dolphins.

But the importance of such captives is based on more than just science. We and the millions who have watched them swim up to a tank window in an ocean exhibit have wondered about the distance between animal and human minds. Without these dolphins to watch and wonder about, few of us, I fear, would care, and the disastrous kill of dolphins out there on the eastern tropical Pacific tuna fishery would have gone on unnoticed.

Of course, these days there is much discussion about whether we should keep dolphins at all. In this debate, *their* contribution to *our* understanding is seldom considered seriously. This leads to a paradoxical situation. The more we learn from captive dolphins, the more people care about them and the louder the cries from some sectors become for us to break the bridge between us. When I have thought about this pattern, and the more experiences I have had with oceanarium animals, the more valuable the few captive dolphins seem to me (there are between four and five hundred in the United States).

The dolphins we hold are, I think, keepers of the bridge, and they deserve every consideration we can give them. To increase that consideration is the task, not to destroy the bridge. This newfound concern for animals (only a few decades ago nobody in the United States cared much) is also a symptom that we are beginning to understand and accept the commonalities of the minds of wild mammals and ourselves.

We want so much to be unique. Some scientists have even proposed that no creature can think without language, but I think this is far off the mark. This view seems to me the remnant of a past intellectual struggle, when the concept of animal intelligence cluttered the intellectual landscape with problems too hard to solve. It was clearer (but not more correct) to avoid the question altogether by deciding we should not discuss it. We are now moving past that blind time.

In the larger frame of our society how much does all this matter? I hope it is not arrogant to say: "It matters."

Especially exciting to me is the emerging view that we, the dolphins, the other mammals, the parrots, and the rest have very much in common. We are altogether of a single piece.

15

The Dolphin's Plight

*T*HE *Hana Nai'a* field effort drew to a close. Money for our work was running out and we knew we must "wrap it up" even though new questions, insights, and answers about the *nai'a* still seemed to come as rapidly as ever. Lack of money almost always limits field studies such as this, and I've spared you the almost constant struggles we went through to keep the coffers filled.

Sadly we turned our backs on the bay, stopped the scans that had been going on since the days of the "field shelter," pulled Melany and the theodolite down off the cliff in a cascade of spiders, and ignored the schools of *nai'a* swimming behind us, as we packed cameras, boats, notebooks, radiotracking gear, anchor lines, outboard motors, and all the rest that it had taken to run our effort.

An incredible pile it was, too. It soon converged upon the Long Marine Laboratory in California, where data reduction began in earnest. Science is only partly the joys of the field, or of conceptualizing at night around the camp table. Probably half of the time is spent trying to make sense of the miles of tape, the tens of thousands of slides, and the almost endless field notes. Then came data reduction time. In our offices we had to grind out the tables of numbers and produce the statistical proofs that would convince colleagues that we spoke sense about what we claimed to have seen.

Finally, our volume-sized report was filed with our National Marine Fisheries Service sponsors. Our work made us a major voice for the oceanic dolphins, since we truly knew them as nobody else did. In our findings there were observations that might free dolphins from nets. We alone had developed some understanding of why they sank in those sorrowful windrows in the backdown channel, and we alone had an intimate idea of how their societies worked and what seining could do to them.

The problem, as always, was to insert such knowledge into the processes of the fishery. That involves workshops and reports to Congress, all of which are things the field biologist would rather not do, given a choice. But I knew these things had to be done, and since *Hana Nai'a* ended I have been one of the very few informed spokespeople the *nai'a* have had in the halls of government. I've felt needed.

When U.S. domination of eastern tropical Pacific tuna fishing ended in the 1980s, matters became rapidly worse for the dolphins. In 1986 at Panama City, Panama, the Inter-American Tropical Tuna Commission released staggering figures showing that the estimated annual dolphin kill in the eastern tropical Pacific yellowfin tuna seine fishery had skyrocketed again, to an estimated 125- to 129,000 dolphins a year. Two-thirds of the trips taken that year (68 percent) were on vessels flying flags other than that of the United States, and therefore only indirectly required to carry out dolphin-saving maneuvers. The dolphin-killing capacity of the fleet continued to hammer the remaining three to four million dolphins of the area.

The 1986 dolphin kill spoke of a problem out of control. This is a remote and statistical statement of what, close-up, is much more simply stated: mindless, senseless slaughter. It is worth noting in a book about dolphins that today the tuna populations are also being exploited without regulation. Only because tuna grow remarkably rapidly—five years of age is a very old tuna—and only because the populations are huge— they girdle the globe in the tropical current systems—have they withstood the onslaught as well as they have. The tunas may need assistance, too.

This bleak history and future is not a onetime thing. In one form or another, the same story has been played over and over for other species of food fish. The story is, in fact, the typical and predictable history of multinational fisheries of the "common ground": far offshore where no nation claims sovereignty over the seas or their resources. It's "get in, get yours, and get out before the resource collapses." The economic engine is no respecter of countries, fishermen, or dolphins.

In this case, where the obviously sentient dolphin is involved—an animal that nurtures and instructs its young—the problem strikes home to us more than it does with any fish. In the expressionless faces of fish we read little of ourselves, but the rules of the tragedy are the same.

Economic forces bear down hard on the fishermen. It costs a bundle just to be a player. Enormously expensive boats, canneries, and the infrastructure of commerce must be established, and behind all this are the banks who lend the money to make the industry go, and then the western market economy itself. That economy is the ultimate pressure that kills dolphins. For nearly every private fisherman in the fleet, there is a bank demanding payments. This pressure translates to rapid trips, to the need to make every set that daylight will allow. Dolphins, sad to say, are chaff in such an equation, and they die caught in the fisherman's social imperatives, even though they show the fisherman where to set his net. The loss no longer matters. The demands upon the fisherman are too insistent to think about such things. The game is to pay off the boat, the house, get the kids through school before the fishery collapses, and then, hopefully, to move on to some new grounds for another round with other players.

That's why canneries are built to be portable. They are designed to be disassembled, lifted up bodily, and shipped to Peru, or Samoa, or wherever. The seiners are no problem. They just top off their tanks with diesel, set out to sea, and follow along into the new reality.

So it's not much of an inconvenience for these fishermen to move their boats to new flags and new shores. They're ready for it, and many have been through it before. We know that Mexico is building a fleet of tuna seiners, but what is not so evident is that many of their fishermen once worked in San Diego, or Wilmington, California.

The dolphins, of course, have no such option. They are stuck with their life patterns, and as long as they serve the purposes of these itinerant fishermen they will be used as thoughtlessly as any other part of the world the fishermen exploit. This pattern has not been a pretty sight in the past and it certainly is not one now. It is run by tough, resolute men who revel in the capture, the weather, and perhaps even the jousting with banks.

Their families troop along behind them, cohesive and often a bit isolated from the society that surrounds them. They are typically insular communities, resigned to the next chess move that may send them to Panama, or Ponape, or wherever.

In the early 1970s my indignation and that of my conservationist colleagues was high. With few qualms we consciously brought the force of society to bear upon the issue. It was a case of "Mr. Smith Goes to Washington," pure and simple. It was all so clear to us! Stories flooded the press about the dolphin kill, and soon the populace was as indignant as we were. With good reason we didn't trust the fishermen's data describing the numbers of dolphins they killed. In such a *we-they* polarized environment, the fishing industry would have been unlikely to provide us with such ammunition.

In time the fishery built up its own staff of fisheries biologists, whose job it was to fight the battle of numbers and population trends—to mute the problem of dolphin mortality while the fishery went on.

As a result of our early work, observers were stationed on seiners to bring back trustworthy data. The resultant figures, and especially the off-the-record stories of these observers, suggested how large the kill really might be. No one knew how much the dolphin populations could stand.

It has been extremely valuable to have these observers hanging over the fishermen. Some reckon that their presence has been the single most important dolphin-saving factor: kills on vessels with observers aboard seem to be lower than those without them.

The fishermen's will also determines the level of dolphin kill. When I first worked on the problem, our goal was to drive the kill down near twenty thousand dolphins per year. That was accomplished, and the level encodified in law. Only so many dolphins could be killed in a single fishing season or the boats would have to stay in port. Today, the same quota is still in effect for U.S. boats, and the number of our vessels has been reduced by two-thirds as I write, but the dolphin kill remains about the same. When the rules are tight, the fishermen will adapt and cut the kill. When the rules are less demanding, the kill will remain at the statutory limit.

With observers aboard, for the first time in their lives the fishermen carried cops along with them. Mind you, these same men have lived their lives at sea in large measure because they could go where they wished, and do what they wanted. In them the buccaneer spirit is as strong as in any group in our society. Some of them knew exactly how to deal with a cop in their midst.

In extreme cases the two-month observer trips became jail sentences for the young observer-biologists. Shunned by everyone aboard, they refused to accede to the improper requests of their skipper to fudge the numbers. They might then be forced to sleep out in the rain on the net pile and to eat cold food after everyone else had finished. The daily round became one of threats—"into the sea you go"—and of seal bombs exploding behind them. These are huge firecrackers that some misguided fishermen used to toss in the water to drive the dolphins away from openings in the net circle. It is an understatement to say that at first our fishermen didn't like the observer arrangement, though the wiser, more visionary ones tried hard to find solutions and didn't seek to influence the data gatherers.

Many of the fishermen, such as those I traveled with on the *Alisa S. J.,* were foreign born. As the general public became more aware of the dolphin kill, the tight structure of their communities were challenged. The fishermen's children heard at school that their fathers were engaged in immoral killing. Only months before, some of these fathers had been held up as near-mythic versions of the American success story. After all, in a few years they had come from mending nets on an Azores dock to being the proud owners of six-million-dollar fishing machines with helicopters atop the wheelhouse.

"But, Daddy," the children said, "those dolphins you kill aren't fish. They have brains like ours."

We in Washington, D.C., had been warned that our efforts could disrupt the fishery. We had rushed in filled with anger and had applied what became overwhelming pressure on the rule makers in the agencies, and upon the federal legislature. But during those battles the lawyers for the fishing fleet repeatedly mentioned that if we forced the industry too far it would simply "go foreign." Few people really listened. After all, none of us would do such a thing, forgetting that our heritage as

Americans typically went very much farther back than that of most fishermen.

As a result, the fleet today is heavily foreign. Mexico, with her overwhelming need for foreign exchange, now sends about 40 percent of the eastern Pacific tuna fleet to sea. She has resolutely refused to become a member of the multination Interamerican Tropical Tuna Commission (IATTC). Nonetheless, in a recent show of cooperation, she has cooperated with various dolphin-saving maneuvers of that group. Perhaps this happened because the IATTC is a creature of the fishery concerned first and foremost with supporting the tuna fishery and not primarily with dolphin welfare. But what is certain is that the conservationist's target had become a scattered and elusive one.

The priorities of Mexicans are very different from those of U.S. citizens. Afflicted with a massive population problem, a huge foreign debt, and grinding poverty, their leaders search hard for sources of revenue. The imperatives of the dolphins pale beside their human problems. Foremost is the problem of providing the barest sort of economic opportunity for their people.

For an ocean-bounded country like Mexico, the sea is an obvious place to turn for development. Fishery schools are now scattered along both coasts, training young people from the countryside for what is hoped will be productive jobs in the fishing industry. As these schools were built, Mexico began to acquire tuna vessels. At first these were castoffs from the United States, where the race was for ever-larger ships with greater speed. Later Mexico began to join the tuna hunt with new "ships of the line," and with subsidized diesel fuel to run them.

None of the IATTC vessels, except those belonging to the U.S., are legally constrained to spend time letting dolphins go, even though most make an effort under a voluntary program of the IATTC. To hedge their bets a little, much of Mexico's exported tuna has been sent to Europe, mostly to Italy. The

U.S. market is probably viewed as being too volatile; it might collapse if it was discovered that Mexico persisted in catching its tuna on dolphin schools.

Vessels from countries other than the United States, such as Costa Rica, El Salvador, Panama, Spain, Venezuela, and Vanuatu converge on the eastern tropical Pacific tuna grounds. In 1989 they accounted for 74 percent of the tuna harvest and a little under 90 percent of the dolphin kill. Most ships now leave from ports much closer to the schools of tuna and dolphins than the U.S. vessels do, and as a result they save a great amount of fuel. There is little likelihood that those owners who have left the United States will return.

In part the exodus of tuna vessels from United States registry was related to Venezuela's guarantee to subsidize diesel fuel for vessels that flew her flag and used her ports. This was a bargain that many vessels could not pass up, given the adverse climate of opinion in the United States, and the much shorter trip to and from the tuna grounds.

What I have said so far deals mostly with tuna and economics. What about the dolphins? Why has the kill skyrocketed? The answer is certainly complex: in part the need for more concerted dolphin-saving efforts, and in part the exigencies of fishing. For example, the fishermen recently discovered a large source of tuna under the schools of common dolphins swimming close to the Central American shore. These were dolphins that had remained largely unexploited, so at first the kill was horrendous, as it has been whenever the fishery netted dolphins that had not experienced seining.

A similar example occurred in the 1970s when fishermen discovered a good supply of tuna far out on the western boundary of the fishing grounds. This stretch of sea was so remote from the mainland that it was as economical for ships to dock at Honolulu as at Manzanillo, Mexico. In that distant sea, when the fishermen set their nets on an unexploited race of dolphins called "whitebelly spinners," thousands upon thousands of the untutored animals panicked, rushed the nets, entangled, and died.

But in time, wherever they are caught, surviving dolphins learn something about the fishery and they become more stoic. In 1986 twenty-five thousand of the inexperienced common dolphins seined off Central America drowned in a single year; their societies had not yet incorporated seining into their experience.

Since no annual quota now regulates non-U.S. fishermen, they are free to engage all year long in a number of practices that we know kill dolphins. For instance, many of the fishermen make their last set at dusk and end up "rolling their net" in the dark. Because they can't see very well to operate a backdown channel, and because the dolphins down in the dark water can see far less, the kill rate is greatly increased.

The curious oceanwide events of an "El Niño year" are involved too. In time of El Niño, which is when the global balance of currents in the tropical Pacific changes, altering sea climate both north and south of the equator, nutrient patterns shift over much of the warmer Pacific.

During the height of El Niño, fishermen have discovered that tuna surface in huge schools—without dolphins—and the fishery shifts toward this new resource, with the result that the overall dolphin kill goes down. In 1986 the events of a recent El Niño were over and the fishermen had returned to netting dolphins in order to catch tuna. The dolphin kill skyrocketed.

So, while the recent increase in dolphin kill cannot be totally ascribed to the fleet's going foreign, some of it can, and the situation deteriorates, especially for the eastern spinner dolphin, the pearl-gray dolphin whose populations were some years ago officially declared as "depleted." Scientists of the U.S. National Marine Fisheries Service estimate the decline of eastern spinners by as much as 80 percent since seining began.

Others say that the density of dolphins in the area seems to remain about the same. That may be, but I think it likely that as the pressure on the eastern spinners has continued, new dolphins have moved in to replace those who have died, so even though the population *seems* to stay the same, it may be under severe fishing pressure. How much more those threatened remnants can take is anybody's guess.

The ominous parallels and portents are already there. The sex ratio between males and females of these dolphins is becoming unbalanced—in this case males have apparently come to outnumber females. This imbalance has preceded population crashes before in other exploited dolphin populations. Somehow the complicated arrangements of courtship, nurture, and protection are shattered, and like Humpty Dumpty it's not simple to glue them together again. It may take decades of protection for such an overexploited population to stabilize and increase again. The problem is especially severe for dolphins, long-lived animals with life spans not so very different from our own.

The tuna fishery and its leadership were given a remarkable chance to solve the dolphin kill when we of the scientific and conservation communities joined forces with them on the dedicated-vessel cruises. It's a pity that the program was not continued long enough to work.

Through all this time a quite remarkable research program of the National Marine Fisheries Service went on, led by Dr. William Perrin. Its goal was to outline the extent and nature of the problem, and, even though they did not have a working seiner to experiment from, to suggest changes in fishing practices when they could. This program provided the scientific foundation upon which regulations were based.

The ocean arena in which Perrin and his team worked was a huge *aqua incognita* when they started, five times the size of the United States, and when they were done, and their program moved over to the IATTC, they knew the species involved, where they moved, about how many there were, what their growth, life spans, food, and population patterns were. They pinpointed the causes of dolphin deaths, and they had begun to evolve new ways of fishing. I never cease to be awed by this scientific tour de force.

Under this unparalleled increase in understanding, and with the regulations that flowed from it, the kill dropped more than tenfold, and could have gone lower had the fishery leadership dedicated itself to solutions with as much good will as did the scientists and technical people. These biologists, gear experts, and, to be fair, a good many enlightened fishermen, showed that the problem held hope of being solved, and that progress hinged on a simple matter of good faith between the parties directly involved.

The question boiled down to this: Did or did not the leadership of the U.S. fishermen want to respond to the wishes of the vast majority of the U.S. public to do something about the dolphin kill? Or did they want to paper over the public concerns with legal maneuvering, and retreat to the hidden reaches of the open sea, just as they always had? There they could carry on with "fishing as usual" and continue their oft-repeated gavotte of exploitation, of building more vessels than the resource could support, and of facing a decline of both the resources upon which they fished and of their fishery itself. Their leadership chose fishing as usual.

In the early 1980s, under pressure from the fishery, the little reforms that together had inched the dolphin kill downward in the 1970s were eroded, as one by one crucial rules were relaxed by the U.S. Government, and as the fleet "went foreign." Dusk sets were allowed again. The need for boats in the water to hold the backdown channel open, or to help the dolphins out, was pushed aside. These and other carefully crafted rules had been shown to work, but because they took time and effort and shortened the fishing day, they were discarded, and the dolphin kill began to climb. Fishing as usual prevailed.

The resurgence of dolphin death that followed did not escape the attention of the conservation community. Especially concerned were the conservationist-biologists Todd Steiner and David Phillips of the Earth Island Institute, who began to document the upward trends, and who spearheaded a long campaign with canners, the fishing industry, and the government.

Their carefully crafted case was greatly strengthened when the activist Sam LaBudde shipped aboard a Panamanian seiner as a seaman and was permitted to videotape events on board. The vessel he chose was run by an inexperienced crew and the carnage was horrendous. He taped dolphins tangled and drowning in the nets, and others going up with the seine through the power block, to drop fifteen feet to the deck below. His footage was made part of a film by director Stan Minasian, and narrated by actor George C. Scott. They called it *Where Have All the Dolphins Gone?* This film featured various interviews, including one with me. It received wide coverage, and it created a furor.

Disheartened by the rising kill, my passions were high during my interview, and I forswore eating further canned tuna—of which I am quite fond—until I felt the fishery had been brought back to a responsible position with regard to the dolphins. This is the first time in my non-activist life I have ever taken such a position. Before, it had been enough for me to be a responsible scientific voice in such encounters.

The film, and other conservationist-led investigations of the time, raised the issue anew with the American public. The demand for change flooded the governmental sphere and new pressures began to assail the fishery.

I was as surprised as anybody by the half-page newspaper ad that flooded U.S. newspapers on April 20, 1990. It said "Thanks StarKist" in bold type, set under a picture of a bottlenose dolphin, mouth open and "smiling." The tag line in this self-congratulatory message was a new logo proclaiming that "StarKist, Dolphin Safe" had placed the ad. Two other tuna canners, Chicken-of-the-Sea and Bumblebee, quickly followed suit. Both of these canners are now foreign-owned, one based in Indonesia and the other in Thailand.

In the 1970s I had believed what the tuna industry had repeatedly told us: that if the conservation-scientific community pushed too hard for dolphin-saving maneuvers, the tuna industry would simply fail. Now that prediction had been invalidated in one swift move. Apparently they could survive OK, and without fishing on dolphins at all!

The announcement was greeted by the conservation community with euphoria. They had won. The dolphins would be saved. It all reminded me of my own feelings in the late 1970s when an administrative law judge had shut the fishery down until it complied with the Marine Mammal Protection Act. My elation of that time proved only a prelude to the somber events of the 1980s when the dolphin kill rose again, in a new and more intractable form. Will that happen again? Maybe.

Why should I be so skeptical about the canners' promise? First, the promise was to the U.S. public, and hence to a major market that consumes at this writing about 32 percent of the world's canned tuna. There would be great economic benefit to any canner who could capture this market. The United States is, in fact, *the* major consumer of canned tuna in the world, although Japan is close with 30 percent and western Europe with about 25 percent of the world tuna pack.

Second, it will not be difficult for the three canners to keep their promise to American consumers without affecting their total commerce. Major sources of tuna not caught on dolphins are available from areas outside the eastern tropical Pacific. For example, much tuna sold in the U.S. market already comes from the western Pacific, which is apparently mostly caught without setting seines around dolphin schools. Only a modest shift in purchasing practices or deployment of boats owned by the canners will be required to satisfy the pledge. Such a shift may not save dolphins though, nor will it necessarily stop seining in the eastern tropical Pacific. A large non–U.S. fleet continues to set seines on dolphins on the eastern tropical Pacific fishing grounds now without competition from the more carefully controlled U.S. boats.

Third, who is going to check up on the canners, and how? There is at the present time a major worldwide commerce in what the canners call "bright cans." These are job lots of tuna canned at a given location and sold wholesale without labels. Since canning practices are now fairly standard in most places, the product is usually indistinguishable from yellowfin straight from the eastern tropical Pacific. The purchaser merely buys such lots of tuna, puts his own label on the cans, and sends them off to market, regardless of how or where they were caught.

Possibly, checks could be run to determine the sources of such tuna. A little sleuthing, assuming that records are available, should reveal the source of a given lot, or perhaps modern chemistry, especially mass spectroscopy, could be used to determine the actual geographical source of a given lot of tuna. But who is to carry out this sleuthing? Who is to pay for it?

Fourth, the dolphin-free pledge to U.S. consumers, from the only U.S.–based tuna canner, erodes the basis upon which the U.S. Government passes laws and promulgates regulations relating to dolphin kill. The Marine Mammal Protection Act, for example, regulates the activities of U.S. fishermen and their vessels, not boats of foreign registry. With all the U.S. boats catching tuna without setting nets on dolphins, the statutory basis of regulating dolphin fishing practices beyond the U.S. has now been made much more difficult. It now rests heavily upon import laws, and upon diplomacy.

In my somewhat cynical view, the maneuver of pledging

dolphin-free tuna to the U.S. consumer seems most likely to be an economic maneuver, pure and simple, designed to capture the U.S. canned tuna market. But perhaps I am wrong.

The decision by U.S. canners to stop catching tuna by seining on dolphins may have evolved in a debate within company leadership that had come to recognize our mutual responsibilities to the earth and the sea. That sort of change is afoot in many places in the business and governmental communities as young leadership replaces old. But regardless of its source, the canners' decision electrified the debate over utilization of open-ocean resources, and has begun to take on a life of its own that is reverberating around the world. Its immediate effect is no longer contained within the tuna canners' boardrooms, and this we can attribute to the awakening world ecological consciousness.

The conservation-scientific community itself has also begun to mature, but it has been a rough road. In the 1960s, when scientists and conservationists found a mission, we typically raced in with flags flying, and raised public concern. Lo and behold, laws were changed, and victories were achieved. Then, just as typically, we dusted off our palms, congratulated each other for a job well done, and went back to the jobs that actually paid the household bills.

Our antagonists soon learned to deal with these surprise attacks. They learned the importance of staying power. If you waited around till the conservationists were gone, it was usually simple to jigger things back the way they were; and that's what happened in the tuna fishery during the 1980s.

I find it unlikely that a sudden uncharacteristic flood of altruism has swept over the leadership of the tuna industry. Such responses, I suspect, will begin to increase in number down the road a piece when the developed nations—and the world more broadly—achieve a citizens' consensus about protecting the world's ecology. It will require a generational change, as all major shifts in cultures seem to. A new generation of young people, concerned about the fate of their world, has to take the place of the elders who operated under different and more primitive rules. Then the citizenry, the commercial sector, and the dolphins will be equal partners of the vision. I believe we are now in the messy center of such a changing of the guards. We and the fishery are both being swept along by an inexorable tide of changing perception that will not be stemmed.

I doubt that the dolphins of the eastern tropical Pacific will be left alone solely because StarKist and the others have pledged not to catch tuna using them. Given our current lack of regard for world ecology, the majority of nations who harvest that multimillion-dollar resource can be expected to use the most economical means of tuna capture, which at this time is the use of the tuna seine set upon dolphin schools. It seems to me to be a last-ditch battle between the world ecologists on one hand and the hunter-gatherers on the other. In the long run, the old guard hasn't a chance in the face of changing world perceptions. Signs of change are everywhere as I write. Some Japanese canners have pledged not to pack dolphin-caught tuna. Canneries in Italy and France have made similar announcements, and a major market chain in the United Kingdom has said that it will not sell tuna caught on dolphins.

Other signs show that the battleground may be shifting, at least in part, from the problems of seine fishing to those of entanglement nets such as gill and drift nets. The world tuna fishery already takes much of its catch from such nets, some twenty miles long, which entangle just about everything in their path, whether it is birds, billfish, sharks, dolphins, or tuna. The effect is no less a rape of the sea than the tuna seine has produced.

Where does this leave all the work of *Hana Nai'a?* Remember that we began to think we could see the reasons for dolphin deaths in seines, and we began to think we could propose solid ways of letting dolphins go. Was this all a dead end?

I think it need not be. There are commonalities between the ways dolphins die in seines and in drift nets. The need for solid research remains as critical as ever for both methods. How might these things be achieved?

First, the world fishery, regardless of what countries it calls home, must shake off its hunter-gatherer mentality, which thus far has led to attempts to hide the deleterious effects of its fishing methods. In the place of such evasion, a solid research and development program must be instituted, with enough staying power and support to find solutions to the industry's problems.

The problem of dolphin kill in tuna seines or in drift nets may not be beyond technical solution. *No thorough ongoing research program to solve the world tuna fishery's problems has ever existed.* There is no group in the tuna industry, or in the drift net fishery, with the necessary support to experiment with methods of capture, net construction, alternative methods of fishing, or dolphin and tuna behavior *at sea* on a seiner or a drift netter where the problems take place, and where they can be tested and refined. No such vessel has ever been permanently dedicated full time to solving the problems of the tuna fishery. What manufacturer of cars, cameras, or computers would think of entering the competitive marketplace without a skilled and well-funded research and development operation at its core? In these oceanic fisheries, research into methods that could solve their problems has never been a priority.

A good deal of money *is* spent by the fishery and the fishery agencies to provide statistics for the lawyers who joust with one another. This tells us where the thinking of the combatants has been focused. Their aim has been mostly to document the kill or to sway the public and the judges and agency heads who devise the rules by which these fisheries must work. Their primary concern has not yet become to learn to deal with the problems their industries create.

If seining continues to be used to capture tuna, it might be modified to reduce the kill using some of our findings. I'd start with our observations of the school's magic envelope, and the *hukilau* tests. The first observations outlined the forces that structure a dolphin's school, and allowed us to perceive why dolphins sink in tuna seines and why they do not help themselves. Our *hukilau* roughly defined what it might take to reinstate the dolphin's normal escape reactions. It also highlighted the fact that tuna and dolphins have very different escape patterns. It is in this difference that the key to release from seines might lie. The great behavioral difference between the fish and dolphins should allow their separation in the net. The subsequent release of dolphins without loss of tuna should be a fairly direct matter.

I hope the time has come for us to truly work together—fishermen, gear specialists, boat owners, cannery owners, fishery biologists, and behaviorists—not in a climate of suspicion and manipulation but with a mutual understanding that the problem must be solved if the fishery is to be accepted in its present form.

Everyone needs to understand that punitive solutions derived from acrimonious debate tend only to paper over the deeper resource issues. Problems then tend to move sideways and reappear in more intractable form than before. Laws alone are simply not enough.

We conservationists and scientists will have to understand that our viewpoint is not the only important one. Mexican nationals and other fishermen need jobs, sometimes desperately, and their countries need capital. Fishermen everywhere will continue to react first to their personal needs and to the imperatives of their families. They will react against having their hard-won accomplishments assailed by outsiders. They should be recognized for having forged a remarkable fishery by dint of experiments as daring and innovative as those of any scientist.

I think that the eastern tropical Pacific tuna seine fishery should not be allowed to carry out "fishing as usual" until a solution is found. The dolphin populations of this battleground-ocean have already suffered too much. It is only because their populations have proven amazingly resilient that they are still there, leading the fishermen to tuna.

The international fishery now works all year so there is no surcease for the dolphins, even during their summer-fall peak calving time. I think it is likely that a given dolphin is caught very frequently, and as their populations have grown smaller, that rate of recapture has inevitably gone up. Those long, high-speed chases, with the little calves somehow keeping up, and then the chaos of the backdown channel, cannot contribute to anything like a normal life in the open sea.

In my view, before fishermen seine further on the eastern tropical Pacific, they should know how to release the dolphins without killing them. There must be regulations that make the summer-fall calving season off limits, so that normal birth and early nurture of dolphin calves can take place undisturbed.

It is crucial, I think, that the fishery should become a limited-entry effort in which only so many licenses to fish are available, probably determined by an international commission whose concerns are the health both of tuna stocks and dolphin populations. These licenses then become the things that determine fishery effort, not the number of fishing boats one can buy. They become the things that are bought and sold. The present proliferation of vessels not only kills dolphins, it also drives fishermen into bankruptcy.

Tuna fishing doesn't necessarily have to involve dolphins at all. One such method, called *log fishing,* should be explored in depth. Tuna gather under floating objects such as the logs that are washed out to sea from tropical rivers. The attracted schools can be remarkable large, and they are frequently "set upon" by today's seine fishermen.

Far out at sea, I once saw a collection of several species of small fish clustered around a knot of hauser weighing perhaps a hundred pounds, and down in the depths I could see the golden flash of a big school of tuna.

Fishermen told me of setting their nets on floating trash such as styrofoam coffee cups, and of bringing up good catches of tuna. This association between fish and floating objects is, in fact, commonplace.

If the seine fishery becomes a limited-entry one, and without the dog-eat-dog competition we see today, it seems to me that artificially constructed tuna attractants, called FADs (Fish Aggregating Devices), might be scattered across the tuna grounds to be located by radio. A tuna seiner might work its own "trapline of logs." A private electronic access code might allow it to locate each one, rather than seeking dolphins at all. Such FADs can even be submerged and brought to the surface for fishing. With refinement, such fishing might be much more fuel-efficient, and faster than the present-day hunting technique.

Fishermen know that FADs work, but at this point only dolphins seem to carry the largest tuna, and the big tuna bring premium prices at the cannery. The causes of that price differential need to be explored, and if possible altered, so that FADs can become the method of choice.

If these things can be done, we have a fighting chance not only of releasing dolphins but of redesigning a fishery that does not fall of its own weight, and one that does not drive the dolphin and fish populations of a vast area of sea into decline.

As I write in the fall of 1990, a new step in this tortured saga has just taken place, and I wonder what it portends for the *nai'a*. A law forbidding the importation of tuna from nations that catch the fish in violation of U.S. law has been invoked by a U.S. federal judge. This means that some nations in Central and South America and in the Pacific islands may be prohibited from exporting tuna to the United States if it is found that they have violated the rules that govern the U.S. fleet. If the embargo is invoked, it could make the United States totally free of dolphin-caught tuna on its shelves. The judge is quoted as saying:

> Under the agency's interpretation [The National Marine Fisheries Service] it is the dolphins and domestic fishermen, not the foreign governments, who bear the burden of the foreign governments' late production of evidence. The continued slaughter and destruction of these innocent victims of the economics of fishing constitutes an irreparable injury to us all.

One can view this development in differing ways. First, it may indeed establish the United States as a model for other nations who import tuna. The effect may be to bring pressure on various tuna seine fleets to conform to U.S. rules, and then the dolphin kill should drop.

But if these nations do not conform, the effect could be to capture the huge U.S. tuna market for the canners who have pledged "dolphin free tuna," while seining in the eastern tropical Pacific goes on as usual, and dolphins continue to die outside the reach of U.S. law. As we have seen, when fishermen work without rules the number of dolphins they kill can be expected to rise, probably to levels threatening the collapse of dolphin populations.

Right now, for tuna canners selling to the U.S. market, these events are very smart economics. Much foreign competition is effectively excluded from the U.S. market, at least for the time being, and they have already moved their operation largely out of the eastern tropical Pacific.

So the battleground shifts over the tropical oceans of the world, and from country to country. One must not forget that since the vessels of "have not" nations such as Mexico are now prominent players, and they fish using subsidized fuel, the consumption patterns for canned tuna could change. Tuna could become a needed protein source for nations nearing nutritional disaster such as Mexico and some other Central and South American countries. If this happens, the problem of dolphin kill will enter a new and still more difficult chapter.

While all this goes on, the *nai'a* of the eastern tropical Pacific try to carry out their life patterns as they always have. They are yet another cipher in the earth-wide struggle within the human mind to understand that the earth is a fragile home that must be tended with care and compassion, because it is we, most of all, who stand to lose everything if we do not. I see strong signs that the newest generation of young people, whether from the United States, Europe, Russia, or Japan, understand this without being told. They know they must pick up the pieces from their parents who regarded the earth's bounty as something without cost, put there for the plucking.

WHAT'S next for us now that *Hana Nai'a* is over? Well, Randy and my graduate student Jan Ostman, and boat-builder friends Tom Lang and Charlie Johnson, have helped to build a successor to the *Maka Ala* that lets us sit upright in a nice swivel chair inside an aluminum cylinder that hangs through the ship's hull. There are big windows all around down there, and we wear a pair of stereo earphones to hear in 3-D the sounds of the Yugoslavian News Report. We can cruise at as much as five or six knots with an observer down below: plenty fast to keep up with most dolphins. Whenever the weather picks up, a little winch pulls the viewing chamber up into the hull, and off we go toward home port like a perfectly normal boat.

We started with an old eighteen-foot boat hull that we found mouldering in the weeds behind our marine station, given us by the relieved lab director, who wanted the place cleaned up. We let Jan name it, and since he is Swedish he chose the almost unpronounceable name of *Smyg Tittar'n,* which means something like "Tiptoing Peeping Tom" in that language.

This craft has just been launched in Hawaii, a worthy successor to the Semisubmersible Seasick Machine and the *Maka Ala.* The *Smyg* is one of the oddest-looking craft I have ever seen, but we love her already. She looks like a little blue drilling rig.

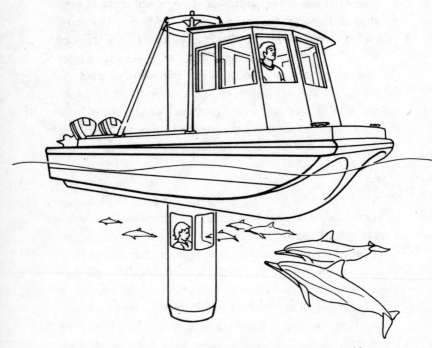

The *Smyg Tittar'n.* Our viewing vehicles keep getting better and better.

Now if I can set up a new camp, we will soon be back with old Four-Nip and old Finger Dorsal. I want to study the magic envelope in more detail, and I want to learn more about shark mimicry. Maybe we can get Randy to jump into the ocean with some spinners while I film from inside the *Smyg Tittar'n*. We can show the results at a *luau* with all the people I talked about in this book in attendance, plus all the neighbors, and any of you who happen to be around.

We learned through our work that a vital part of protecting an animal is knowing who it is. The more we have learned about spinner dolphins, the more remarkable they seem to us. Because we know them a little, we have come to care for them a great deal. I feel it in my bones that this will lead to their salvation out on the open Pacific.

Epilogue

WHAT a wonderful crew I had in *Hana Nai'a!* My two leaders both completed doctor's degrees long ago and have gone on to do fine work on their own. Bernd Würsig is now in charge of a major marine program at the Texas Tech Marine Station, in Galveston, Texas. He continues to be involved in marine mammal studies in places as distant as Argentina, New Zealand, and China. He and Mel have a second child, Paul. Randy Wells, whose work has also taken him to faraway places, is best known for his splendid study of Florida bottlenose dolphins, the most complete such work on any cetacean population. He is a full-time behavioral ecologist at the Brookfield Zoo, in Chicago.

Jody Solow is now a doctoral candidate in cultural ecology at Cambridge University in England. She now works in the New Hebrides of the South Pacific. Chris Johnson, a doctoral candidate in cognitive psychology at Cornell University, is investigating the ability of bottlenose dolphins to perform analogies: the basic stuff of our own kind of reasoning and communication.

Shortly after *Hana Nai'a* was completed, Shannon Brownlee became a researcher and then a writer for the science magazine

Discover. She won the American Institute of Physics award for best American science writing in 1987, for a story on the science of earthquakes. She now writes about science for *U.S. News and World Report,* in Washington, D.C., and in 1990 won the General Motors Cancer Research Foundation Prize for International Biomedical Science Journalism.

In my career I can look back to the very beginnings of our understanding about wild dolphins. And I watch with great pleasure as some of my students combine that understanding with the more recent science of animal behavior ashore, especially with the findings of primate biologists. Rachel Smolker, who set up camp on our lawn, is one. For her doctoral degree she is working on the group relations of the dolphins of Monkey Mia; and Richard Connor has completed his doctoral studies, observing the same animals and studying the role of the male in dolphin society.

Bibliography

THE following are some books, articles, and scientific papers about the general subject of dolphins, with particular emphasis on spinners. These were selected to amplify the material in the book.

Au, D. W., and D. Weihs 1980. At high speeds dolphins save energy by leaping. *Nature* 284 (5756): 548–50.
A paper that ties hydrodynamic theory and observations of wild dolphins together to explain why they make long, low-angle leaps when swimming fast.

Au, W. W. L., R. W. Floyd, R. H. Penner, and A. E. Murchison 1978. Propagation of Atlantic bottlenose dolphin echolocation signals. *Jour. Acoustical Society of America* 64 (2): 411–22.
A report that describes the extremely high intensity clicks that echolocating dolphins sometimes make. This set me to thinking about the possibility of prey stunning by dolphins.

Bateson, G. 1974. Observations of a cetacean community. In *Mind in the Waters*, edited by J. McIntyre. 146–65. New York: Scribner.
This is all Gregory ever published of his long study of the spinner and spotted dolphin community at Sea Life Park. His mind had turned to his other books by that time.

Bateson, G. 1972. *Steps to an Ecology of Mind*. San Francisco: Chandler.
Gregory wrote this after he had abandoned dolphin study and retreated down the beach. It's full of those metalogues of his.

Bateson, G. 1979. *Mind and Nature: A Necessary Unity*. New York: Dutton.
Gregory's final book. It evolved naturally from *Steps to an Ecology of Mind*.

Caldwell, M. C., and D. K. Caldwell 1965. Individualized whistle contours in bottlenose dolphins *(Tursiops truncatus)*. *Nature* 207: 434–35.
This is the paper that showed the basis for the sensory integration system of dolphin schools, which is the whistle matrix. The subject has since been extended a great deal by the work of Peter Tyack.

Caldwell, M. C., and D. K. Caldwell 1968. Vocalizations of native captive dolphins in small groups. *Science* 159: 1121–123.
This interesting paper shows how the sensory integration system of a school can integrate its activities, and how, without words, it can transmit a great deal of information between dolphins. To me, it was the first demonstration that dolphins do not have anything like a human language. Instead, they use a here-and-now system of signs, some of them metaphors of ongoing events, to get across their information and intent. Such a system is vastly more ponderous than language, and leads dolphins to going through the "Yugoslavian News Report" every afternoon to get their points across.

Caldwell, M. C., D. K. Caldwell, and P. Tyack 1990. Review of the signature whistle hypothesis for the Atlantic Bottlenose Dolphin, Ch. 10. In *The Bottlenose Dolphin*, edited by S. Leatherwood and R. R. Reeves. New York: Academic.
A detailed statistical analysis of signature whistles by the two research programs that have studied them most: the Caldwells in Florida and Peter Tyack's group at Woods Hole, Mass.

Clay, C. S., and H. Medwin 1977. *Acoustical Oceanography: Principles and Applications*. New York: Wiley Interscience.
This book contains the basic physics of bubble behavior, which we came to think was so important to dolphins. Bubbles produce markers upon reentry from leaps, and when rough weather comes they make an inverted, acoustically opaque topography underwater.

Conference on the shark-porpoise relationship. American Institute of Biological Sciences, Symposium Proceedings, Washington, D.C., 1967.
This "gray literature" pamphlet is the only source I know to some important anecdotes about sharks and dolphins. Some of the relevant parts are abstracted in Norris et al. *The Hawaiian Spinner Dolphin* (in press), cited below.

Dawson, W., L. Birndorf, and J. Perez 1972. Gross anatomy and optics of the dolphin eye. *Cetology* 10: 1–12.
A study by the major students of dolphin vision.

Delius, J. D. 1970. Irrelevant behavior, information processing and arousal homeostasis. *Psych. Forschung* 33: 165–88.
This paper puts forth the theory that we used to explain why dolphins sink helplessly in the backdown channel of a tuna seine.

Doty, M. S. 1968. Biological and physical features of Kealakekua Bay, Hawaii. Univ. Hawaii Botanical Sci. Paper 8: 1–34.
After *Hana Nai'a* was over we found a reference in this paper to a plan to put an exhibit on Kealakekua Bay that would exhibit the *nai'a* as they came in to rest. No wonder the local folks were nervous with us and wanted us out of the bay! The idea that we were just nosy biologists is not easy to explain to people who must "work for a living."

Estes, R. D., and J. Goddard 1967. Prey selection and hunting behavior of the African wild dog. *Jour. Wildlife Management* 31: 52–70.
This is one of the papers that set me to thinking about why dolphins should burst into the "Yugoslavian News Report" when they head for sea at dusk.

Fitch, J. E., and R. L. Brownell, Jr. 1968. Fish otoliths and their importance in interpreting feeding habits. *Jour. Fish. Res. Bd. Canada* 25: 2561–574.
Two marine sleuths join forces to show how one can interpret the behavior of spinner and spotted dolphins by cataloguing what the animals have eaten. The scientists used the tiny ear bones and beaks of squid found in dolphin stomachs as markers. For example, if they knew how deep beneath the surface a certain species of squid lived, and it showed up in a dolphin stomach, they had a clue to what the dolphin must have done to find dinner.

Ford, J. K. B. 1984. Call traditions and dialects of killer whales (*Orcinus orca*) in British Columbia. Ph.D. diss., University of British Columbia, Vancouver, B.C.
This is John Ford's seminal study of the dialects of killer whales. He did the work at the same time we were forming our ideas about the structure of spinner dolphin communications matrices. We traded notes and ideas, as we visited each other's camps.

Gawain, E. 1981. *The Dolphin's Gift*. Mill Valley, Calif.: Whatever Publishing.
This graceful little volume resulted from "Chi-uh" Gawain's visits to my laboratory at Santa Cruz. I encouraged her to publish her highly original observations of the "tame" bottlenose dolphin population at Monkey Mia, in Shark Bay, Australia.

Herman, L., ed. 1980. *Cetacean behavior: Mechanism and Functions*. New York: Wiley Interscience.
This is my favorite book showing how the behavioral systems of dolphins

work. Amongst other things, it describes the remarkable and voluminous works of Louis Herman and his colleagues on dolphin cognition and language acquisition. For me, it finally lays to rest the idea that dolphins have a spoken syntactic language like ours. They can be taught strings of symbols, and they may use a few isolated ones of their own, but they do not seem to combine them by themselves, or think abstractly with them, as we do. But, like a number of other higher social mammals, they teeter on the evolutionary brink of such capability.

Holbrook, J. R. 1980. Dolphin mortality related to the yellowfin tuna purse seine fishery in the eastern tropical Pacific. An annotated bibliography. Tech. Bull. 2, Porpoise Rescue Foundation. 131 pp.

This compilation lists a great many papers and government reports dealing with all aspects of the tuna–dolphin problem up through the late 1970s.

Jakobson, R. 1960. Linguistics and Poetics. In *Style in Language,* edited by T. A. Sebeok. Cambridge, Mass.: MIT Press.

Though seldom quoted or used by animal behaviorists, this work better describes the communications matrices of dolphin, and those of other mammal and bird groups, than any other work with which I am familiar. Perhaps the problem is that Jakobson is a linguist, not an animal behaviorist. Like most branches of science, these two divisions of behavioral study are careful not to read each other's material most of the time.

Johnson, R. H., and D. R. Nelson 1973. Agonistic display in the gray reef shark, *Carcharhinus menisorah,* and its relation to attacks on man. *Copeia* 1: 70–83.

The paper that set my mind to thinking that spinner dolphins might mimic the aggressive patterns of sharks.

Kooyman, G. L., and L. H. Cornell 1981. Flow properties of expiration and inspiration in a trained bottlenose porpoise. *Physiol. Zool.* 54(1): 55–61.

The work that resulted in Chris Johnson's and my conceptualization of how dolphins may clear the water over their heads as they rise to the surface for a breath.

Lang, T. G. 1966. Hydrodynamic analysis of cetacean performance. In *Whales, Dolphins and Porpoises,* 410–32, edited by K. S. Norris. Berkeley, Calif.: University of California Press.

The best paper I know at explaining the physical constraints upon the locomotion of a dolphin, or a fish, or a human, or a sailboat, moving in water.

Leatherwood, S., and R. R. Reeves 1983. *The Sierra Club Handbook of Whales and Dolphins.* Sierra Club Books.

The best guidebook to the dolphins and whales of the world. It is very carefully illustrated by Larry Foster, the one artist who has taken the time to get everything right, and to measure his animals before he painted them. Before he produced these portraits, we hardly knew how long and thin blue whales really are.

Miyazaki, N. 1977. School structure of *Stenella coeruleoalba*. Rept. Int. Whaling Commission No. 27, Paper L, 18: 498–99.

This work used the capture of entire schools of dolphins in a Japanese fishery to tell us how dolphin schools were structured. I was especially struck by the sometimes very large, nearly pure juvenile groups he found. It was especially thought-provoking that these juvenile groups were accompanied by cadres of adult male dolphins that I think could have been teachers. Are we seeing here the mechanism for cultural transmission in dolphin societies? That is, is such male accompaniment of the young a normal thing? Our work suggests that this might be the case.

McFarland, W. N., and E. R. Loew 1983. Wave produced changes in underwater light and their relations to vision. *Env. Biol. Fishes.* 8: 3 / 4, 173–84.

A paper that shows how the curved surface of the sea can focus light and make a remarkably difficult visual environment for animals that live just beneath the sea surface. These two authors extend these findings to speculate on the origins of terrestrial vertebrate vision.

Norris, K. S. 1974. *The Porpoise Watcher.* New York: Norton.

A book describing my experiences with dolphins before I began *Hana Nai'a,* and all the work described here.

Norris, K. S., W. E. Stuntz, and W. Rogers 1978. The behavior of porpoises and tuna in the eastern tropical Pacific yellowfin tuna fishery: Preliminary studies. U.S. Marine Mammal Commission Rept., Contract MM6ACO22.

This 78-page volume is buried deep in the institutional literature. It is the result of our fifteen cruises aboard a tuna seiner, and contains a good deal of the thinking about what goes on in tuna seines.

Norris, K. S., and T. P. Dohl 1980a. The structure and functions of cetacean schools. In *Cetacean Behavior: Mechanisms and Processes,* edited by L. M. Herman, 211–61. New York: Wiley Interscience.

Tom's and my earlier thinking about how dolphin schools work.

Norris, K. S., and T. P. Dohl 1980b. Behavior of the Hawaiian spinner dolphin, *Stenella longirostris.* U.S. National Marine Fisheries Service, Fisheries Bulletin 77 (4): 821–49.

This paper contains our early findings about how spinner dolphin societies may function. Though it is just a start at understanding the lives of wild dolphins, I have been pleased at how well the conclusions we reached and the ideas we proposed have stood up as new information has accumulated. But the great majority still lies ahead for future workers to uncover.

Norris, K. S., and B. Møhl 1983. Can odontocetes debilitate prey with sound? *American Naturalist* 122 (1): 85–104.

This controversial paper has continued to receive support from new observations, especially from recent experiments that showed that machine-made sounds similar to those the dolphins use can kill fish. Included are new recordings that show how very lengthy and very different the gunshotlike sounds recorded amidst dolphin feeding schools are from their normal navigation sounds. These long-duration sounds were *not* what Kehaulani and Kahe used when they disrupted the fish schools. Theirs were normal echolocation sounds, played over and over against the fish.

Norris, K. S., B. Würsig, R. S. Wells, M. Würsig, S. Brownlee, C. Johnson, and J. Solow. The behavior of the Hawaiian spinner dolphin. Administrative Rept., LJ-85-06C. National Marine Fisheries Service, Southwest Fisheries Laboratory, La Jolla, California, 1–213.

This is the report of *Hana Nai'a*. It has since been much expanded and submitted to the University of California Press as a volume entitled *The Hawaiian Spinner Dolphin*. We expect it to be published soon.

Norris, K. S., and C. R. Schilt 1987. Cooperative societies in three-dimensional space: On the origins of aggregations, flocks, and schools, with special reference to dolphins and fish. *Ethol. Sociobiol.* 9: 149–79.

Here we flesh out our theory of the sensory integration system of schools and discuss how being a schooling organism affects behavior.

Pabst, D. Ann 1990. Axial muscles and connective tissues of the bottlenose dolphin. In *The Bottlenose Dolphin,* edited by S. Leatherwood and R. R. Reeves, ch. 3. New York: Academic.

This is the article that shows how a dolphin's propulsive muscles work, and how they are rerouted by connective tissue sheaths to allow the great power of a dolphin's swimming strokes.

Perrin, W. F. 1968. The porpoise and the tuna. *Sea Frontiers* 14(3): 166–74.

A little paper, but one that showed the extent of the dolphin kill in tuna seining. It unleashed a storm of protest.

Perrin, W. F. 1975. Distribution and differentiation of populations of dolphins of the genus *Stenella* in the eastern tropical Pacific. *Jour. Fish. Bd. Canada* 32 (7), 1059–67.

Just one of great many papers by this remarkable scientist. Many are cited in the Holbrook bibliography cited earlier.

Perrin, W. F., and W. F. Gilpatrick (in press). Spinner dolphin *Stenella longirostris* (Gray, 1828). In *Handbook of Marine Mammals,* vol. 5, edited by S. H. Ridgway and R. J. Harrison. New York: Academic.

This article will be the accepted systematic treatment of spinner dolphins. It will define in detail the distribution and other features of spinner dolphins.

Pryor, K. W. 1975. *Lads Before the Wind.* New York: Harper & Row.

For the reader who wants to know more about Karen Pryor's adventures in putting together the Sea Life Park dolphin show, this is the book.

Pryor, K. W., and I. Kang 1978. Social behavior and school structure in pelagic porpoises (*Stenella attenuata* and *S. longirostris*) during purse seining for tuna. Rept. Southwest Fish. Lab. (Nat. Mar. Fish. Serv.), Contract 01-78-027-1043, 86 pp.

Another one of those difficult-to-find cruise reports. This one describes what Karen Pryor and Ingrid Kang found when they dove in the tuna nets, directly following my cruise. We didn't always see the same things, but there was never another cruise to let us resolve such matters.

Tyack, P. 1986. Whistle repertoires of two bottlenose dolphins, *Tursiops truncatus:* mimicry of signature whistles? *Behav. Ecology and Sociobiology* 18: 251–57.

Tyack has pioneered studies of the use of mimicry by wild dolphins, and here he begins to show how it can knit their communications together.

Watkins, W. A., and W. E. Schevill 1974. Listening to Hawaiian spinner porpoises, *Stenella* cf. *longirostris*, with a 3-dimensional hydrophone array. *Jour. Mammal* 55: 319–28.

These are the results of the Schevill and Watkins test of putting a listening array in Kealake'akua Bay. We wish they'd stayed longer.

Wells, R. S. 1984. Reproductive behavior and hormonal correlates in Hawaiian spinner dolphins, *Stenella longirostris.* In *Reproduction in Whales, Dolphins and Porpoises,* edited by W. F. Perrin, R. L. Brownell, Jr., and D. P. DeMaster, Report International Whaling Commission, Special Issue No. 6. Cambridge, England.

This is the complete scientific version of Randy's studies of spinner reproductive patterns.

Würsig, B., and M. Würsig 1977. The photographic determination of group size, composition and stability of coastal porpoises (*Tursiops truncatus*) in an Argentine bay. *Science* 198: 755–56.

The first description of what scars and marks analysis could tell us about dolphin life patterns.

Index

Page numbers in *italics* refer to illustrations.